The Conflict of the Faculties

THE JANUS LIBRARY

IMMANUEL KANT • The Conflict of the Faculties

Der Streit der Fakultäten

TRANSLATION AND INTRODUCTION BY MARY J. GREGOR

*Dedicated by the Translator
to Her Son, Ian*

Contents

TRANSLATOR'S INTRODUCTION

With the exception of his lectures on anthropology, *The Conflict of the Faculties* was the last book Kant published. Although it appeared in the autumn of 1798, its three parts—dealing with the conflict between the "lower" or philosophical faculty on the one hand and the three "higher" faculties of theology, law, and medicine on the other—were written on different occasions and originally intended to be issued separately. Publication of the first two parts had to be postponed, however, because of the repressive measures of Frederick William II, which Kant refers to in his Preface to this work.

The theme of a conflict between the philosophical and theological faculties appears in Kant's correspondence as early as 1793. Having expressed his distrust of the biblical theologian who wants to overstep the limits of his authority and pronounce upon purely philosophical writings, he notes that the worst thing about the affair is that the philosopher, instead of resisting the theologian's claim, comes to an understanding with him. In a letter to J.G. Kiesewetter of December 13, 1793, he says that this sort of coalition and the false peace resulting from it "must come up for discussion one day" (XI, 456 [this system of notation refers to the *Koniglich Preussische Akademie der Wissenschaften* edition of Kant's works]). Kant had, in fact, discussed the subject briefly, earlier that year, in his Preface to the first edition

of *Religion within the Limits of Mere Reason*. Since "The Conflict of the Philosophical Faculty with the Theology Faculty" was written before October 1794, we can look to the events of that period to account for his decision to continue the discussion promptly rather than "one day" in the indefinite future. The Preface to *Religion* arose out of the circumstances surrounding its publication, and the situation had not improved by the following year: if anything, it had deteriorated even further. Moreover, the "biblical theologians," to no one's great surprise, had reacted sharply and adversely to what they regarded as the philosopher's invasion of their territory. The precarious position into which the philosophical faculty was being forced made it imperative for Kant to define more clearly his faculty's rights in its inevitable conflict with the theological faculty. The conflict, as Kant would put it, had become an "illegal" one, in which one of the parties was resorting to force and fraud to silence the other and secure an amicable accommodation with it. He must, therefore, make it clear to both parties that the philosophical faculty has the right and the duty to keep the conflict going, to accept no such settlement but rather press for a verdict on the part of reason.

Kant wrote to the liberal theologian C.F. Staeudlin on May 4, 1793 (XI, 429-30) that his "rather violent" Preface to *Religion* was occasioned by the obstacles that the Censorship Commission in Berlin had put in the way of its publication, answering his arguments not with reason but with "anathemas launched from the clouds over officialdom." Like many of his colleagues, Kant had not adjusted to the change in the intellectual climate of Prussia that followed upon the death of Frederick the Great in 1786. Despite his veiled criticism of kings who spend on war the money that might better be used for education, Kant was well aware that the academic community enjoyed a unique status under Frederick. Everywhere else, he wrote in 1784, man is kept

under intellectual tutelage, discouraged from using his own reason in matters that concern him most closely. The guardians of the people are only too glad to do their thinking for them, admonishing them not to argue but only believe: "Only one prince in the world says, 'Argue as much as you will, about what you will, but obey' " (*What Is Enlightenment?* VII, 36). Discussing Frederick's motto, Kant drew a distinction that he would invoke in later, less fortunate times, between the private and the public use of one's reason. A man makes private use of his reason when, as a civil servant, he performs the functions for which he was hired. So the clergyman, as a representative of the state, is not free to argue with the tenets of the church when he addresses his congregation: here obedience, not argument, is called for. But the same man, as a scholar, has complete freedom to argue, to communicate to the learned public of the world the use of his own reason in religious matters. In his sermons he speaks in the name of the church and at its dictation: in his scholarly writings he speaks freely in his own name.

Although the mechanism of censorship did exist under Frederick the Great, it was, at his express order, applied very mildly in scholarly affairs, only "to prevent public scandal." But within two years after he was succeeded by his religiously orthodox and mystically inclined nephew, Frederick William II, the situation had changed drastically. In 1788 Baron von Zedlitz—to whom Kant had dedicated the *Critique of Pure Reason*—was dismissed, and the notorious Woellner was appointed Minister of Justice and head of the state departments of church and schools. Together, the King, his favorite minister, and the coterie of likeminded officials they gathered around them launched a campaign to "stamp out the Enlightenment." Six days after his appointment, Woellner's Edict on Religion paid lip service to freedom of conscience while effectively silencing any criticism of orthodox ecclesiastical tenets:

A subject of the Prussian state is declared free to hold what religious views he likes, so long as he quietly performs his duties as a good citizen of the state and so long as he keeps any peculiar opinion to himself and carefully guards himself from spreading it or persuading others, making them uncertain in their faith or leading them astray.

To ensure that Prussian subjects kept their opinions to themselves, a new Censorship Edict was enacted which would limit "the impetuosity of today's so-called enlighteners" by censoring all writings dealing in any way with religious matters, whether published within Prussia or exported for publication outside Prussia.

The antics of this Censorship Commission, especially of one Hermann Daniel Hermes, soon became a subject for concern as well as ridicule. In one of his gossipy letters from Berlin, J.G. Kiesewetter—a former pupil of Kant who had become tutor to the royal children—reported that the first issue of his new journal, *Philosophische Bibliothek,* was returned with so many corrections that he had decided in favor of foreign publication. [1] "His [Hermes'] corrections are masterpieces: they would deserve to be published as an official document of the Berlin Censorship Commission, if I were not so lazy." He had treated the distinguished Professor Grillo "like a schoolboy, writing doggerel in the margins of his manuscript" (November 23, 1793, XI, 450-52). By the following year, Hermes and his colleague Hillmer had been appointed overseers of secondary schools, and Kant foresaw trouble for the universities. Commenting to J.E. Biester on Rehberg's essay grounding the principle of right on the powers that be, Kant remarked that it would be too dangerous to answer that view. "As a matter of fact, an essay of that sort forbids one at the outset to say anything against it. That injunction will presumably be felt with full force, since Herr Hermes and Herr Hillmer have taken their positions as overseers

of secondary schools and have thereby acquired influence on the universities with respect to how and what is to be taught there" (April 10, 1794, XI, 496-97). In 1795 Kant personally experienced their direct influence on the universities when Woellner and Hillmer issued an order to the academic senate in Koenigsberg, forbidding any professor to lecture on Kant's philosophy of religion (XIII, 371).

Some such action was not entirely unexpected. Although Woellner at first tried to appear friendly to Kant, Kant was so obviously the embodiment of what the government was committed to destroy that rumors of a conflict were circulating three years before it actually materialized. The fact that Kant's expected book on moral philosophy (presumably the frequently postponed *Metaphysic of Morals*) had failed to appear at the 1791 book fair in Berlin created a stir. "People around here are saying . . . that Woltersdorf, the new *Oberkonsistorialrath,* has managed to get the King to forbid you to write any more" (from Kiesewetter, June 14, 1791, XI, 173). Although the rumor was premature, Kant had only to direct his attention to the subject of Christianity to precipitate the crisis.

Kant was not looking for trouble when he wrote *Religion within the Limits of Mere Reason,* though he might reasonably have expected it. Long before, he had declared that pure philosophy has to deal with three problems: 1) what can I know? (metaphysics); 2) what ought I to do? (moral philosophy); and 3) what may I hope? (philosophy of religion). The *Critique of Pure Reason* had dealt with the first question and, by the restriction it placed on the legitimate use of theoretical reason, left the sphere of morality open for the practical use of reason. The *Critique of Practical Reason* had investigated the second problem and, in the most abstract terms, laid the foundations for the solution of the third. The essence of morality, Kant had argued, lies in the adoption of a pure rational motive in our principle of action. But

action is essentially purposive; and if the motive we adopt into our principle of action is the thought of its rational validity, the final end at which we aim must be the systematic totality of rational ends, the highest good. This consists in the happiness of rational beings proportioned to their virtue; and since the only way we can conceive of this as possible is through a moral author of nature, we are entitled on moral grounds to postulate the existence of God. In this way morality leads to religion, "the recognition of all one's duties as divine commands."

If Kant's discussion of religion had remained on this level of abstraction, it seems unlikely that he would have come into conflict with the Censorship Commission. In fact, even after the second *Critique* had been published, some of Kant's friends feared that his denial of reason's ability to achieve knowledge of the supersensible might be claimed by the fanatics in Berlin as support for their insistence on blind faith in matters of religion, and asked him to make an emphatic declaration of his position (from the bookdealer Meyer, September 5, 1788, X, 518-19).[2] Kant apparently thought it unnecessary to make such a declaration. But he had not finished with the subject of religion.

Kant may well have been dissatisfied with the extrinsic and tenuous connection between morality and religion he had tried to establish through his doctrine of the *summum bonum*. Although the argument of the second *Critique* is summarized again at the beginning of *Religion,* the command to strive for the *summum bonum* seems to be tacitly replaced, as the work develops, by considerations of the obstacles to the realization of moral ends in general and, more particularly, to the development of virtue. Moreover, man does not exist merely as an imperfectly rational being oriented through morality to the Idea of God. Although the essence of religion is moral, this "one, universal and necessary" religion has always co-existed, if we consider man concretely, with certain ecclesiastical forms. To the "invisible

church,'' the ethical community whose realization would counteract men's inherent tendency to corrupt one another in society, there is added a visible church; to the tenets of pure moral religion, ecclesiastical dogmas. The most relevant example of this interrelationship is Christianity, the study of which is, accordingly, a legitimate undertaking for the philosopher of religion.

Elaborating on the title *Religion within the Limits of Mere Reason,* Kant distinguishes his function as ''philosophical theologian'' from his role of pure philosopher in the second *Critique.* We can think of the pure religion of reason as the smaller of two concentric circles and revelation as the larger circle containing it—larger because it includes empirical, historical material which is foreign to the a priori principles of the first. The pure philosopher must confine himself within the narrower circle, waiving consideration of what has been historically revealed. As philosophical theologian, however, he can perform the experiment of beginning with some allegedly divine revelation and examining it, as a historical system, in the light of moral concepts, ''to see whether it does not lead back to the very same pure rational system of religion.'' If the experiment is successful, we can say that reason is not only in harmony with Scripture, but even at one with it, ''so that he who follows one (under the guidance of moral concepts) will not fail to conform to the other.'' From Kant's point of view, the experiment was successful. As he would later explain to Frederick William, this book in no way disparaged Christianity, but, on the contrary, established its credentials as divine revelation in the only way this can be established, by demonstrating its consistency with pure moral religion.

Yet, he added, biblical theologians might not always be pleased with this philosophical interpretation of the Scriptures. They were not. When Kant wrote this Preface he had already

experienced the displeasure of Hermes, the biblical theologian on the Censorship Commission. The reaction of biblical theologians at large, following the publication of *Religion,* would call forth "The Conflict of the Philosophy Faculty with the Theology Faculty."

In 1791 Kant sent the manuscript of *Religion* to Biester, editor of the *Berliner Monatsschrift,* who planned to publish its four sections in four consecutive issues of his journal. The first section was submitted to the censor, received the imprimatur, and was published in the April 1792 issue. As for the fate of the remaining three sections, we can best quote Kant's account of the affair, from the letter to Staeudlin cited earlier:

> The first part, "On the Radical Evil in Human Nature," went all right: the censor of philosophy, Herr Privy Counselor Hillmer, took it as falling under his department's jurisdiction. The second part was not so fortunate, since Herr Hillmer thought it ventured into the area of biblical theology (for some unknown reason he thought the first part did not), and he therefore thought it advisable to confer with the biblical censor, *Oberkonsistorialrath* Hermes, who then of course took it as falling under his own jurisdiction (when did a mere priest ever decline any power?), and so he expropriated it and refused to approve it.

Biester twice appealed the decision, once to the Censorship Commission and once directly to the King. Both times he was curtly notified that the decision stood. Informed of this, Kant asked Biester to return his manuscript promptly, since he had other plans for it. "To satisfy all the demands of justice," he first submitted the manuscript to the theological faculty of "a domestic [i.e., Prussian] university," presumably Koenigsberg, not for censorship, but for a decision as to whether the book invaded the territory of biblical theology or whether it came under the jurisdiction of the philosophical faculty, "which is how it turned out." The philosophical and theological faculties

of several German universities outside Prussia had the right to authorize publication of books dealing with questions of religion. Kant accordingly submitted his manuscript for censorship to the Philosophy Faculty of the University of Jena, received the imprimatur from J.C. Hennings, its dean, and had the four sections published together as a book in Koenigsberg in 1793.

As might be expected, biblical theologians on the whole were less than enthusiastic. "I hear the voices of biblical theologians cry out in unison against the very idea of a philosophical interpretation of the scriptures," Kant remarks in *The Conflict*, as he prepares to answer their objections. His remark contains some exaggeration: the outcry was not unanimous. But it was prompt and widespread. Writing to Kant on March 8, 1794, C.F. Ammon listed professors of theology from Jena, Goettingen, Altdorf, and Leipzig who were offended by the book and compared Kant to "the long derided Origen" (XI, 494). It was apparently this outcry that led Staeudlin to solicit from Kant an article for the theological journal he edited in Goettingen, promising him "unlimited freedom of the press" (June 14, 1794, XI, 488).

Kant's reply to Staeudlin's invitation, dated December 4, 1794 (XI, 513-15), is the most important reference we have to "The Conflict of the Philosophy Faculty with the Theology Faculty." Although he would not make full use of the freedom of expression promised him, Kant writes, this freedom would be most welcome in view of the dangerous hyperorthodoxy in Prussia. With a view to accepting the invitation, he wrote a treatise entitled *The Conflict of the Faculties,* which he finished "some time ago." He then goes on to outline the contents of this treatise in a way which indicates that it is, in fact, the second and third sections of "The Conflict of the Philosophy Faculty with the Theology Faculty," along with its appendix, the "General

Note on Religious Sects." But, he concludes, although this treatise is, properly speaking, merely political and not theological (*eigentlich bloss publicistisch und nicht theologisch* [*de jure principis circa religionem et ecclesiam*]), he must withhold it for the time being, because he has had to adduce examples that the censors in Prussia, who now wield great power, might take as referring to them, and thus censure. More specifically, there was only one example he could use to clarify his argument that a mystical sect can, at best, be tolerated but not sanctioned by a government as a state religion, and this example was too relevant not to be taken personally. If, as he hopes, peace is soon concluded and brings with it greater freedom of judgment in Prussia,[3] he will send the treatise to Staeudlin so that he may, in any case, decide whether it is really theological or merely political. Kant's dedication of *The Conflict of the Faculties* to Staeudlin was by way of apology for not having sent him the treatise that, eventually, became its first and most important part (July 1, 1798, XII, 245).

This letter is important for two reasons. First, it enables us to date the treatise in question fairly accurately. Staeudlin's invitation was issued in June 1794, and Kant, in December of that year, had had the treatise finished "for some time." What led him to withhold the treatise was, presumably, the Cabinet Order which he received on October 12, 1794. Threatened with "unpleasant measures" should he continue to "distort and disparage" the basic teachings of Christianity as he had done in *Religion* and other, shorter treatises, Kant, though defending himself vigorously against the charge, gave his promise "as Your Majesty's most loyal subject" not to write anything more on the subject of religion.[4] "The Conflict of the Philosophy Faculty with the Theology Faculty" was, then, written between June and October of 1794. Since Kant later refers to this work as "the one censored by Hermes and Hillmer," it would seem that he wrote it

shortly after receiving Staeudlin's invitation, in time to submit it to the censors, who refused the imprimatur, before October 1794.

What doubt remains on the subject stems from the second important point in Kant's letter to Staeudlin, his characterization of the treatise as "properly speaking merely political and not theological." It could be argued that, since Kant did not consider the treatise a theological work, he might have submitted it for censorship some time after promising the King to refrain from writing on religion. In this case, his decision to withhold the manuscript for the time being could mean to withhold it from the censors rather than from Staeudlin. But this seems most unlikely. The subject of the treatise is, indeed, the rights of the respective faculties. But—even apart from other considerations—the inevitable examples Kant uses delve so deeply and so extensively into theological questions that it would have required an almost incredible naïveté on Kant's part to imagine that the censors would not take it as dealing with theological questions.[5]

Quite apart from its possible significance in dating the events relevant to this treatise, Kant's statement that it is, properly speaking, merely political and not theological is important for the orientation it gives the reader. The extensive nature of the examples Kant uses might well make the reader forget that they are, in fact, examples, and distract him from the theme they are intended to illustrate. This theme is, precisely, that of the rights of the government and of the theological and philosophical faculties in questions of religious teachings.

Kant is far from denying the right of the government to sanction certain doctrines which it is then the duty of the clergy, as civil servants, to preach to the people. Elaborating on the theme he had introduced in *What Is Enlightenment?* Kant argues that, religion being a powerful instrument for securing obedience to the laws of the state, the government's legitimate interest

entitles it to require that certain doctrines, rather than their contraries, be expounded to the people. For the government to be indifferent to what sort of teachings are preached from the pulpits and to permit the clergy to decide this for themselves would be to authorize anarchy, to give its officials the legal title to win the people away from its own influence, since the clergy will try to increase *its* influence by accommodating its teachings to the people's inclination to laziness and comfort. But what teachings the government is to sanction cannot be decided capriciously. In making this decision the government is entitled to the advice of the learned community, most obviously, of the scholars of the theological faculty, to whom it entrusts the training of its civil servants, the clergy. In short. the function of the clergy is simply to preach what it is told to preach. It is for the scholars of the theological faculty to examine and rectify the tenets of ecclesiastical faith which, once sanctioned by the government, they will hand down to the clergy.

One concern running through Kant's discussion of rights in matters of religious teaching, then, relates to the rights of the government and of the faculties in relation to the "businessmen" of the church, that is, the clergy. It would be quite incorrect to regard this theme as topical in its origin: Kant is, in fact, elaborating on his earlier discussion of Frederick the Great's dictum, "argue but obey." On the other hand, the activities of Hermes and other "mere priests" may account for the vigor with which the theme is developed here. Under Frederick the Great there was little danger of the clergy's getting out of control, or of the government's mistaking its own interests in matters of religion. Frederick was well aware that it was not his business to lead his subjects to heaven but only to secure their obedience to the laws of the state. Under Frederick William II, however, the clergy had got out of control and, with the government's approval, usurped some of the functions of the faculties. It was

necessary to spell out for him who ought to be doing what, as well as to clarify the nature of the government's interest in religion: he had to be reminded that the government would be acting against its own interests were it to sanction a mystical sect that, in relying on private inspiration rather than public dogma, escaped the government's control.

His discussion of what is in the government's legitimate interest, and what it therefore has the right to demand, brings Kant to the central theme of this work. Because it is in the government's interest to have a people it can rely upon, the government has the right to require that the faculties set forth their views on the doctrines it sanctions for the clergy to expound to the people, and the faculties have the corresponding duty to publish their views on the subject. Clearly, the crucial role here belongs to the philosophical faculty. If the "one, universal and necessary" religion is moral in its essence, it is up to the philosophers to examine the tenets of ecclesiastical faith and determine whether they are conducive to, or at least compatible with, the aim of religion, which is man's moral improvement. Confronted, for example, with a scriptural text such as "he who believes and is baptized will be saved," the philosopher must argue that it cannot be taken literally since the literal meaning is contrary to morality. Driving home his point that the philosopher is thereby doing the government an indispensable service, Kant asks whether the government will be better able to trust the people if they are taught that salvation is attained by obedience to the moral law or merely by belief in dogma and performance of certain rites. Nor, as he is quick to point out, can this sort of open criticism of dogmas weaken the government's influence on the people. As he replied to Frederick William's Cabinet Order, a work such as *Religion* does no harm to the religion of the land, since, for the people, it is an unintelligible, closed book, "only a debate among scholars of the faculty," to which they pay no attention.

The theological faculty, however, has an unfortunate tendency to panic when the philosopher wants to put ecclesiastical dogma to the test of reason. Conflict is built into the relations of the two faculties by virtue of their natures, since one appeals to a priori principles, the other to the empirical fact of an allegedly divine revelation, as the highest authority. The proper tools of the biblical theologian are, accordingly, the methods of historical and literary criticism used in the study of a historical document: as a biblical theologian his function is to determine what the author of the text meant by his words. Since the document in question is supposed to be the vehicle of religion, however, the philosopher claims the right to interpret it consistently with the principles of morality, from which religion springs. Hence the biblical theologian accuses the philosopher of wanting to philosophize away the very essence of the Bible as an act of revelation.

Moreover, the close alliance between the theological faculty and the government, which sanctions its teachings, presents a standing temptation for the theological faculty to appeal to force, to end the debate by silencing the philosophical faculty through censorship. The Theological Faculty of Koenigsberg had behaved with admirable self-restraint toward Kant's book on religion—he had been prepared to take the matter to the academic senate had the higher faculty claimed jurisdiction over the work. But this was not always the case. In 1792, for example, Fichte had sought Kant's advice on how to salvage his *Critique of Revelation,* which had been denied the imprimatur by the Theological Faculty in Halle (February 2, 1792, XI, 321-22). Although the decision was later reversed, Kant saw clearly that the inevitability of conflict between the two faculties, together with the protection extended by the government to the teachings of the higher faculty, presented a constant danger of intimidation and corruption to his own

faculty. Under a clear-sighted government the threat might be held in abeyance. But enlightened governments can be succeeded by benighted ones, as Kant well knew, and under them the right of the philosophical faculty, "through which reason is authorized to speak out publicly," will be trampled underfoot.

"The Conflict of the Philosophy Faculty with the Theology Faculty," then, is essentially a vindication of the right of the philosophical faculty to freedom of expression, the right to have its rational arguments answered by rational arguments rather than by force. It is one of Kant's most personal writings, a direct continuation and development of the points by which he defended himself against the charges directed at him by the King and Woellner. Because of this it is also, I think, one of his most attractive writings—and, incidentally, the occasion for one of the better displays of his dry humor, at the expense of the clergy and the biblical theologian. If it sometimes cuts deep, it is at least a more civilized weapon than what they had used against him.

From Kant's letter to Staeudlin, it is clear that *The Conflict of the Faculties* was the original title for the treatise that eventually became Part I of the work by that name. We must now consider how this treatise came to be joined by two other essays before it was finally published.

The history of the essay that became Part III, entitled "The Conflict of the Philosophy Faculty with the Faculty of Medicine," is fairly straightforward. On December 12, 1796, Professor C.W. Hufeland of the University of Jena sent Kant a copy of his book *Macrobiotics, or the Art of Prolonging Human Life*. Thanking him, Kant mentioned his intention of writing an essay revealing how the results of the regimen he had long practiced confirm Hufeland's "bold but elevating idea of the power man's moral disposition has to animate even the physical element in him" (XII, 148). Hufeland replied enthusiastically

promising that such an essay would quickly be made available to the medical profession. Kant's essay, which takes the form of a letter to Hufeland, was written in January 1798 and published the same year in Jena, in Hufeland's *Journal of Practical Pharmacology and Surgery.*

With the help of Kant's title and his remarks in the general introduction to *The Conflict of the Faculties,* which he wrote in order to tie the three parts together, it is possible to find the theme of a conflict between the philosophy faculty and the medical faculty in Part III. In the Introduction, Kant envisaged the people, with their inherent aversion to working for the ends they naturally desire, approaching the philosophy faculty for advice on how to achieve salvation, protect their property, and live a long and healthy life. Its advice can only be to behave rationally: live righteously, commit no injustice, and be moderate in one's pleasures. So the people, in disgust, turn to the practitioners of the higher faculties, attributing magical powers to the clergyman, the lawyer, and the doctor. More specifically, they want from the doctor miraculous drugs and feats of surgery which will enable them to live as they please and still enjoy a long and healthy life.

From the content of Kant's essay it is clear that Hufeland does not represent the medical faculty with which the philosophical faculty is in conflict. On the contrary, both Hufeland and Kant adopt a merely "rational" view of medicine, advocating discipline of man's sensuous nature by reason as distinguished from an "empirical and mechanical" medicine which relies on the external aid of drugs and surgery. As Klaus Reich points out,[7] however, Kant's ironic closing remarks suggest another area in which philosophy and medicine could come into conflict, although here the philosophical viewpoint is to be distinguished not only from the "empirical" viewpoint in medicine, but also from the "rational" teaching on "the art of

prolonging human life." As Kant notes in one of his reflections:

> The conformity to law of an organic being by which it maintains itself in the same form while continuously sloughing off and restoring its parts is health. As far as the whole of organic nature as such is concerned, this conformity to law of an organic being and alteration of the vital force imply that the creature, after it has produced offspring like itself, mingles as an individual with unorganized matter and only the species endures. Growing old and death. This is not disease, but consummation of the vital force.
>
> (Reflection #1538, XV 2, 964-65)

To the extent that medical science, of whatever kind, regards the patient's death as a process to be postponed indefinitely, it is then in conflict with a philosophical view of nature.

If the theme of a conflict of faculties seems rather strained in Part III, the implicit "Conflict of the Philosophy Faculty with the Faculty of Law" does not emerge clearly until Section 8 of Part II. The essay that was finally published as Part II of *The Conflict of the Faculties*—"An Old Question Raised Again: Is the Human Race Constantly Progressing?"—appears to have been written in 1795. Agreeing to Tieftrunk's proposal to publish a collection of his minor writings, Kant tells him, on October 13, 1797, about two essays which he entrusted for safekeeping to Professor Gensichen, one of his dinner companions, more than two years ago. Should Kant die "before these matters are settled," Gensichen will tell him how to make use of these essays. But, Kant concludes, "keep this matter confidential, for it is possible that I shall still publish them myself while I live" (XII, 207-8 and XIII, 463). These essays, one of which was said to be finished, the other almost finished, were apparently the treatises that were to become Parts I and II of *The Conflict of the Faculties*.

It was not until October 1797, shortly before Frederick William's death and the subsequent relaxation of his repressive measures, that Kant sent Biester the second of these essays. Biester duly submitted the manuscript for censorship, but his letter informing Kant of the outcome has not been preserved, and it is not altogether clear what happened. According to Kant, the manuscript was presented to *Stadtpraesident* Eisenberg on October 23, before the King's death, and was refused the imprimatur, but Biester did not inform him of it until February 28, 1798 (to J. H. Tieftrunk, April 5, 1798, XII, 240-41). In the meantime Frederick William had died, but Kant was, apparently, too annoyed to start the process all over again. "Everyone knows how conscientiously I have kept my writings within the limits of the law; but I am not willing to have the products of my careful efforts thrown away for no reason at all." Since Kant's promise to refrain from publishing anything on the subject of religion had been a personal promise to Frederick William II ("as Your Majesty's most loyal subject"), he was now free to release "The Conflict of the Philosophy Faculty with the Theology Faculty":

> Therefore I have decided, after inquiring of a lawyer, to send this work, together with the one censored by Eisenberg, to Halle via my publisher Nicolovius, and to ask you to be so kind as to have it submitted to the censor there. I am sure it will not be condemned, and I shall try to write the Introduction to it in such a way that the two parts will compose one book. If you like, you may then include the latter separately in your collection of my minor essays.
>
> (April 5, 1798, XII, 240-41)

It must have been very shortly after writing this letter to Tieftrunk that Kant conceived the idea of adding his essay for Hufeland to these other two essays, writing the Introduction with a view to all three higher faculties, and publishing it as a whole.

Replying on May 9 to a letter from Nicolovius on May 2, Kant confirms that he did in fact give Hufeland permission to publish "On the Power of the Mind to Master Its Morbid Feelings by Sheer Resolution," either in his medical journal or separately, because he had not yet conceived the plan of publishing a book, *The Conflict of the Faculties,* in three parts "as I agreed upon with you before your journey " (XII, 241). Though no record has been found of the first two essays having been submitted for censorship in Halle, Nicolovius apparently carried out his commission to deliver copies of them to Tieftrunk. With that begins the final chapter in the complicated career of *The Conflict of the Faculties.*

Before going into these final developments, let us revert for a moment to Kant's decision to publish the book in three parts. That it was a sudden inspiration is clear from his correspondence. That the parts do not fuse into an integral whole is clear from even a superficial reading of the work: only the first part is primarily and explicitly concerned with a conflict of faculties. One's impression is that Kant found himself with three essays, one dealing with medicine, one concerned in part with political philosophy, and one dealing with the conflict between the philosophical and theological faculties. Since the three higher faculties of a university are theology, law, and medicine, and since each of the essays represents a philosopher examining one of these fields, he wrote an introduction that tries to establish a connection among them. The trouble is that the essays were ready-made, written "for different purposes and at different times," and they do not fit together well. What I want to suggest is that Kant was, in fact, concerned with the relation of the philosophy faculty to the other three faculties, and that he could well have written a genuine "Conflict of the Faculties."

That he was seriously concerned with the problem is

apparent from his correspondence. Curiously enough, his clearest statement of the problem occurs in the area where one would least expect it. On August 10, 1795, Kant replied to a letter from S. T. Soemmerring requesting his comments on Soemmerring's book *The Organ of the Soul* (XII, 30-35). Kant notes that this request, made to him as one "not altogether unversed in natural history," is embarrassing because the question also involves metaphysics, so that the medical faculty and the philosophical faculty could come into conflict regarding their jurisdiction over it. When this happens, unpleasantness arises, as in all attempts at coalition between those who want to base everything on empirical principles and those who require a priori grounds. It happens whenever attempts are made to unite pure doctrine of law with politics, as empirically conditioned doctrine of law, or pure doctrine of religion with revealed doctrine, which is also empirically conditioned. Such questions posed to a university bring its faculties into conflict, since they can be answered both by the philosophical faculty and by one of the higher faculties, "though according to quite different principles." Kant's comment on Rehberg's essay, mentioned earlier in another context, specifies the dangers of such a coalition:

> Herr Rehberg wants to unite the actual *lawyer* . . . with the *philosopher of right,* and the inevitable result is that the *application* [*Praxis*] extolled as so necessary in order to render the theory adequate . . . will turn out to be *trickery* [*Praktiken*].

The theme is familiar. Only the context in which Kant develops it is new.

The theme in question is Kant's methodological principle that the philosopher's first task is to separate out the a priori elements in experience and examine them in isolation from the empirical. Whether in metaphysics, in moral philosophy (ethics

and philosophy of law), or in philosophy of religion, only confusion results from a failure to distinguish the a priori from the empirical. And where issues involving moral philosophy are at stake, there is added to this confusion the danger of corrupting morality. Only after a priori principles have been isolated and examined in themselves can we think of applying them, by systematically bringing in the empirical elements from which we have first abstracted.[8] That the *Critique of Pure Reason* must precede the *Metaphysical First Principles of Natural Science* is not directly relevant to our purposes.[9] What is directly relevant is that the *Groundwork of the Metaphysic of Morals* and the *Critique of Practical Reason* must precede the *Metaphysic of Morals,* and—although the parallel is not exact—that the second *Critique* must precede *Religion within the Limits of Mere Reason.* To reverse the procedure—to try to derive normative principles from empirical facts—is to court confusion, and, worse yet, to corrupt morality and religion at their source.

Now the function of the philosophy faculty, in its "department of pure rational knowledge," is precisely to set forth the a priori principles involved in knowledge and action. The faculties of theology and law, on the other hand, take as their authority something empirically given: the historical document that we call the Bible, and the law of the land. (The case of the medical faculty is more complicated: it both teaches an empirical science and administers the given code of medical regulations. But in his praise of Hufeland as "a legislative member of the body of doctors drawn from pure reason, who has . . . the wisdom to prescribe what is also duty in itself," Kant suggests that the "rational" approach to medicine coincides to some extent with the philosopher's derivation of duties to oneself, more specifically, duties to oneself as a being at once animal and rational.) Confronted, for example, with the question "what is right?" the philosopher and the jurist will

appeal to very different principles. The philosopher will try to determine, in accordance with the principle of autonomy, the principle of juridical legislation and thereby obtain a norm for testing the empirically given laws of the land. In other words, he will apply the a priori principle of moral philosophy. The jurist, on the other hand, will identify "right" with the laws of the land and regard this as the norm. Genuine peace among the faculties can come only if the ecclesiastical faith and the law of the land are purified to the point where they are completely consistent with a priori principles of reason and can be regarded as applications of them. But since this can happen only through the philosophical faculty's criticism of the religion and legal code of the state, the government and the higher faculties must be made to realize that it is in their own interests to leave the philosophy faculty free to speak out publicly in criticism of any existing statutes. This is, in fact, the theme enunciated in the general introduction to *The Conflict of the Faculties,* and, but for historical circumstances that made the book an aggregate of essays, it would presumably have been developed systematically in relation to each of the three higher faculties.

To return, now, to what Warda calls "The Conflict about *The Conflict of the Faculties,*" Nicolovius knew that Hufeland had Kant's permission to publish Part III of the work. Since Nicolovius's letter of May 2 is missing, it is not clear whether he knew that Kant had given Tieftrunk permission to include Part II in his collection of Kant's minor writings. Tieftrunk, however, had assumed permission to include in his collection all of Kant's minor writings, so that volume III of the collection, which appeared in 1799, contained, though not in serial order, all three parts of *The Conflict of the Faculties.* Nicolovius promptly brought a lawsuit against Tieftrunk, whose defense was, essentially, that he had, as Kant requested in his letter of April 5, 1798, sent him proofs of the collection two or three months

before publication and Kant had raised no objection. In evidence, Tieftrunk submitted what he said was a copy of his letter to Kant of March 12, 1799, accompanying the proofs. Nicolovius, for his part, maintained that Kant's letter of April 5, 1798, gave Tieftrunk permission to include only Part II of *The Conflict,* not the entire work.

The suit dragged on until well after Kant's death, and it is not clear how, or whether, it was finally settled.[10] From the letters and documents submitted as evidence, it appears that neither Tieftrunk nor Kant was entirely without fault, though Kant's age and ill health by this time make his oversight understandable. Tieftrunk, on the other hand, appears to have behaved rather badly throughout the affair. Perhaps it was fitting that a work whose separate parts had such difficulties getting into print should continue to be plagued by complications even after its publication.

Bibliographical Note

The text used in this translation is that contained in volume VII of the edition of Kant's works by the *Koniglich Preussische Akademie der Wissenschaften* (Berlin, 1902-38). Occasionally, when the sense of the text seems contrary to Kant's meaning, I have followed Klaus Reich's emendations of the *Akademie* text in the *Philosophische Bibliothek* series, pointing out the emendations in footnotes. Kant's footnotes are indicated by asterisks, mine by numerals. In explaining Kant's references to persons and historical events, I have often relied on Vorlaender's notes to the *Akademie* edition of the text. References to Kant's correspondence in my Introduction are to the volume and page of the *Akademie* edition. Arnulf Zweig has translated and edited selections from Kant's correspondence in his volume *Kant: Philosophical Correspondence 1759-1799* (Berkeley and Los Angeles, University of California Press, 1967), and in some quotations I have used his translations, with occasional emendations.

The translation of Part II of *The Conflict of the Faculties* is by Robert E. Anchor and is reprinted from the collection *Kant: On History,* edited by Lewis W. Beck (Indianapolis and New York, Bobbs-Merrill, 1963).

For readers who wish to pursue further the topics discussed in this work, a brief bibliography may be helpful. The main sources for Kant's philosophy of religion are the *Critique of Practical Reason* and *Religion within the Limits of Mere Reason.* The former has been translated by Lewis W. Beck (Chicago, University of Chicago Press, 1949), who also wrote *A Commentary on Kant's Critique of Practical Reason* (Chicago, University of Chicago Press, 1960). The latter has been translated by T.M. Greene and H.H. Hudson (Chicago, Open Court, 1934). Two of the most helpful works on the subject are Allen Wood's *Kant's Moral Religion* (Ithaca, Cornell University

Press, 1970) and Jean-Louis Bruch's *La philosophie religieuse de Kant* (Paris, Aubier-Montaigne, 1968). James D. Collins's *The Emergence of Philosophy of Religion* (New Haven, Yale University Press, 1967) contains an important chapter on Kant. Studies of Kant's philosophy of history have, on the whole, been confined to articles in philosophical journals and chapters in works on the philosophy of history. A bibliography is given in the collection *Kant: On History,* referred to above. Mention should be made of a few recent books and articles on the subject: Michel Dupland, *Kant on History and Religion* (Montreal-McGill, Queen's University Press, 1973); William A. Galston, *Kant and the Problem of History* (Chicago, University of Chicago Press, 1975); Peter Burg, *Kant und die franzoesische Revolution* (Berlin, Duncker und Humblot, 1974), and Lewis W. Beck, "Kant and the Right of Revolution," *Journal of the History of Ideas,* volume 32 (1971), pp. 411-22. Material relevant to Part III of *The Conflict of the Faculties* is very sparse. Kant discusses hypochondria and other psychiatric topics more fully in his *Anthropology from a Pragmatic Point of View,* which I have translated (The Hague, Nijhoff, 1974), and discussions of his own medical problems are scattered through his correspondence. I have been unable to find any serious studies of the subject in English. There are a few in German, notably in Klaus Dorner's *Burger und Irre* (Frankfurt/Main, 1969), and in W. Leibbrand's and A. Wetley's *Der Wahnsinn* (Freiburg, 1961), as well as an article by K.P. Kisker, "Kant's psychiatrische Systematik," in *Psychiatria et Neurologia* 133:24 (1957).

I should like to express my gratitude to Professor Lewis W. Beck, whose critical reading of my manuscript resulted in both substantive and stylistic improvements in a number of passages.

NOTES

1. Not all authors were as conscientious as Kant in securing the imprimatur for their writings. Although censorship was supposed to be imposed on writings published outside Prussia, it was apparently easier to evade the censors by resorting to foreign publication.

2. In the same letter Meyer adds his voice to the request of a group of distinguished authors in Berlin that Kant write a treatise on freedom of the press. Kant did not respond to the request directly, but argued the subject thoroughly in *The Conflict of the Faculties.*

3. Kant was unduly optimistic. The first coalition war ended with the Peace of Basel in 1795, but it was not until Frederick William's death in 1797 that there was any improvement in the situation. In 1793 Kiesewetter had told Kant: "Hermes himself said to my publisher that he is only waiting for the war to be over before issuing more cabinet orders, which he has in his desk" (XI, 468-70).

4. Although Woellner usually gets the blame for this Cabinet Order, Paulsen cites a letter from Frederick William to Woellner, of March 30, 1794: "At Frankfort there is Steinbart, who must be driven out; at Koenigsberg, Hasse, who is a chief radical; of such things as well as of the disgraceful writings of Kant there must be an end . . . . There must be an absolute stop put to this disorder before we are good friends again." From this Paulsen concludes that Woellner was proceeding too slowly and gently for the King, who personally insisted on proceedings against Kant. (See Friedrick Paulsen: *Immanuel Kant, His Life and Doctrine,* translated from the revised German edition by J.E. Creighton and A. Lefevre (New York, Ungar, 1963). This is not to be

taken as a character reference for Woellner: it says nothing about his motives for proceeding slowly and gently. Frederick the Great's description of Woellner as "a deceitful and intriguing parson" is echoed by Kiesewetter: "I talked with Woellner recently and his flattery made me blush. He tried to appear very favorably disposed toward me, but I don't trust him at all." (June 14, 1791, XI, 264-66)

5. The time at which Kant submitted this work for censorship was the subject of a heated debate between Arthur Warda and Otto Schoendorfer. On the basis of this letter to Staeudlin, Warda argues that it could have been submitted for censorship after Kant's promise to the King, since Part II of *The Conflict* was submitted in 1797, during Frederick William's lifetime. Schoendorfer takes this as impugning Kant's honesty and replies that there is no comparison between the extensive theological content of Part I and the passing reference to the Jewish prophets in Part II. See Arthur Warda, "Der Streit um den 'Streit der Fakultaten,'" *Kantstudien* XXIII (1919): 385-405 and Otto Schoendorfer "Zur Entstehungsgeschichte des 'Streit des Fakultaeten': *Eine Erurderung,"* *Kantstudien* XXIV (1920): 389-93. Erorterung Vorlaender's notes to the *Akademie* edition of *The Conflict* are in essential agreement with Schoendorfer's view.

6. It is interesting to compare Kant's position with the policies of Frederick the Great, who, as Gerhard Ritter puts it, "without hesitation . . . made use of the parson as a kind of spiritual control agent, who acted as spokesman for the authorities." But this control was exercised for purely secular ends, and implied no concern for the people's spiritual welfare, no attempt to lead them to heaven. "The Frederician monarchy was a purely temporal state" which "did not claim to control all aspects of life. Because of this it did not view the autonomy of religious ideology as a restriction of its own power, as a limitation to the authority it claimed over man. The state was enlightened, but not opposed to religion. It had no need for such opposition since it felt too secure to demand more than the ready obedience of its subjects in concrete matters. . . . The soul of the people could belong to another supragovernmental community so long as this allegiance did not alienate them from their temporal fatherland." With regard to Kant's principle that man cannot be used as a mere means, Ritter remarks: "Had Frederick been told of this he

would presumably have agreed in theory. . . . '' If Frederick did not hear of it, it was, at least in part, because Kant wrote in a "barbaric language" which Frederick used only to the extent necessary for the conduct of government. See Gerhard Ritter, *Frederick the Great,* trans. Peter Paret (Berkeley and Los Angeles, University of California Press, 1968), especially chapter 9, "The Character of Frederician Government and Society." The quotations above are taken from pp. 167-68 of this book.

7. In the Introduction to his *Philosophische Bibliothek* edition of *Der Streit der Fakultaten,* pp. XXV-XXVI.

8. As Kant puts it in Part III of the present work: "Hence it is not surprising if metaphysicians are incapacitated sooner than scholars in other fields or in applied philosophy. Yet some people must devote themselves entirely to metaphysics [i.e., to the study of the a priori elements in theoretical and practical knowledge], because otherwise there would be no philosophy at all."

9. "I have placed the main point of enlightenment—the escape of men from their self-incurred tutelage—in matters of religion because our rulers have no interest in playing the guardian with respect to the arts and sciences . . . ." (VIII, 40)

10. All the documents preserved by the University Courts of Koenigsberg and Halle are reproduced in Arthur Warda's article "Der Streit um den 'Streit der Fakultaten,'" *Kantstudien* XXIII (1919): 385 ff.

Vorrede.

Gegenwärtige Blätter, denen eine aufgeklärte, den menschlichen Geist seiner Feſſeln entſchlagende und eben durch dieſe Freiheit im Denken deſto bereitwilligern Gehorſam zu bewirken geeignete Regierung jetzt den Ausflug verſtattet, — mögen auch zugleich die Freiheit verantworten, die der Verfaſſer ſich nimmt, von dem, was bei dieſem Wechſel der Dinge ihn ſelbſt angeht, eine kurze Geſchichtserzählung voran zu ſchicken.

König Friedrich Wilhelm II., ein tapferer, redlicher, menſchenliebender und — von gewiſſen Temperamentseigenſchaften abgeſehen — durchaus vortrefflicher Herr, der auch mich perſönlich kannte und von Zeit zu Zeit Äußerungen ſeiner Gnade an mich gelangen ließ, hatte auf Anregung eines Geiſtlichen, nachmals zum Miniſter im geiſtlichen Departement erhobenen Mannes, dem man billigerweiſe auch keine andere, als auf ſeine innere Überzeugung ſich gründende gut gemeinte Abſichten unterzulegen Urſache hat, — im Jahr 1788 ein Religionsedict, bald nachher ein die Schriftſtellerei überhaupt ſehr einſchränkendes, mithin auch jenes mit ſchärfendes Cenſuredict ergehen laſſen. Man kann nicht in Abrede ziehen: daß gewiſſe Vorzeichen, die der Exploſion, welche nachher erfolgte, vorhergingen, der Regierung die Nothwendigkeit einer Reform in jenem Fache anräthig machen mußten; welches auf dem ſtillen Wege des akademiſchen Unterrichts künftiger öffentlicher Volkslehrer zu erreichen war: denn dieſe hatten als junge Geiſtliche ihren Kanzelvortrag auf ſolchen Ton geſtimmt, daß, wer Scherz verſteht, ſich durch ſolche Lehrer eben nicht wird bekehren laſſen.

Indeſſen daß nun das Religionsedict auf einheimiſche ſowohl als auswärtige Schriftſteller lebhaften Einfluß hatte, kam auch meine Abhandlung unter dem Titel: „Religion innerhalb den Gränzen der bloßen

Preface

An enlightened government, which is releasing the human spirit from its chains and deserves all the more willing obedience because of the freedom of thought it allows, permits this work to be published now. This accounts for the freedom I take to add, as a preface, a brief account of what concerns me personally in this turn of events.

King Frederick William II—a courageous, sincere, benevolent and (except for certain peculiarities of temperament)[1] and altogether excellent ruler, who knew me personally[2] and, from time to time, gave me expressions of his favor—issued in 1788 a *religious edict,* followed shortly afterward by an edict of censorship which sharply restricted literary activity in general and so reinforced the earlier decree. This he did at the instigation of a clergyman,[3] later promoted to Minister of Spiritual Affairs; and to him, again, we have no just grounds for imputing any but good intentions based on his inner convictions. It cannot be denied that certain signs, which preceded this explosion, must have warned the government that reform was needed in that field—a reform that should have been carried out quietly, through the academic instruction of those who were to become the people's public teachers; for young clergymen had been preaching their sermons in such a tone that no one with a sense of humor would let himself be converted by teachers like *that.*

It was while the religious edict was exercising a lively influence on native as well as foreign writers that my treatise entitled *Religion within the Limits of Mere Reason** appeared.

*My purpose in formulating this title was to prevent a misinterpretation to the effect that the treatise deals with religion *from* mere reason (without

9

Vernunft" heraus,*) und da ich, um keiner Schleichwege beschuldigt zu werden, allen meinen Schriften meinen Namen vorsetze, so erging an mich im Jahr 1794 folgendes Königl. Rescript, von welchem es merkwürdig ist, daß es, da ich nur meinem vertrautesten Freunde die Existenz desselben bekannt machte, auch nicht eher als jetzt öffentlich bekannt wurde.

Von Gottes Gnaden Friedrich Wilhelm, König von Preußen 2c. 2c.

Unsern gnädigen Gruß zuvor. Würdiger und Hochgelahrter, lieber Getreuer! Unsere höchste Person hat schon seit geraumer Zeit mit großem Mißfallen ersehen: wie Ihr Eure Philosophie zu Entstellung und Herab- würdigung mancher Haupt= und Grundlehren der heiligen Schrift und des Christenthums mißbraucht; wie Ihr dieses namentlich in Eurem Buch: „Religion innerhalb der Gränzen der bloßen Vernunft," desgleichen in anderen, kleineren Abhandlungen gethan habt. Wir haben Uns zu Euch eines Besseren versehen, da Ihr selbst einsehen müsset, wie unverantwort- lich Ihr dadurch gegen Eure Pflicht als Lehrer der Jugend und gegen Unsere Euch sehr wohl bekannte landesväterliche Absichten handelt. Wir verlangen des ehsten Eure gewissenhafteste Verantwortung und gewärtigen Uns von Euch bei Vermeidung Unserer höchsten Ungnade, daß Ihr Euch künftighin Nichts dergleichen werdet zu Schulden kommen lassen, sondern vielmehr Eurer Pflicht gemäß Euer Ansehen und Eure Talente dazu an- wenden, daß Unsere landesväterliche Intention je mehr und mehr erreicht werde; widrigenfalls Ihr Euch bei fortgesetzter Renitenz unfehlbar unan- genehmer Verfügungen zu gewärtigen habt.

Sind Euch mit Gnade gewogen. Berlin, den 1. October 1794.

Auf Seiner Königl. Majestät
allergnädigsten Specialbefehl.
Woellner.

_____

*) Diese Betitelung war absichtlich so gestellt, damit man jene Abhandlung nicht dahin deutete: als sollte sie die Religion aus bloßer Vernunft (ohne Offenbarung) bedeuten; denn das wäre zu viel Anmaßung gewesen: weil es doch sein könnte, daß die Lehren derselben von übernatürlich inspirirten Männern herrührten; sondern daß ich nur dasjenige, was im Text der für geoffenbart geglaubten Religion, der Bibel, auch durch bloße Vernunft erkannt werden kann, hier in einem Zusammenhange vorstellig machen wollte.

And since I sign my name to all my writings, so that I cannot be accused of using underhanded means, the following royal proclamation was issued to me in the year 1794. It should be noted that, since I let only my most trusted friend know of its existence,[4] it has never been made public before.

Frederick William, by the Grace of God King of Prussia, etc., etc.,

First, our gracious greetings, worthy, most learned, dear and loyal subject! Our most high person has long observed with great displeasure how you misuse your philosophy to distort and disparage many of the cardinal and basic teachings of the Holy Scriptures and of Christianity; how you have done this particularly in your book *Religion within the Limits of Mere Reason,* as well as in other shorter treatises. We expected better things of you, as you yourself must realize how irresponsibly you have acted against your duty as a teacher of youth and against our paternal purpose, which you know very well. We demand that you give at once a most conscientious account of yourself, and expect that in the future, to avoid our highest disfavor, you will be guilty of no such fault, but rather, in keeping with your duty, apply your authority and your talents to the progressive realization of our paternal purpose. Failing this, you must expect unpleasant measures for your continuing obstinacy.

With our favorable regards.

Berlin, 1 October 1794
By *special,* most gracious order
of His Majesty
Woellner

revelation). That would be claiming too much, since reason's teachings could still come from men who are supernaturally inspired. The title incicates that I intended, rather, to set forth as a coherent whole everything in the Bible—the text of the religion believed to be revealed—that can *also* be recognized *by mere reason.*

ab extra — Dem würdigen und hochgelahrten, Unserem Professor, auch lieben, getreuen Kant

zu

Königsberg

in Preußen.

praesentat. d. 12. Oct. 1794.

Worauf meinerseits folgende allerunterthänigste Antwort abgestattet wurde.

Allergnädigster ꝛc. ꝛc.

Ew. Königl. Maj. allerhöchster den 1sten October c. an mich ergangener und den 12ten eiusd. mir gewordener Befehl legt es mir zur devotesten Pflicht auf: Erstlich „wegen des Mißbrauchs meiner Philosophie in Entstellung und Herabwürdigung mancher Haupt= und Grundlehren der heil. Schrift und des Christenthums, namentlich in meinem Buch: „Religion innerhalb den Gränzen der bloßen Vernunft," desgleichen in anderen, kleineren Abhandlungen und der hiedurch auf mich fallenden Schuld der Übertretung meiner Pflicht als Lehrer der Jugend und gegen die höchste, mir sehr wohl bekannte landesväterliche Absichten eine gewissenhafte Verantwortung beizubringen." Zweitens auch, „nichts dergleichen künftighin mir zu Schulden kommen zu lassen." — In Ansehung beider Stücke ermangle nicht den Beweis meines allerunterthänigsten Gehorsams Ew. Königl. Maj. in folgender Erklärung zu Füßen zu legen:

Was das Erste, nämlich die gegen mich erhobene Anklage, betrifft, so ist meine gewissenhafte Verantwortung folgende:

Daß ich als Lehrer der Jugend, d. i., wie ich es verstehe, in akademischen Vorlesungen, niemals Beurtheilung der heil. Schrift und des Christenthums eingemischt habe, noch habe einmischen können, würden schon die von mir zum Grunde gelegte Handbücher Baumgartens, als welche allein einige Beziehung auf einen solchen Vortrag haben dürften, beweisen: weil in diesen nicht einmal ein Titel von Bibel und Christenthum enthalten ist und als bloßer Philosophie auch nicht enthalten sein kann; der Fehler aber, über die Gränzen einer vorhabenden Wissenschaft auszuschweifen, oder sie in einander laufen zu lassen, mir, der ich ihn jederzeit gerügt und dawider gewarnt habe, am wenigsten wird vorgeworfen werden können.

Daß ich auch nicht etwa als Volkslehrer, in Schriften, namentlich

addressed—To our worthy and most learned Professor, dear and
     loyal Kant

at
Koenigsberg in Prussia
delivered 12 October 1794

To which, for my own part, I replied most obediently as
follows: [5]

    Most Gracious etc., etc.

    The supreme order of Your Majesty, issued on October 1
and delivered to me on October 12, charges me, as my most
humble duty: *first,* "to give a most conscientious account of
myself for having misused my philosophy to distort and
disparage many of the cardinal and basic teachings of the Holy
Scriptures and of Christianity, particularly in my book *Religion
within the Limits of Mere Reason,* as well as in other shorter
treatises, and for having, by this, incurred the guilt of
transgressing my duty as a teacher of youth and opposing the
highest paternal purpose, which I know very well"; and,
secondly, "to be guilty of nothing of the sort in the future." With
regard to both these points I shall not fail to put before Your
Majesty proof of my most submissive obedience, by the
following declaration.

    As for the *first*—that is, the charge brought against me—my
conscientious account is as follows:

    As a *teacher of youth*—that is, I take it, in my academic
lectures—I never have and never could have mixed any
evaluation of the Holy Scriptures and of Christianity into my
lectures. The texts of Baumgarten, which are the basis of my
lectures and the only thing that could be at all relevant to such a
discourse, are sufficient to prove this. For, being purely
philosophical, these texts do not and cannot contain a single
heading referring to the Bible or to Christianity; and since I have
always censured and warned against the mistake of straying
beyond the limits of the science at hand or mixing one science
with another, this is the last fault I could be reproached with.

13

nicht im Buche: „Religion innerhalb den Gränzen u. f. w.," mich gegen
die allerhöchste, mir bekannte landesväterliche Absichten vergangen,
d. i. der öffentlichen Landesreligion Abbruch gethan habe; welches schon
daraus erhellt, daß jenes Buch dazu gar nicht geeignet, vielmehr für das
Publicum ein unverständliches, verschlossenes Buch und nur eine Ver-
handlung zwischen Facultätsgelehrten vorstellt, wovon das Volk keine Notiz nimmt; in Ansehung deren aber die Facultäten selbst frei bleiben, nach
ihrem besten Wissen und Gewissen öffentlich zu urtheilen, und nur die ein-
gesetzte Volkslehrer (in Schulen und auf Kanzeln) an dasjenige Resultat
jener Verhandlungen, was die Landesherrschaft zum öffentlichen Vortrage
für diese sanctionirt, gebunden werden, und zwar darum, weil die letztere
sich ihren eigenen Religionsglauben auch nicht selbst ausgedacht, sondern
ihn nur auf demselben Wege, nämlich der Prüfung und Berichtigung durch
dazu sich qualificirende Facultäten (die theologische und philosophische),
hat überkommen können, mithin die Landesherrschaft diese nicht allein zu-
zulassen, sondern auch von ihnen zu fordern berechtigt ist, alles, was sie
einer öffentlichen Landesreligion zuträglich finden, durch ihre Schriften zur
Kenntniß der Regierung gelangen zu lassen.

Daß ich in dem genannten Buche, weil es gar keine Würdigung
des Christenthums enthält, mir auch keine Abwürdigung desselben habe
zu Schulden kommen lassen: denn eigentlich enthält es nur die Würdigung
der natürlichen Religion. Die Anführung einiger biblischer Schriftstellen
zur Bestätigung gewisser reiner Vernunftlehren der Religion kann allein
zu diesem Mißverstande Veranlassung gegeben haben. Aber der sel. Michaelis, der in seiner philosophischen Moral eben so verfuhr, erklärte sich
schon hierüber dahin, daß er dadurch weder etwas Biblisches in die Philosophie hinein, noch etwas Philosophisches aus der Bibel heraus zu bringen
gemeint sei, sondern nur seinen Vernunftsätzen durch wahre oder vermeinte
Einstimmung mit Anderer (vielleicht Dichter und Redner) Urtheile Licht
und Bestätigung gäbe. — Wenn aber die Vernunft hiebei so spricht, als
ob sie für sich selbst hinlänglich, die Offenbarungslehre also überflüssig
wäre (welches, wenn es objectiv so verstanden werden sollte, wirklich für
Abwürdigung des Christenthums gehalten werden müßte), so ist dieses
wohl nichts, als der Ausdruck der Würdigung ihrer selbst; nicht nach ihrem
Vermögen, nach dem, was sie als zu thun vorschreibt, sofern aus ihr allein
Allgemeinheit, Einheit und Nothwendigkeit der Glaubenslehren
hervorgeht, die das Wesentliche einer Religion überhaupt ausmachen,

Again, as a *teacher of the people*—in my writings and particularly in my book *Religion within the Limits etc.*—I have not in any way offended against the highest paternal purpose, which I know: in other words, I have done no harm to the public *religion of the land*. This is already clear from the fact that the book in question is not at all suitable for the public: to them it is an unintelligible, closed book, only a debate among scholars of the faculty, of which the people take no notice. But the faculties themselves remain free to judge it publicly, according to the best of their knowledge and their conscience. It is only those who are appointed to teach the people (in the schools and from the pulpits) who are bound to uphold whatever outcome of the debate the crown sanctions for them to expound *publicly;* for they cannot think out their own religious belief *by themselves,* but can only have it handed down to them by the same route—namely, its examination and rectification by the competent faculties (of theology and philosophy). Accordingly, the crown is entitled not only to permit but even to require the faculties to let the government know, by their writings, everything they consider beneficial to a public religion of the land.

Since, in the book mentioned, I make no *appraisal* of Christianity, I cannot be guilty of *disparaging* it. In fact, it is only natural religion that I appraise. The only possible occasion for this misunderstanding is the fact that I cite some biblical texts to corroborate certain purely rational teachings in religion. But the late *Michaelis,*[6] who uses the same practice in his moral philosophy, explains that his purpose in doing this is neither to put anything biblical into philosophy nor to draw anything philosophical out of the Bible, but only to clarify and confirm his rational propositions by their real or supposed agreement with the judgments of others (poets, perhaps, and orators). But when reason speaks, in these matters, as if it were sufficient to itself and as if revealed teachings were therefore superfluous (an assertion which, were it to be taken objectively, would have to be considered a real disparagement of Christianity), it is merely expressing its appraisal of itself—not in terms of its [theoretical] ability [but] in terms of what it commands us to do,[7] in so far as it

welches im Moralisch=Praktischen (dem, was wir thun sollen) besteht, wogegen das, was wir auf historische Beweisgründe zu glauben Ursache haben (denn hiebei gilt kein Sollen), d. i. die Offenbarung als an sich zufällige Glaubenslehre, für außerwesentlich, darum aber doch nicht für unnöthig und überflüssig angesehen wird; weil sie den theoretischen Mangel des reinen Vernunftglaubens, den dieser nicht abläugnet, z. B. in den Fragen über den Ursprung des Bösen, den Übergang von diesem zum Guten, die Gewißheit des Menschen im letzteren Zustande zu sein u. dgl., zu ergänzen dienlich und als Befriedigung eines Vernunftbedürfnisses da= zu nach Verschiedenheit der Zeitumstände und der Personen mehr oder weniger beizutragen behülflich ist.

Daß ich ferner meine große Hochachtung für die biblische Glaubens= lehre im Christenthum unter anderen auch durch die Erklärung in demselben obbenannten Buche bewiesen habe, daß die Bibel, als das beste vorhandene, zur Gründung und Erhaltung einer wahrhaftig seelenbessernden Landes= religion auf unabsehliche Zeiten taugliche Leitmittel der öffentlichen Reli= gionsunterweisung darin von mir angepriesen und daher auch die Unbe= scheidenheit gegen die theoretische, Geheimnißenthaltende Lehren derselben in Schulen oder auf Kanzeln, oder in Volksschriften (denn in Facultäten muß es erlaubt sein), Einwürfe und Zweifel dagegen zu erregen von mir getadelt und für Unfug erklärt worden; welches aber noch nicht die größte Achtungsbezeigung für das Christenthum ist. Denn die hier aufgeführte Zusammenstimmung desselben mit dem reinsten moralischen Vernunft= glauben ist die beste und dauerhafteste Lobrede desselben: weil eben dadurch, nicht durch historische Gelehrsamkeit das so oft entartete Christenthum immer wieder hergestellt worden ist und ferner bei ähnlichen Schicksalen, die auch künftig nicht ausbleiben werden, allein wiederum hergestellt wer= den kann.

Daß ich endlich, so wie ich anderen Glaubensbekennern jederzeit und vorzüglich gewissenhafte Aufrichtigkeit, nicht mehr davon vorzugeben und anderen als Glaubensartikel aufzudringen, als sie selbst davon gewiß sind, empfohlen, ich auch diesen Richter in mir selbst bei Abfassung meiner Schriften jederzeit als mir zur Seite stehend vorgestellt habe, um mich von jedem nicht allein seelenverderblichen Irrthum, sondern selbst jeder Anstoß erregenden Unbehutsamkeit im Ausdruck entfernt zu halten; weshalb ich auch jetzt in meinem 71sten Lebensjahre, wo der Gedanke leicht aufsteigt, es könne wohl sein, daß ich für alles dieses in Kurzem einem Weltrichter

alone is the source of the *universality, unity,* and *necessity* in the tenets of faith that are the essence of any religion as such, which consists in the morally practical (in what we *ought* to do). On the other hand, what we have cause to believe on historical grounds (where *"ought"* does not hold at all)—that is, revelation as contingent tenets of faith—it regards as nonessential. But this does not mean that reason considers it idle and superfluous; for revelation is useful in making up the theoretical deficiency which our pure rational belief admits it has (in the questions, for example, of the origin of evil, the conversion from evil to good, man's assurance that he has become good, etc.) and helps—more or less, depending on the times and the person concerned—to satisfy a rational need.

Further, I have evidenced my great respect for Christianity in many ways—among others, by my account of the Bible in the book mentioned, where I praised it as the best and most adequate means of public instruction available for establishing and maintaining indefinitely a state religion that is truly conducive to the soul's improvement. Accordingly I censured the temerity of raising objections and doubts, in the schools and pulpits and in popular writings, about the theoretical teachings of the Bible and the mysteries these contain (for in the faculties this must be permitted). But this is not yet the highest tribute of respect to Christianity. Its best and most lasting eulogy is its harmony, which I demonstrated in this book, with the purest moral belief of religion. For it is by this, and not by historical scholarship, that Christianity, so often debased, has always been restored; and only by this can it again be restored when, in the future, it continues to meet a similar fate.

Finally, as I have always and above all recommended to other believers a conscientious sincerity in not professing or obtruding on others, as articles of faith, more than they themselves are sure of, so, when composing my writings, I have always pictured this judge as standing at my side to keep me not only from error that corrupts the soul, but even from any careless expression that might give offense. And this is why now, in my seventy-first year, when I can hardly help thinking that I may well have to answer for this very soon to a judge of the world

als Herzenskündiger Rechenschaft geben müsse, die gegenwärtige mir wegen meiner Lehre abgeforderte Verantwortung als mit völliger Gewissen=haftigkeit abgefaßt freimüthig einreichen kann.

Was den zweiten Punkt betrifft, mir keine dergleichen (ange=schuldigte) Entstellung und Herabwürdigung des Christenthums künftighin zu Schulden kommen zu lassen: so halte ich, um auch dem mindesten Ver=dachte darüber vorzubeugen, für das Sicherste, hiemit, als Ew. Königl. Maj. getreuester Unterthan,*) feierlichst zu erklären: daß ich mich fernerhin aller öffentlichen Vorträge die Religion betreffend, es sei die natürliche oder geoffenbarte, sowohl in Vorlesungen als in Schriften gänz=lich enthalten werde.

In tiefster Devotion ersterbe ich u. s. w.

Die weitere Geschichte des fortwährenden Treibens zu einem sich immer mehr von der Vernunft entfernenden Glauben ist bekannt.

Die Prüfung der Candidaten zu geistlichen Ämtern ward nun einer Glaubenscommission anvertraut, der ein Schema Examinationis nach pietistischem Zuschnitte zum Grunde lag, welche gewissenhafte Candidaten der Theologie zu Schaaren von geistlichen Ämtern verscheuchte und die Juristenfacultät übervölkerte; eine Art von Auswanderung, die zufälliger=weise nebenbei auch ihren Nutzen gehabt haben mag. — Um einen kleinen Begriff vom Geiste dieser Commission zu geben: so ward nach der Forde=rung einer vor der Begnadigung nothwendig vorhergehenden Zerknirschung noch ein tiefer reuiger Gram (maeror animi) erfordert und von diesem nun gefragt, ob ihn der Mensch sich auch selbst geben könne. Quod negan-dum ac pernegandum, war die Antwort; der reuvolle Sünder muß sich diese Reue besonders vom Himmel erbitten. — Nun fällt ja in die Augen: daß den, welcher um Reue (über seine Übertretung) noch bitten muß, seine That wirklich nicht reuet; welches eben so widersprechend aussieht, als wenn es vom Gebet heißt: es müsse, wenn es erhörlich sein soll, im Glauben geschehen. Denn wenn der Beter den Glauben hat, so braucht er nicht darum zu bitten: hat er ihn aber nicht, so kann er nicht erhörlich bitten.

Diesem Unwesen ist nunmehr gesteuret. Denn nicht allein zum bürgerlichen Wohl des gemeinen Wesens überhaupt, dem Religion ein

*) Auch diesen Ausdruck wählte ich vorsichtig, damit ich nicht der Freiheit meines Urtheils in diesem Religionsproceß auf immer, sondern nur so lange Se. Maj. am Leben wäre, entsagte.

who scrutinizes men's hearts, I can frankly present this account of my teachings, which you demand of me, as composed with the utmost *conscientiousness*.

Regarding the second point—not to be guilty in the future of (as I am charged) distorting and disparaging Christianity—I believe the surest way, which will obviate the least suspicion, is for me to declare solemnly, *as Your Majesty's most loyal subject,* *that I will hereafter refrain altogether from discoursing publicly, in lectures or writings, on religion, whether natural or revealed.

With deepest devotion I remain for life, etc.

The further history of this incessant drive toward a faith ever more estranged from reason is well known.

The examination of candidates for ecclesiastical offices was now entrusted to a *Commission of Faith,* which based the examination on a Pietistic *Schema Examinationis.* This drove conscientious candidates in theology away from ecclesiastical offices in flocks and overpopulated the faculty of law—a kind of emigration which, by the way, may have had its advantages. To give some idea of the spirit of this Commission: their claim that an overwhelming remorse must precede forgiveness required a profound affliction of repentance (*maeror animi*) on man's part, and they asked whether man could attain this grief by himself. *Quod negandum ac pernegandum,* was the answer: the repentant sinner must especially beg this repentance from heaven. Now it seems perfectly obvious that anyone who still has to beg for this *repentance* (for his transgressions) does not really *repent* of his deeds. And this looks just as contradictory as the statement about prayer: if it is to be heard, it must be made in faith. For if the petitioner has faith, he does not need to ask for it; but if he does not have faith, his petition cannot be heard.

This nonsense has now been brought under control. A happy event has recently taken place that will not only promote

---

*This expression, too, I chose carefully, so that I would not renounce my freedom to judge in this religious suit *forever,* but only during His Majesty's lifetime.

höchstwichtiges Staatsbedürfniß ist, sondern besonders zum Vortheil der Wissenschaften vermittelst eines diesen zu befördern eingesetzten Oberschul= collegiums — hat sich neuerdings das glückliche Eräugniß zugetragen, daß die Wahl einer weisen Landesregierung einen erleuchteten Staats= mann getroffen hat, welcher nicht durch einseitige Vorliebe für ein beson= deres Fach derselben (die Theologie), sondern in Hinsicht auf das ausge= breitete Interesse des ganzen Lehrstandes zur Beförderung desselben Be= ruf, Talent und Willen hat und so das Fortschreiten der Cultur im Felde der Wissenschaften wider alle neue Eingriffe der Obscuranten sichern wird.

*   *   *

Unter dem allgemeinen Titel: „der Streit der Facultäten" erscheinen hier drei in verschiedener Absicht, auch zu verschiedenen Zeiten von mir abgefaßte, gleichwohl aber doch zur systematischen Einheit ihrer Verbin= dung in einem Werk geeignete Abhandlungen, von denen ich nur späterhin inne ward, daß sie als der Streit der unteren mit den drei oberen (um der Zerstreuung vorzubeugen) schicklich in Einem Bande sich zusammen finden können.

the civil good of the commonwealth in general, for which religion is a primary political need, but benefit the sciences in particular, by means of a Higher School Commission established for their advancement. The choice of a wise government has fallen upon an enlightened statesman [8] who has, not a one-sided predilection for a special branch of science (theology), but the vocation, the talent, and the will to promote the broad interests of the entire scholastic profession and who will, accordingly, secure the progress of culture in the field of the sciences against any new invasions of obscurantism.

*   *

*

Under the general title *The Conflict of the Faculties* I am now issuing three essays that I wrote for different purposes and at different times. They are, however, of such a nature as to form a systematic unity and combine in one work, though it was only later that I realized I could avoid scattering them by bringing them together in one volume, as the conflict of the *lower* faculty with the three *higher* faculties.

Dritter Abschnitt.

Der Streit der philosophischen Facultät mit der medicinischen.

The Conflict of the Philosophy Faculty with the Theology Faculty

Einleitung.

Es war kein übeler Einfall desjenigen, der zuerst den Gedanken faßte und ihn zur öffentlichen Ausführung vorschlug, den ganzen Inbegriff der Gelehrsamkeit (eigentlich die derselben gewidmeten Köpfe) gleichsam fabrikenmäßig, durch Vertheilung der Arbeiten, zu behandeln, wo, so viel es Fächer der Wissenschaften giebt, so viel öffentliche Lehrer, Professoren, als Depositeure derselben angestellt würden, die zusammen eine Art von gelehrtem gemeinen Wesen, Universität (auch hohe Schule) genannt, ausmachten, die ihre Autonomie hätte (denn über Gelehrte als solche können nur Gelehrte urtheilen); die daher vermittelst ihrer Facultäten*) (kleiner, nach Verschiedenheit der Hauptfächer der Gelehrsamkeit, in welche sich die Universitätsgelehrte theilen, verschiedener Gesellschaften) theils die aus niedern Schulen zu ihr aufstrebende Lehrlinge aufzunehmen, theils auch freie (keine Glieder derselben ausmachende) Lehrer, Doctoren genannt, nach vorhergehender Prüfung aus eigner Macht mit einem von jedermann anerkannten Rang zu versehen (ihnen einen Grad zu ertheilen), d. i. sie zu creiren, berechtigt wäre.

---

*) Deren jede ihren Decan als Regenten der Facultät hat. Dieser aus der Astrologie entlehnte Titel, der ursprünglich einen der 3 Astralgeister bedeutete, welche einem Zeichen des Thierkreises (von 30°) vorstehen, deren jeder 10 Grade anführt, ist von den Gestirnen zuerst auf die Feldläger (ab astris ad castra. vid. Salmasius de annis climacteriis pag. 561) und zuletzt gar auf die Universitäten gezogen worden; ohne doch hiebei eben auf die Zahl 10 (der Professoren) zu sehen. Man wird es den Gelehrten nicht verdenken, daß sie, von denen fast alle Ehrentitel, mit denen sich jetzt Staatsleute ausschmücken, zuerst ausgedacht sind, sich selbst nicht vergessen haben.

Introduction

Whoever it was that first hit on the notion of a university and proposed that a public institution of this kind be established, it was not a bad idea to handle the entire content of learning (really, the thinkers devoted to it) by *mass production,* so to speak — by a division of labor, so that for every branch of the sciences there would be a public teacher or *professor* appointed as its trustee, and all of these together would form a kind of learned community called a *university* (or higher school). The university would have a certain autonomy (since only scholars can pass judgment on scholars as such), and accordingly it would be authorized to perform certain functions through its *faculties** (smaller societies, each comprising the university specialists in one main branch of learning): to admit to the university students seeking entrance from the lower schools and, having conducted examinations, by its own authority to grant degrees or confer the universally recognized status of "doctor" on free teachers (that is, teachers who are not members of the university)—in other words, *to create doctors.*

---

*Each of which has its Dean, who is the head of the faculty. This title, taken from astrology, originally meant one of the three astral spirits that preside over a sign of the zodiac (of 30 degrees), each governing 10 degrees. From the stars it was transferred to the military camp (*ab astris ad castra;* see *Salmasius de annis climacteriis,* page 561), [9] and finally to the university, where, however, the number 10 (of professors) was not taken into account. Since it was the scholars who first thought up most of the honorific titles with which state officials now adorn themselves, they can hardly be blamed for not having forgotten themselves.

Außer diesen zünftigen kann es noch zunftfreie Gelehrte geben, die nicht zur Universität gehören, sondern, indem sie blos einen Theil des großen Inbegriffs der Gelehrsamkeit bearbeiten, entweder gewisse freie Corporationen (Akademien, auch Societäten der Wissenschaften genannt) als so viel Werkstätten ausmachen, oder gleichsam im Naturzustande der Gelehrsamkeit leben und jeder für sich ohne öffentliche Vorschrift und Regel sich mit Erweiterung oder Verbreitung derselben als Liebhaber beschäftigen.

Von den eigentlichen Gelehrten sind noch die Litteraten (Studirte) zu unterscheiden, die als Instrumente der Regierung, von dieser zu ihrem eigenen Zweck (nicht eben zum Besten der Wissenschaften) mit einem Amte bekleidet, zwar auf der Universität ihre Schule gemacht haben müssen, allenfalls aber Vieles davon (was die Theorie betrifft) auch können vergessen haben, wenn sie nur so viel, als zu Führung eines bürgerlichen Amts, das seinen Grundlehren nach nur von Gelehrten ausgehen kann, erforderlich ist, nämlich empirische Kenntniß der Statuten ihres Amts (was also die Praxis angeht), übrig behalten haben; die man also Geschäftsleute oder Werkundige der Gelehrsamkeit nennen kann. Diese, weil sie als Werkzeuge der Regierung (Geistliche, Justizbeamte und Ärzte) aufs Publicum gesetzlichen Einfluß haben und eine besondere Klasse von Litteraten ausmachen, die nicht frei sind, aus eigener Weisheit, sondern nur unter der Censur der Facultäten von der Gelehrsamkeit öffentlichen Gebrauch zu machen, müssen, weil sie sich unmittelbar ans Volk wenden, welches aus Idioten besteht (wie etwa der Klerus an die Laiker), in ihrem Fache aber zwar nicht die gesetzgebende, doch zum Theil die ausübende Gewalt haben, von der Regierung sehr in Ordnung gehalten werden, damit sie sich nicht über die richtende, welche den Facultäten zukommt, wegsetzen.

Eintheilung der Facultäten überhaupt.

Nach dem eingeführten Brauch werden sie in zwei Klassen, die der drei obern Facultäten und die einer untern, eingetheilt. Man sieht wohl, daß bei dieser Eintheilung und Benennung nicht der Gelehrtenstand, sondern die Regierung befragt worden ist. Denn zu den obern werden nur diejenigen gezählt, deren Lehren, ob sie so oder anders beschaffen sein, oder öffentlich vorgetragen werden sollen, es die Regierung selbst interessirt; da hingegen diejenige, welche nur das Interesse der

In addition to these *incorporated* scholars, there can also be scholars *at large,* who do not belong to the *university* but simply work on part of the great content of learning, either forming independent organizations, like various workshops (called *academies* or *scientific societies*), or living, so to speak, in a state of nature so far as learning is concerned, each working by himself, as an *amateur* and without public precepts or rules, at extending and propagating [his field of] learning.

We must distinguish, further, between scholars proper and those members of the *intelligentsia* (university graduates) who are instruments of the government, invested with an office for its own purpose (which is not exactly the progress of the sciences). As such, they must indeed have been educated at the university; but they may well have forgotten much of what they learned (about theory), so long as they retain enough to fill a civil office. While only the scholar can provide the principles underlying their functions, it is enough if they retain empirical knowledge of the statutes relevant to their office (hence what has to do with practice). Accordingly they can be called the *businessmen* or technicians of learning. As tools of the government (clergymen, magistrates, and physicians), they have legal influence on the public and form a special class of the intelligentsia, who are not free to make public use of their learning as they see fit, but are subject to the censorship of the faculties. So the government must keep them under strict control, to prevent them from trying to exercise judicial power, which belongs to the faculties; for they deal directly with the people, who are incompetent (like the clergyman in relation to the layman), and share in the executive, though certainly not the legislative, power in their field.

General Division of the Faculties

The faculties are traditionally divided into two ranks: *three higher* faculties and *one lower* faculty. It is clear that this division is made and this nomenclature adopted with reference to the government rather than the learned professions; for a faculty is considered higher only if its teachings—both as to their content and the way they are expounded to the public—interest the government itself, while the faculty whose function is only to look after the interests of science is called lower because it may

Wissenschaft zu besorgen hat, die untere genannt wird, weil diese es mit ihren Sätzen halten mag, wie sie es gut findet. Die Regierung aber interessirt das am allermeisten, wodurch sie sich den stärksten und daurendsten Einfluß aufs Volk verschafft, und dergleichen sind die Gegenstände der oberen Facultäten. Daher behält sie sich das Recht vor, die Lehren der oberen selbst zu sanctioniren; die der untern überläßt sie der eigenen Vernunft des gelehrten Volks. — Wenn sie aber gleich Lehren sanctionirt, so lehrt sie (die Regierung) doch nicht selbst; sondern will nur, daß gewisse Lehren von den respectiven Facultäten in ihren öffentlichen Vortrag aufgenommen und die ihnen entgegengesetzte davon ausgeschlossen werden sollen. Denn sie lehrt nicht, sondern befehligt nur die, welche lehren (mit der Wahrheit mag es bewandt sein, wie es wolle), weil sie sich bei Antretung ihres Amts*) durch einen Vertrag mit der Regierung dazu verstanden haben. — Eine Regierung, die sich mit den Lehren, also auch mit der Erweiterung oder Verbesserung der Wissenschaften befaßte, mithin selbst in höchster Person den Gelehrten spielen wollte, würde sich durch diese Pedanterei nur um die ihr schuldige Achtung bringen, und es ist unter ihrer Würde, sich mit dem Volk (dem Gelehrtenstande desselben) gemein zu machen, welches keinen Scherz versteht und alle, die sich mit Wissenschaften bemengen, über einen Kamm schiert.

Es muß zum gelehrten gemeinen Wesen durchaus auf der Universität noch eine Facultät geben, die, in Ansehung ihrer Lehren vom Befehle der Regierung unabhängig**), keine Befehle zu geben, aber doch alle zu

---

*) Man muß es gestehen, daß der Grundsatz des großbritannischen Parlaments: die Rede ihres Königes vom Thron sei als ein Werk seines Ministers anzusehen (da es der Würde eines Monarchen zuwider sein würde, sich Irrthum, Unwissenheit oder Unwahrheit vorrücken zu lassen, gleichwohl aber das Haus über ihren Inhalt zu urtheilen, ihn zu prüfen und anzufechten berechtigt sein muß), daß, sage ich, dieser Grundsatz sehr fein und richtig ausgedacht sei. Eben so muß auch die Auswahl gewisser Lehren, welche die Regierung zum öffentlichen Vortrage ausschließlich sanctionirt, der Prüfung der Gelehrten ausgesetzt bleiben, weil sie nicht als das Product des Monarchen, sondern eines dazu befehligten Staatsbeamten, von dem man annimmt, er könne auch wohl den Willen seines Herrn nicht recht verstanden oder auch verdreht haben, angesehen werden muß.

**) Ein französischer Minister berief einige der angesehensten Kaufleute zu sich und verlangte von ihnen Vorschläge, wie dem Handel aufzuhelfen sei: gleich als ob er darunter die beste zu wählen verstände. Nachdem Einer dies, der Andere das in Vorschlag gebracht hatte, sagte ein alter Kaufmann, der so lange geschwiegen

2*

use its own judgment about what it teaches. Now the government is interested primarily in means for securing the strongest and most lasting influence on the people, and the subjects which the higher faculties teach are just such means. Accordingly, the government reserves the right itself to *sanction* the teachings of the higher faculties, but those of the lower faculty it leaves up to the scholars' reason. But even when the government sanctions teachings, it does not itself *teach;* it requires only that the respective faculties, *in expounding a subject publicly,* adopt certain teachings and exclude their contraries. For the government does not teach, but it commands those who, in accepting its offices,* have contracted to teach what it wants (whether this be true or not). If a government were to concern itself with [the truth of] these teachings, and so with the growth or progress of the sciences, then it would, in the highest person, be trying to play the role of scholar, and its pedantry would only undermine the respect due it. It is beneath the government's dignity to mingle with the people (in this case, the people in the learned professions), who cannot take a joke and deal impartially with everyone who meddles in the sciences.

It is absolutely essential that the learned community at the university also contain a faculty that is independent of the government's command with regard to its teachings;** one that, having no commands to give, is free to evaluate everything, and

---

*It is a principle in the British Parliament that the monarch's speech from the throne is to be considered the work of his ministers (since the House must be entitled to judge, examine, and attack the content of the speech and it would be beneath the monarch's dignity to let himself be charged with error, ignorance, or untruth). And this principle is quite acute and correct. It is in the same way that the choice of certain teachings which the government expressly sanctions for public exposition must remain subject to scholarly criticism; for this choice must not be ascribed to the monarch but to a state official whom he appoints to do it—an official who, it is supposed, could have misunderstood or misrepresented his ruler's will.

**A minister of the French government summoned a few of the most eminent merchants and asked them for suggestions on how to stimulate trade—as if he would know how to choose the best of these. After one had suggested this and another that, an old merchant who had kept quiet so far said: "Build good roads, mint sound money, give us laws for exchanging money readily, etc.;

beurtheilen die Freiheit habe, die mit dem wissenschaftlichen Interesse, d. i. mit dem der Wahrheit, zu thun hat, wo die Vernunft öffentlich zu sprechen berechtigt sein muß: weil ohne eine solche die Wahrheit (zum Schaden der Regierung selbst) nicht an den Tag kommen würde, die Vernunft aber ihrer Natur nach frei ist und keine Befehle etwas für wahr zu halten (kein crede, sondern nur ein freies credo) annimmt. — Daß aber eine solche Facultät unerachtet dieses großen Vorzugs (der Freiheit) dennoch die untere genannt wird, davon ist die Ursache in der Natur des Menschen anzutreffen: daß nämlich der, welcher befehlen kann, ob er gleich ein demüthiger Diener eines andern ist, sich doch vornehmer dünkt als ein anderer, der zwar frei ist, aber niemanden zu befehlen hat.

---

hatte: Schafft gute Wege, schlagt gut Geld, gebt ein promptes Wechselrecht u. d. gl., übrigens aber „laßt uns machen"! Dies wäre ungefähr die Antwort, welche die philosophische Facultät zu geben hätte, wenn die Regierung sie um die Lehren befrüge, die sie den Gelehrten überhaupt vorzuschreiben habe: den Fortschritt der Einsichten und Wissenschaften nur nicht zu hindern.

---

concerns itself with the interests of the sciences, that is, with truth: one in which reason is authorized to speak out publicly. For without a faculty of this kind, the truth would not come to light (and this would be to the government's own detriment); but reason is by its nature free and admits of no command to hold something as true (no imperative "Believe!" but only a free "I believe"). The reason why this faculty, despite its great prerogative (freedom), is called the lower faculty lies in human nature; for a man who can give commands, even though he is someone else's humble servant, is considered more distinguished than a free man who has no one under his command.

but as for the rest, leave us alone!" [10] If the government were to consult the Philosophy Faculty about what teachings to prescribe for scholars in general, it would get a similar reply: just don't interfere with the progress of understanding and science.

I.

Vom Verhältniſſe der Facultäten.

Erſter Abſchnitt.

Begriff und Eintheilung der oberen Facultäten.

Man kann annehmen, daß alle künſtliche Einrichtungen, welche eine
Vernunftidee (wie die von einer Regierung iſt) zum Grunde haben, die
ſich an einem Gegenſtande der Erfahrung (dergleichen das ganze gegen=
wärtige Feld der Gelehrſamkeit) praktiſch beweiſen ſoll, nicht durch blos
zufällige Aufſammlung und willkürliche Zuſammenſtellung vorkommender
Fälle, ſondern nach irgend einem in der Vernunft, wenn gleich nur dunkel,
liegenden Princip und darauf gegründetem Plan verſucht worden ſind,
der eine gewiſſe Art der Eintheilung nothwendig macht.

Aus dieſem Grunde kann man annehmen, daß die Organiſation
einer Univerſität in Anſehung ihrer Klaſſen und Facultäten nicht ſo ganz
vom Zufall abgegangen habe, ſondern daß die Regierung, ohne deshalb
eben ihr frühe Weisheit und Gelehrſamkeit anzudichten, ſchon durch ihr
eignes gefühltes Bedürfniß (vermittelſt gewiſſer Lehren aufs Volk zu
wirken) a priori auf ein Princip der Eintheilung, was ſonſt empiriſchen
Urſprungs zu ſein ſcheint, habe kommen können, das mit dem jetzt ange=
nommenen glücklich zuſammentrifft; wiewohl ich ihr darum, als ob ſie
fehlerfrei ſei, nicht das Wort reden will.

Nach der Vernunft (d. h. objectiv) würden die Triebfedern, welche
die Regierung zu ihrem Zweck (auf das Volk Einfluß zu haben) benutzen
kann, in folgender Ordnung ſtehen: zuerſt eines jeden ewiges Wohl
dann das bürgerliche als Glied der Geſellſchaft, endlich das Leibes=
wohl (lange leben und geſund ſein). Durch die öffentlichen Lehren in
Anſehung des erſten kann die Regierung ſelbſt auf das Innere der Ge=

I.

On the Relation of the Faculties

First Section
The Concept and Division of the Higher Faculties

Whenever a man-made institution is based on an Idea of reason (such as that of a government) which is to prove itself practical in an object of experience (such as the entire field of learning at the time), we can take it for granted that the experiment was made according to some principle contained in reason, even if only obscurely, and some plan based on it—not by merely contingent collections and arbitrary combinations of cases that have occurred. And a plan of this sort makes a certain kind of division necessary.

We can therefore assume that the organization of a university into ranks and classes did not depend entirely on chance. Without attributing premature wisdom and learning to the government, we can say that by its own felt need (to influence the people by certain teachings) it managed to arrive a priori at a principle of division which seems otherwise to be of empirical origin, so that the a priori principle happily coincides with the one now in use. But this does not mean that I shall advocate [the present system] as if it had no faults.

According to reason (that is, objectively), the following order exists among the incentives that the government can use to achieve its end (of influencing the people): first comes the *eternal* well-being of each, then his *civil* well-being as a member of society, and finally his *physical* well-being (a long life and health). By public teachings about the *first* of these, the government can exercise very great influence to uncover the

31

danken und die verschlossensten Willensmeinungen der Unterthanen, jene
zu entdecken, diese zu lenken, den größten Einfluß haben; durch die, so sich
aufs zweite beziehen, ihr äußeres Verhalten unter dem Zügel öffentlicher
Gesetze halten; durch die dritte sich die Existenz eines starken und zahl=
reichen Volks sichern, welches sie zu ihren Absichten brauchbar findet. —
— Nach der Vernunft würde also wohl die gewöhnlich angenommene
Rangordnung unter den oberen Facultäten Statt finden; nämlich zuerst
die theologische, darauf die der Juristen und zuletzt die medicinische
Facultät. Nach dem Naturinstinct hingegen würde dem Menschen
der Arzt der wichtigste Mann sein, weil dieser ihm sein Leben fristet, dar=
auf allererst der Rechtserfahrne, der ihm das zufällige Seine zu erhalten
verspricht, und nur zuletzt (fast nur, wenn es zum Sterben kommt), ob es
zwar um die Seligkeit zu thun ist, der Geistliche gesucht werden: weil auch
dieser selbst, so sehr er auch die Glückseligkeit der künftigen Welt preiset,
doch, da er nichts von ihr vor sich sieht, sehnlich wünscht, von dem Arzt in
diesem Jammerthal immer noch einige Zeit erhalten zu werden.

*   *
*

Alle drei obere Facultäten gründen die ihnen von der Regierung an=
vertraute Lehren auf Schrift, welches im Zustande eines durch Gelehr=
samkeit geleiteten Volks auch nicht anders sein kann, weil ohne diese es
keine beständige, für jedermann zugängliche Norm, darnach es sich richten
könnte, geben würde. Daß eine solche Schrift (oder Buch) Statute, d.i.
von der Willkür eines Obern ausgehende (für sich selbst nicht aus der
Vernunft entspringende) Lehren, enthalten müsse, versteht sich von selbst,
weil diese sonst nicht als von der Regierung sanctionirt schlechthin Ge=
horsam fordern könnte, und dieses gilt auch von dem Gesetzbuche selbst in
Ansehung derjenigen öffentlich vorzutragenden Lehren, die zugleich aus
der Vernunft abgeleitet werden könnten, auf deren Ansehen aber jenes
keine Rücksicht nimmt, sondern den Befehl eines äußeren Gesetzgebers zum
Grunde legt. — Von dem Gesetzbuch, als dem Kanon, sind diejenigen
Bücher, welche als (vermeintlich) vollständiger Auszug des Geistes des
Gesetzbuchs zum faßlichern Begriff und sicherern Gebrauch des gemeinen
Wesens (der Gelehrten und Ungelehrten) von den Facultäten abgefaßt
werden, wie etwa die symbolischen Bücher, gänzlich unterschieden.
Sie können nur verlangen als Organon, um den Zugang zu jenem zu

32

inmost thoughts and guide the most secret intentions of its subjects. By teachings regarding the *second,* it helps to keep their external conduct under the reins of public laws, and by its teachings regarding the *third,* to make sure that it will have a strong and numerous people to serve its purposes. So the ranks customarily assigned to the higher faculties—*theology* first, *law* second, and *medicine* third—are in accordance with reason. According to *natural instinct,* however, men consider the physician most important, because he prolongs their *life.* Next to him comes the jurist, who promises to secure their contingent *possessions.* And only last (almost at the point of death) do they send for the clergyman, though it is their salvation that is in question; for even the clergyman, no matter how highly he commends the happiness of the world to come, actually perceives nothing of it and hopes fervently that the doctor can keep him in this vale of tears a while longer.

* *
*

All three higher faculties base the teachings which the government entrusts to them on *writings,* as is necessary for a people governed by learning, since otherwise there would be no fixed and universally accessible norm for their guidance. It is self-evident that such a text (or book) must comprise *statutes,* that is, teachings that proceed from an act of choice on the part of an authority (that do not issue directly from reason); for otherwise it could not demand obedience simply, as something the government has sanctioned. And this holds true of the entire code of laws, even those of its teachings, to be expounded to the public, which could also be derived from *reason:* the code takes no notice of their rational ground, but bases itself on the command of an external legislator. The code of laws is the çanon, and as such it is quite distinct from those books which the faculties write as (supposedly) complete summaries of the spirit of the code, so that the community (of the learned and the ignorant) may grasp its concepts more easily and use them more safely—the *symbolic books,* for example. These can claim only the respect due to the *organon,* which gives easier access to the

erleichtern, angesehen zu werden und haben gar keine Autorität; selbst dadurch nicht, daß sich etwa die vornehmsten Gelehrten von einem gewissen Fache darüber geeinigt haben, ein solches Buch statt Norm für ihre Facultät gelten zu lassen, wozu sie gar nicht befugt sind, sondern sie einstweilen als Lehrmethode einzuführen, die aber nach Zeitumständen veränderlich bleibt und überhaupt auch nur das Formale des Vortrags betreffen kann, im Materialen der Gesetzgebung aber schlechterdings nichts ausmacht.

Daher schöpft der biblische Theolog (als zur obern Facultät gehörig) seine Lehren nicht aus der Vernunft, sondern aus der Bibel, der Rechtslehrer nicht aus dem Naturrecht, sondern aus dem Landrecht, der Arzneigelehrte seine ins Publicum gehende Heilmethode nicht aus der Physik des menschlichen Körpers, sondern aus der Medicinalordnung. — So bald eine dieser Facultäten etwas als aus der Vernunft Entlehntes einzumischen wagt: so verletzt sie die Autorität der durch sie gebietenden Regierung und kommt ins Gehege der philosophischen, die ihr alle glänzende von jener geborgte Federn ohne Verschonen abzieht und mit ihr nach dem Fuß der Gleichheit und Freiheit verfährt. — Daher müssen die obern Facultäten am meisten darauf bedacht sein, sich mit der untern ja nicht in Mißheirath einzulassen, sondern sie fein weit in ehrerbietiger Entfernung von sich abzuhalten, damit das Ansehen ihrer Statute nicht durch die freien Vernünfteleien der letzteren Abbruch leide.

A.

Eigenthümlichkeit der theologischen Facultät.

Daß ein Gott sei, beweiset der biblische Theolog daraus, daß er in der Bibel geredet hat, worin diese auch von seiner Natur (selbst bis dahin, wo die Vernunft mit der Schrift nicht Schritt halten kann, z. B. vom unerreichbaren Geheimniß seiner dreifachen Persönlichkeit) spricht. Daß aber Gott selbst durch die Bibel geredet habe, kann und darf, weil es eine Geschichtssache ist, der biblische Theolog als ein solcher nicht beweisen; denn das gehört zur philosophischen Facultät. Er wird es also als Glaubenssache auf ein gewisses (freilich nicht erweisliches oder erklärliches) Gefühl der Göttlichkeit derselben selbst für den Gelehrten gründen, die Frage aber wegen dieser Göttlichkeit (im buchstäblichen Sinne genommen) des Ursprungs derselben im öffentlichen Vortrage ans Volk gar nicht auf-

canon, and have no authority whatsoever. Even if the most eminent scholars in a certain field should agree to give such a book the weight of norm for their faculty, it would derive no authority from this: for the scholars are not entitled to do this, but only to establish the book as a pedagogical method for the time being—a method that can always be changed to suit the times and, in any case, concerns only the way they lecture [on the code], without in any way affecting the content of the legislation.

So the biblical theologian (as a member of a higher faculty) draws his teachings not from reason but from the *Bible*; the professor of law gets his, not from natural law, but from the *law of the land;* and the professor of medicine does not draw his *method of therapy as practiced on the public* from the physiology of the human body but from *medical regulations.* As soon as one of these faculties presumes to mix with its teachings something it treats as derived from reason, it offends against the authority of the government that issues orders through it and encroaches on the territory of the philosophy faculty, which mercilessly strips from it all the shining plumes that were protected by the government and deals with it on a footing of equality and freedom. The higher faculties must, therefore, take great care not to enter into a misalliance with the lower faculty, but must keep it at a respectful distance, so that the dignity of their statutes will not be damaged by the free play of reason.

A.

The Distinctive Characteristic of the Theology Faculty

The biblical theologian proves the existence of God on the grounds that He spoke in the Bible, which also discusses His nature (and even goes so far into it that reason cannot keep up with the text, as when, for example, it speaks of the incomprehensible mystery of His threefold personality). But the biblical theologian as such cannot and need not prove that God Himself spoke through the Bible, since that is a matter of history and belongs to the philosophy faculty. [Treating it] as a matter of faith, he will therefore base it—even for the scholar—on a certain (indemonstrable and inexplicable) *feeling* that the Bible is divine. But the question of the divine origin of the Bible (in the literal sense) must not be raised at all in public discourses directed

werfen müssen: weil dieses sich darauf als eine Sache der Gelehrsamkeit doch gar nicht versteht und hiedurch nur in vorwitzige Grübeleien und Zweifel verwickelt werden würde; da man hingegen hierin weit sicherer auf das Zutrauen rechnen kann, was das Volk in seine Lehrer setzt. — Den Sprüchen der Schrift einen mit dem Ausdruck nicht genau zusammentreffenden, sondern etwa moralischen Sinn unterzulegen, kann er auch nicht befugt sein, und da es keinen von Gott autorisirten menschlichen Schriftausleger giebt, muß der biblische Theolog eher auf übernatürliche Eröffnung des Verständnisses durch einen in alle Wahrheit leitenden Geist rechnen, als zugeben, daß die Vernunft sich darin menge und ihre (aller höheren Autorität ermangelnde) Auslegung geltend mache. — Endlich was die Vollziehung der göttlichen Gebote an unserem Willen betrifft, so muß der biblische Theolog ja nicht auf die Natur, d. i. das eigne moralische Vermögen des Menschen (die Tugend), sondern auf die Gnade (eine übernatürliche, dennoch zugleich moralische Einwirkung) rechnen, deren aber der Mensch auch nicht anders, als vermittelst eines inniglich das Herz umwandelnden Glaubens theilhaftig werden, diesen Glauben selbst aber doch wiederum von der Gnade erwarten kann. — Bemengt der biblische Theolog sich in Ansehung irgend eines dieser Sätze mit der Vernunft, gesetzt daß diese auch mit der größten Aufrichtigkeit und dem größten Ernst auf dasselbe Ziel hinstrebte, so überspringt er (wie der Bruder des Romulus) die Mauer des allein seligmachenden Kirchenglaubens und verläuft sich in das offene, freie Feld der eigenen Beurtheilung und Philosophie, wo er, der geistlichen Regierung entlaufen, allen Gefahren der Anarchie ausgesetzt ist. — Man muß aber wohl merken, daß ich hier vom reinen (purus, putus) biblischen Theologen rede, der von dem verschrieenen Freiheitsgeist der Vernunft und Philosophie noch nicht angesteckt ist. Denn so bald wir zwei Geschäfte von verschiedener Art vermengen und in einander laufen lassen, können wir uns von der Eigenthümlichkeit jedes einzelnen derselben keinen bestimmten Begriff machen.

B.
Eigenthümlichkeit der Juristenfacultät.

Der schriftgelehrte Jurist sucht die Gesetze der Sicherung des Mein und Dein (wenn er, wie er soll, als Beamter der Regierung verfährt) nicht in seiner Vernunft, sondern im öffentlich gegebenen und höchsten

to the people; since this is a scholarly matter, they would fail completely to understand it and, as a result, would only get entangled in impertinent speculations and doubts. In such matters it is much safer to rely on the people's confidence in their teachers. The biblical theologian can also have no authority to ascribe a nonliteral—for example, a moral—meaning to statements in the text. And since there is no human interpreter of the Scriptures authorized by God, he must rather count on a supernatural opening of his understanding by a spirit that guides to all truth than allow reason to intervene and (without any higher authority) maintain its own interpretation. Finally, as far as our will and its fulfillment of God's commands is concerned, the biblical theologian must not rely on nature—that is, on man's own moral power (virtue)—but on grace (a supernatural but, at the same time, moral influence), which man can obtain only by an ardent faith that transforms his heart—a faith that itself, in turn, he can expect only through grace. If the biblical theologian meddles with his reason in any of these tenets, then, even granting that reason strives most sincerely and earnestly for that same objective, he leaps (like Romulus's brother) over the wall of ecclesiastical faith, the only thing that assures his salvation, and strays into the free and open fields of private judgment and philosophy. And there, having run away from the Church's government, he is exposed to all the dangers of anarchy. But note well that I am here speaking only of the *pure* (*purus, putus*) biblical theologian, who is not yet contaminated by the ill-reputed spirit of freedom that belongs to reason and philosophy. For as soon as we allow two different callings to combine and run together, we can form no clear notion of the characteristic that distinguishes each by itself.

B.

The Distinctive Characteristic of the Faculty of Law

The jurist, as an authority on the text, does not look to his reason for the laws that secure the *Mine* and *Thine,* but to the code of laws that has been publicly promulgated and sanctioned by the highest authority (if, as he should, he acts as a civil servant). To require him to prove the truth of these laws and their

Orts sanctionirten Gesetzbuch. Den Beweis der Wahrheit und Recht=
mäßigkeit derselben, ingleichen die Vertheidigung wider die dagegen ge=
machte Einwendung der Vernunft kann man billigerweise von ihm nicht
fordern. Denn die Verordnungen machen allererst, daß etwas recht ist,
und nun nachzufragen, ob auch die Verordnungen selbst recht sein mögen,
muß von den Juristen als ungereimt gerade zu abgewiesen werden. Es
wäre lächerlich, sich dem Gehorsam gegen einen äußern und obersten Wil=
len darum, weil dieser angeblich nicht mit der Vernunft übereinstimmt,
entziehen zu wollen. Denn darin besteht eben das Ansehen der Regierung,
daß sie den Unterthanen nicht die Freiheit läßt, nach ihren eigenen Be=
griffen, sondern nach Vorschrift der gesetzgebenden Gewalt über Recht und
Unrecht zu urtheilen.

In einem Stücke aber ist es mit der Juristenfacultät für die Praxis
doch besser bestellt, als mit der theologischen: daß nämlich jene einen sicht=
baren Ausleger der Gesetze hat, nämlich entweder an einem Richter, oder
in der Appellation von ihm an einer Gesetzcommission und (in der höch=
sten) am Gesetzgeber selbst, welches in Ansehung der auszulegenden
Sprüche eines heiligen Buchs der theologischen Facultät nicht so gut wird.
Doch wird dieser Vorzug andererseits durch einen nicht geringeren Nach=
theil aufgewogen, nämlich daß die weltlichen Gesetzbücher der Verände=
rung unterworfen bleiben müssen, nachdem die Erfahrung mehr oder bessere
Einsichten gewährt, dahingegen das heilige Buch keine Veränderung (Ver=
minderung oder Vermehrung) statuirt und für immer geschlossen zu sein
behauptet. Auch findet die Klage der Juristen, daß es beinah vergeblich
sei, eine genau bestimmte Norm der Rechtspflege (ius certum) zu hoffen,
beim biblischen Theologen nicht statt. Denn dieser läßt sich den Anspruch
nicht nehmen, daß seine Dogmatik nicht eine solche klare und auf alle
Fälle bestimmte Norm enthalte. Wenn überdem die juristischen Praktiker
(Advocaten oder Justizcommissarien), die dem Clienten schlecht gerathen
und ihn dadurch in Schaden versetzt haben, darüber doch nicht verant=
wortlich sein wollen (ob consilium nemo tenetur), so nehmen es doch die
theologischen Geschäftsmänner (Prediger und Seelsorger) ohne Bedenken
auf sich und stehen dafür, nämlich dem Tone nach, daß alles so auch in
der künftigen Welt werde abgeurtheilt werden, als sie es in dieser ab=
geschlossen haben; obgleich, wenn sie aufgefordert würden, sich förmlich zu
erklären, ob sie für die Wahrheit alles dessen, was sie auf biblische Autori=
tät geglaubt wissen wollen, mit ihrer Seele Gewähr zu leisten sich ge=

conformity with right, or to defend them against reason's objections, would be unfair. For these decrees first determine what is right, and the jurist must straightaway dismiss as nonsense the further question of whether the decrees themselves are right. To refuse to obey an external and supreme will on the grounds that it allegedly does not conform with reason would be absurd; for the dignity of the government consists precisely in this: that it does not leave its subjects free to judge what is right or wrong according to their own notions, but [determines right and wrong] for them by precepts of the legislative power.

In one respect, however, the faculty of law is better off in practice than the theology faculty: it has a visible interpreter of the law—namely, a judge or, if his decision is appealed, a legal commission, and (as the highest appeal) the legislator himself. The theological faculty is not so well provided for, when the sayings of its sacred book have to be interpreted. But this advantage is offset by a disadvantage at least equal to it: namely, that any secular code of laws always remains subject to change, as experience brings more or better insight, whereas the sacred code decrees that there will be no change (either by subtraction or addition), and maintains that it is closed forever. Furthermore, biblical theologians do not join in the jurist's complaint that it is all but vain to hope for a precisely determined norm for the administration of justice (*ius certus*); for they reject the claim that their dogma lacks a norm that is clear and determined for every case. Moreover, if the practicing lawyer (counsel or attorney-at-law) has harmed a client by giving him bad advice, he refuses to be held responsible for it (*ob consilium nemo tenetur* ["no one is bound by the advice he receives"]); but the practicing theologian (preacher or spiritual adviser) does not hesitate to take the responsibility on himself and to guarantee—at least to hear him talk—that any decision passed in the next world will correspond exactly with his decisions in this one. But he will probably decline if he is invited to declare formally that he will stake his soul on the truth of everything he would have us believe on the Bible's authority. And yet, the nature of the principles maintained by these public teachers

traueten, sie wahrscheinlicher Weise sich entschuldigen würden. Gleichwohl liegt es doch in der Natur der Grundsätze dieser Volkslehrer, die Richtig= keit ihrer Versicherung keinesweges bezweifeln zu lassen, welches sie freilich um desto sicherer thun können, weil sie in diesem Leben keine Widerlegung derselben durch Erfahrung befürchten dürfen.

C.
Eigenthümlichkeit der medicinischen Facultät.

Der Arzt ist ein Künstler, der doch, weil seine Kunst von der Natur unmittelbar entlehnt und um deswillen von einer Wissenschaft der Natur abgeleitet werden muß, als Gelehrter irgend einer Facultät untergeordnet ist, bei der er seine Schule gemacht haben und deren Beurtheilung er unterworfen bleiben muß. — Weil aber die Regierung an der Art, wie er die Gesundheit des Volks behandelt, nothwendig großes Interesse nimmt: so ist sie berechtigt durch eine Versammlung ausgewählter Geschäftsleute dieser Facultät (praktischer Ärzte) über das öffentliche Verfahren der Ärzte durch ein Obersanitätscollegium und Medicinalverordnungen Auf= sicht zu haben. Die letzteren aber bestehen wegen der besondern Beschaf= fenheit dieser Facultät, daß sie nämlich ihre Verhaltungsregeln nicht, wie die vorigen zwei obern, von Befehlen eines Oberen, sondern aus der Natur der Dinge selbst hernehmen muß — weshalb ihre Lehren auch ursprüng= lich der philosophischen Facultät, im weitesten Verstande genommen, an= gehören müßten —, nicht sowohl in dem, was die Ärzte thun, als was sie unterlassen sollen: nämlich erstlich, daß es fürs Publicum überhaupt Ärzte, zweitens, daß es keine Afterärzte gebe (kein ius impune occidendi nach dem Grundsatz: fiat experimentum in corpore vili). Da nun die Regierung nach dem ersten Princip für die öffentliche Bequemlich= keit, nach dem zweiten für die öffentliche Sicherheit (in der Gesund= heitsangelegenheit des Volks) sorgt, diese zwei Stücke aber eine Polizei ausmachen, so wird alle Medicinalordnung eigentlich nur die medici= nische Polizei betreffen.

Diese Facultät ist also viel freier als die beiden ersten unter den obern und der philosophischen sehr nahe verwandt; ja was die Lehren derselben betrifft, wodurch Ärzte gebildet werden, gänzlich frei, weil es für sie keine durch höchste Autorität sanctionirte, sondern nur aus der Natur geschöpfte Bücher geben kann, auch keine eigentlichen Gesetze (wenn man darunter

permits no doubt whatsoever that their assurances are correct—assurances they can give all the more safely because they need not fear that experience will refute them in this life.

C.
The Distinctive Characteristic of the Faculty of Medicine

Although medicine is an art, it is an art that is drawn directly from nature and must therefore be derived from a science of nature. So the physician, as a man of learning, must come under some faculty by which he must have been trained and to whose judgment he must remain subject. But since the way physicians deal with the people's health must be of great interest to the government, it is entitled to supervise their dealings with the public through an assembly chosen from the businessmen of this faculty (practicing doctors)—*a board of public health*—and through medical regulations. Unlike the other higher faculties, however, the faculty of medicine must derive its rules of procedure not from orders of the authorities but from the nature of things themselves, so that its teachings must have also belonged originally to the philosophy faculty, taken in its widest sense. And because of this special characteristic of the medical faculty, medical regulations deal not so much with what doctors should do as with what they should not do: they ensure, *first,* that there will be doctors for the public and, *secondly,* that there will be no spurious doctors (no *ius impune occidendi* ["law of killing with impunity"], according to the principle: *fiat experimentum in corpori vili* ["let experiments be made on worthless bodies"]). By the first of these principles, the government watches over the public's *convenience*, and by the second, over the public's *safety* (in the matter of the people's health). And since these two services are the function of a *police force,* all medical regulations really have to do only with *policing the medical profession.*

The medical faculty is, therefore, much freer than the other two higher faculties and closely akin to the Philosophy Faculty. Indeed, it is altogether free with regard to the teachings by which it *trains* doctors, since its texts cannot be sanctioned by the highest authorities but can be drawn only from nature. It can also have no laws strictly speaking (if by laws we mean the unalterable

den unveränderlichen Willen des Gesetzgebers versteht), sondern nur Verordnungen (Edicte), welche zu kennen nicht Gelehrsamkeit ist, als zu der
ein systematischer Inbegriff von Lehren erfordert wird, den zwar die Facultät besitzt, welchen aber (als in keinem Gesetzbuch enthalten) die Re-
5 gierung zu sanctioniren nicht Befugniß hat, sondern jener überlassen muß,
indessen sie durch Dispensatorien und Lazarethanstalten den Geschäftsleuten derselben ihre Praxis im öffentlichen Gebrauch nur zu befördern bedacht ist. — Diese Geschäftsmänner (die Ärzte) aber bleiben in Fällen,
welche als die medicinische Polizei betreffend die Regierung interessiren,
10 dem Urtheile ihrer Facultät unterworfen.

Zweiter Abschnitt.
Begriff und Eintheilung der untern Facultät.

Man kann die untere Facultät diejenige Klasse der Universität nennen,
die oder so fern sie sich nur mit Lehren beschäftigt, welche nicht auf den
15 Befehl eines Oberen zur Richtschnur angenommen werden. Nun kann es
zwar geschehen, daß man eine praktische Lehre aus Gehorsam befolgt; sie
aber darum, weil es befohlen ist (de par le Roi), für wahr anzunehmen,
ist nicht allein objectiv (als ein Urtheil, das nicht sein sollte), sondern
auch subjectiv (als ein solches, welches kein Mensch fällen kann) schlechter-
20 dings unmöglich. Denn der irren will, wie er sagt, irrt wirklich nicht und
nimmt das falsche Urtheil nicht in der That für wahr an, sondern giebt
nur ein Fürwahrhalten fälschlich vor, das in ihm doch nicht anzutreffen
ist. — Wenn also von der Wahrheit gewisser Lehren, die in öffentlichen
Vortrag gebracht werden sollen, die Rede ist, so kann sich der Lehrer des-
25 falls nicht auf höchsten Befehl berufen, noch der Lehrling vorgeben, sie auf
Befehl geglaubt zu haben, sondern nur wenn vom Thun geredet wird.
Alsdann aber muß er doch, daß ein solcher Befehl wirklich ergangen, im-
gleichen daß er ihm zu gehorchen verpflichtet oder wenigstens befugt sei,
durch ein freies Urtheil erkennen, widrigenfalls seine Annahme ein leeres
30 Vorgeben und Lüge ist. — Nun nennt man das Vermögen, nach der Autonomie, d. i. frei (Principien des Denkens überhaupt gemäß), zu urtheilen,
die Vernunft. Also wird die philosophische Facultät darum, weil sie für
die Wahrheit der Lehren, die sie aufnehmen oder auch nur einräumen
soll, stehen muß, in so fern als frei und nur unter der Gesetzgebung der
35 Vernunft, nicht der der Regierung stehend gedacht werden müssen.

will of the legislator), but only regulations (*edicts*); and since learning requires [as its object] a systematic content of teachings, knowledge of these regulations does not constitute the learning [of the medical faculty]. This faculty does indeed possess such learning; but since the government does not have the authority to sanction it (because it is not contained in any *code of laws*), it must leave this to the faculty's discretion and concern itself only with helping medical practitioners to be of service to the public, by establishing dispensaries and hospitals. These practitioners (physicians), however, remain subject to the judgment of their faculty in matters which concern the medical police and so interest the government.

Second Section
The Concept and Division of the Lower Faculty

The lower faculty is the rank in the university that occupies itself with teachings which are not adopted as directives by order of a superior, or in so far as they are not so adopted. Now we may well comply with a practical teaching out of obedience, but we can never accept it as true simply because we are ordered to (*de par le Roi*). This is not only objectively impossible (a judgment that *ought not* to be made), but also subjectively quite impossible (a judgment that no one *can* make). For the man who, as he says, wants to err does not really err and, in fact, accept the false judgment as true; he merely declares, falsely, an assent that is not to be found in him. So when it is a question of the *truth* of a certain teaching to be expounded in public, the teacher cannot appeal to a supreme command nor the pupil pretend that he believed it by order. This can happen only when it is a question of *action,* and even then the pupil must recognize by a *free* judgment that such a command was really issued and that he is obligated or at least entitled to obey it; otherwise, his acceptance of it would be an empty pretense and a lie. Now the power to judge autonomously—that is, freely (according to principles of thought in general)—is called reason. So the philosophy faculty, because it must answer for the truth of the teachings it is to adopt or even allow, must be conceived as free and subject only to laws given by reason, not by the government.

43

Auf einer Universität muß aber auch ein solches Departement ge=
stiftet, d. i. es muß eine philosophische Facultät sein. In Ansehung der
drei obern dient sie dazu, sie zu controlliren und ihnen eben dadurch nütz=
lich zu werden, weil auf Wahrheit (die wesentliche und erste Bedingung
der Gelehrsamkeit überhaupt) alles ankommt; die Nützlichkeit aber, welche
die oberen Facultäten zum Behuf der Regierung versprechen, nur ein
Moment vom zweiten Range ist. — Auch kann man allenfalls der theolo=
gischen Facultät den stolzen Anspruch, daß die philosophische ihre Magd
sei, einräumen (wobei doch noch immer die Frage bleibt: ob diese ihrer
gnädigen Frau die Fackel vorträgt oder die Schleppe nachträgt),
wenn man sie nur nicht verjagt, oder ihr den Mund zubindet; denn eben
diese Anspruchlosigkeit, blos frei zu sein, aber auch frei zu lassen, blos die
Wahrheit zum Vortheil jeder Wissenschaft auszumitteln und sie zum be=
liebigen Gebrauch der oberen Facultäten hinzustellen, muß sie der Regie=
rung selbst als unverdächtig, ja als unentbehrlich empfehlen.

Die philosophische Facultät enthält nun zwei Departemente, das eine
der historischen Erkenntniß (wozu Geschichte, Erdbeschreibung, ge=
lehrte Sprachkenntniß, Humanistik mit allem gehört, was die Naturkunde
von empirischem Erkenntniß darbietet), das andere der reinen Ver=
nunfterkenntnisse (reinen Mathematik und der reinen Philosophie,
Metaphysik der Natur und der Sitten) und beide Theile der Gelehrsam=
keit in ihrer wechselseitigen Beziehung auf einander. Sie erstreckt sich eben
darum auf alle Theile des menschlichen Wissens (mithin auch historisch
über die obern Facultäten), nur daß sie nicht alle (nämlich die eigenthüm=
lichen Lehren oder Gebote der obern) zum Inhalte, sondern zum Gegen=
stande ihrer Prüfung und Kritik in Absicht auf den Vortheil der Wissen=
schaften macht.

Die philosophische Facultät kann also alle Lehren in Anspruch nehmen,
um ihre Wahrheit der Prüfung zu unterwerfen. Sie kann von der Regie=
rung, ohne daß diese ihrer eigentlichen, wesentlichen Absicht zuwider handle,
nicht mit einem Interdict belegt werden, und die obern Facultäten müssen
sich ihre Einwürfe und Zweifel, die sie öffentlich vorbringt, gefallen lassen,
welches jene zwar allerdings lästig finden dürften, weil sie ohne solche
Kritiker in ihrem, unter welchem Titel es auch sei, einmal inne habenden
Besitz ungestört ruhen und dabei noch despotisch hätten befehlen können.
— Nur den Geschäftsleuten jener oberen Facultäten (den Geistlichen,
Rechtsbeamten und Ärzten) kann es allerdings verwehrt werden, daß sie

But a department of this kind, too, must be established at a university; in other words, a university must have a faculty of philosophy. Its function in relation to the three higher faculties is to control them and, in this way, be useful to them, since *truth* (the essential and first condition of learning in general) is the main thing, whereas the *utility* the higher faculties promise the government is of secondary importance. We can also grant the theology faculty's proud claim that the philosophy faculty is its handmaid (though the question remains, whether the servant is the mistress's *torchbearer* or *trainbearer*), provided it is not driven away or silenced. For the very *modesty* [of its claim]—merely to be free, as it leaves others free, to discover the truth for the benefit of all the sciences and to set it before the higher faculties to use as they will—must commend it to the government as above suspicion and, indeed, indispensable.

Now the philosophy faculty consists of two departments: a department of *historical knowledge* (including history, geography, philology and the humanities, along with all the empirical knowledge contained in the natural sciences), and a department of *pure rational knowledge* (pure mathematics and pure philosophy, the metaphysics of nature and of morals). And it also studies the relation of these two divisions of learning to each other. It therefore extends to all parts of human knowledge (including, from a historical viewpoint, the teachings of the higher faculties), though there are some parts (namely, the distinctive teachings and precepts of the higher faculties) which it does not treat as its own content, but as objects it will examine and criticize for the benefit of the sciences.

The philosophy faculty can, therefore, lay claim to any teaching, in order to test its truth. The government cannot forbid it to do this without acting against its own proper and essential purpose; and the higher faculties must put up with the objections and doubts it brings forward in public, though they may well find this irksome, since, were it not for such critics, they could rest undisturbed in possession of what they have once occupied, by whatever title, and rule over it despotically. Only the businessmen of the higher faculties (clergymen, legal officials, and doctors) can be prevented from contradicting in public the teachings that the government has entrusted to them to expound in fulfilling

45

den ihnen in Führung ihres respectiven Amts von der Regierung zum
Vortrage anvertrauten Lehren nicht öffentlich widersprechen und den Philo=
sophen zu spielen sich erkühnen; denn das kann nur den Facultäten, nicht
den von der Regierung bestellten Beamten erlaubt sein: weil diese ihr
Wissen nur von jenen her haben. Die letztern nämlich, z. B. Prediger und
Rechtsbeamte, wenn sie ihre Einwendungen und Zweifel gegen die geist=
liche oder weltliche Gesetzgebung ans Volk zu richten sich gelüsten ließen,
würden es dadurch gegen die Regierung aufwiegeln; dagegen die Facul=
täten sie nur gegen einander, als Gelehrte, richten, wovon das Volk prak=
tischerweise keine Notiz nimmt, selbst wenn sie auch zu seiner Kenntniß ge=
langen, weil es sich selbst bescheidet, daß Vernünfteln nicht seine Sache sei,
und sich daher verbunden fühlt, sich nur an dem zu halten, was ihm durch
die dazu bestellte Beamte der Regierung verkündigt wird. — Diese Frei=
heit aber, die der untern Facultät nicht geschmälert werden darf, hat den
Erfolg, daß die obern Facultäten (selbst besser belehrt) die Beamte immer
mehr in das Gleis der Wahrheit bringen, welche dann ihrerseits, auch über
ihre Pflicht besser aufgeklärt, in der Abänderung des Vortrags keinen An=
stoß finden werden; da er nur ein besseres Verständniß der Mittel zu eben
demselben Zweck ist, welches ohne polemische und nur Unruhe erregende
Angriffe auf bisher bestandene Lehrweisen mit völliger Beibehaltung des
Materialen derselben gar wohl geschehen kann.

Dritter Abschnitt.
Vom gesetzwidrigen Streit der oberen Facultäten mit der unteren.

Gesetzwidrig ist ein öffentlicher Streit der Meinungen, mithin ein
gelehrter Streit entweder der Materie wegen, wenn es gar nicht erlaubt
wäre, über einen öffentlichen Satz zu streiten, weil es gar nicht erlaubt
ist, über ihn und seinen Gegensatz öffentlich zu urtheilen; oder blos der
Form wegen, wenn die Art, wie er geführt wird, nicht in objectiven Grün=
den, die auf die Vernunft des Gegners gerichtet sind, sondern in subjectiven,
sein Urtheil durch Neigung bestimmenden Bewegursachen besteht, um
ihn durch List (wozu auch Bestechung gehört) oder Gewalt (Drohung) zur
Einwilligung zu bringen.

Nun wird der Streit der Facultäten um den Einfluß aufs Volk ge=

their respective offices, and from venturing to play the philosopher's role; for the faculties alone, not the officials appointed by the government, can be allowed to do this, since these officials get their knowledge from the faculties. If, that is to say, these officials—for example, clergymen and legal officials—should want to put before the public their objections and doubts about ecclesiastical and civil laws that have been given, they would be inciting the people to rebel against the government. The faculties, on the other hand, put their objections and doubts only to one another, as scholars, and the people pay no attention to such matters in a practical way, even if they should hear of them; for, agreeing that these subtleties are not their affair, they feel obliged to be content with what the government officials, appointed for this purpose, announce to them. But the result of this freedom, which the philosophy faculty must enjoy unimpaired, is that the higher faculties (themselves better instructed) will lead these officials more and more onto the way of truth. And the officials, for their own part, also more enlightened about their duty, will not be repelled at changing their exposition, since the new way involves nothing more than a clearer insight into means for achieving the same end. And such a change can well come about without polemics and attacks, that only stir up unrest, on the traditional way of teaching, when [it is seen that] the content to be taught is preserved in its entirety.

Third Section
On the Illegal Conflict of the Higher Faculties with the Lower Faculty

A public conflict of views, hence a scholarly debate, can be illegal by reason of its matter or its form. It would be illegal by reason of its *matter* if it were not permissible to *debate*, in this way, about a public proposition because it was not permissible to *judge* publicly this proposition and its opposite. It would be illegal by reason of its *form*, or the way in which the debate is carried on, if one of the parties relied, not on objective grounds directed to his adversary's reason, but on subjective grounds, trying to determine his judgment through his *inclinations* and so to gain his assent by fraud (including bribery) or force (threats).

Now the faculties engage in public conflict in order to influence the people, and each can acquire this influence only by

führt, und diesen Einfluß können sie nur bekommen, so fern jede derselben das Volk glauben machen kann, daß sie das Heil desselben am besten zu befördern verstehe, dabei aber doch in der Art, wie sie dieses auszurichten gedenken, einander gerade entgegengesetzt sind.

Das Volk aber setzt sein Heil zu oberst nicht in der Freiheit, sondern in seinen natürlichen Zwecken, also in diesen drei Stücken: nach dem Tode selig, im Leben unter andern Mitmenschen des Seinen durch öffentliche Gesetze gesichert, endlich des physischen Genusses des Lebens an sich selbst (d. i. der Gesundheit und langen Lebens) gewärtig zu sein.

Die philosophische Facultät aber, die sich auf alle diese Wünsche nur durch Vorschriften, die sie aus der Vernunft entlehnt, einlassen kann, mithin dem Princip der Freiheit anhänglich ist, hält sich nur an das, was der Mensch selbst hinzuthun kann und soll: rechtschaffen zu leben, keinem Unrecht zu thun, sich mäßig im Genusse und duldend in Krankheiten und dabei vornehmlich auf die Selbsthülfe der Natur rechnend zu verhalten; zu welchem Allem es freilich nicht eben großer Gelehrsamkeit bedarf, wobei man dieser aber auch größtentheils entbehren kann, wenn man nur seine Neigungen bändigen und seiner Vernunft das Regiment anvertrauen wollte, was aber als Selbstbemühung dem Volk gar nicht gelegen ist.

Die drei obern Facultäten werden nun vom Volk (das in obigen Lehren für seine Neigung zu genießen und Abneigung sich darum zu bearbeiten schlechten Ernst findet) aufgefordert, ihrerseits Propositionen zu thun, die annehmlicher sind: und da lauten die Ansprüche an die Gelehrten, wie folgt: Was ihr Philosophen da schwatzet, wußte ich längst von selbst; ich will aber von euch als Gelehrten wissen: wie, wenn ich auch ruchlos gelebt hätte, ich dennoch kurz vor dem Thorschlusse mir ein Einlaßbillet ins Himmelreich verschaffen, wie, wenn ich auch Unrecht habe, ich doch meinen Proceß gewinnen, und wie, wenn ich auch meine körperlichen Kräfte nach Herzenslust benutzt und mißbraucht hätte, ich doch gesund bleiben und lange leben könne. Dafür habt ihr ja studirt, daß ihr mehr wissen müßt als unser einer (von euch Idioten genannt), der auf nichts weiter als auf gesunden Verstand Anspruch macht. — Es ist aber hier, als ob das Volk zu dem Gelehrten wie zum Wahrsager und Zauberer ginge, der mit übernatürlichen Dingen Bescheid weiß; denn der Ungelehrte macht sich von einem Gelehrten, dem er etwas zumuthet, gern übergroße Begriffe. Daher ist es natürlicherweise vorauszusehen, daß, wenn sich jemand für einen solchen Wundermann auszugeben nur dreust genug ist,

convincing the people that it knows best how to promote their welfare. But as for the way they propose to accomplish this, the lower faculty is diametrically opposed to the higher faculties.

The people conceive of their welfare, not primarily as freedom, but as [the realization of] their natural ends and so as these three things: being *happy* after death, having their *possessions* guaranteed by public laws during their life in society, and finally, looking forward to the physical enjoyment of *life* itself (that is, health and a long life).

But the philosophy faculty can deal with all these wishes only by precepts it derives from reason. It depends, accordingly, on the principle of freedom and limits itself to saying what man himself can and should do toward fulfilling these wishes—live *righteously,* commit no *injustice,* and, by being *moderate* in his pleasures and patient in his illnesses, rely primarily on the self-help of nature. None of this, indeed, requires great learning; but in these matters we can, for the most part, dispense with learning if we would only restrain our inclinations and be ruled by our reason. But since this requires self-exertion, it does not suit the people.

So the people (who find the philosophy faculty's teaching a poor substitute for their inclination to *enjoyment* and their aversion from *working* for it) invite the higher faculties to make them more acceptable proposals. And the demands they make on these scholars run like this. "As for the *philosophers'* twaddle, I've known that all along. What I want you, as men of learning, to tell me is this: if I've been a *scoundrel* all my life, how can I get an eleventh-hour ticket to heaven? If I've *broken* the law, how can I still win my case? And even if I've used and *abused* my physical powers as I've pleased, how can I stay healthy and live a long time? Surely this is why you have studied—so that you would know more than someone like ourselves (you call us laymen), who can claim nothing more than sound understanding." But now the people are approaching these scholars as if they were soothsayers and magicians, with knowledge of supernatural things; for if an ignorant man expects something from a scholar, he readily forms exaggerated notions of him. So we can naturally expect that if someone has the effrontery to give himself out as such a miracle-worker, the

49

ihm das Volk zufallen und die Seite der philosophischen Facultät mit Ver=
achtung verlassen werde.

Die Geschäftsleute der drei oberen Facultäten sind aber jederzeit
solche Wundermänner, wenn der philosophischen nicht erlaubt wird, ihnen
öffentlich entgegen zu arbeiten, nicht um ihre Lehren zu stürzen, sondern
nur der magischen Kraft, die ihnen und den damit verbundenen Obser=
vanzen das Publicum abergläubisch beilegt, zu widersprechen, als wenn es
bei einer passiven Übergebung an solche kunstreiche Führer alles Selbst=
thuns überhoben und mit großer Gemächlichkeit durch sie zu Erreichung
jener angelegenen Zwecke schon werde geleitet werden.

Wenn die obern Facultäten solche Grundsätze annehmen (welches frei=
lich ihre Bestimmung nicht ist), so sind und bleiben sie ewig im Streit mit
der unteren; dieser Streit aber ist auch gesetzwidrig, weil sie die Über=
tretung der Gesetze nicht allein als kein Hinderniß, sondern wohl gar als
erwünschte Veranlassung ansehen, ihre große Kunst und Geschicklichkeit zu
zeigen, alles wieder gut, ja noch besser zu machen, als es ohne dieselbe ge=
schehen würde.

Das Volk will geleitet, d. i. (in der Sprache der Demagogen) es
will betrogen sein. Es will aber nicht von den Facultätsgelehrten (denn
deren Weisheit ist ihm zu hoch), sondern von den Geschäftsmännern der=
selben, die das Machwerk (savoir faire) verstehen, von den Geistlichen,
Justizbeamten, Ärzten, geleitet sein, die als Praktiker die vortheilhafteste
Vermuthung für sich haben; dadurch dann die Regierung, die nur durch
sie aufs Volk wirken kann, selbst verleitet wird, den Facultäten eine
Theorie aufzudringen, die nicht aus der reinen Einsicht der Gelehrten der=
selben entsprungen, sondern auf den Einfluß berechnet ist, den ihre Ge=
schäftsmänner dadurch aufs Volk haben können, weil dieses natürlicher=
weise dem am meisten anhängt, wobei es am wenigsten nöthig hat, sich
selbst zu bemühen und sich seiner eigenen Vernunft zu bedienen, und wo
am besten die Pflichten mit den Neigungen in Verträglichkeit gebracht
werden können; z. B. im theologischen Fache, daß buchstäblich „Glauben“,
ohne zu untersuchen (selbst ohne einmal recht zu verstehen), was geglaubt
werden soll, für sich heilbringend sei und daß durch Begehung gewisser vor=
schriftmäßigen Formalien unmittelbar Verbrechen können abgewaschen
werden; oder im juristischen, daß die Befolgung des Gesetzes nach den
Buchstaben der Untersuchung des Sinnes des Gesetzgebers überhebe.

Hier ist nun ein wesentlicher, nie beizulegender gesetzwidriger Streit

people will flock to him and contemptuously desert the philosophy faculty.

But the businessmen of the three higher faculties will always be such miracle-workers, unless the philosophy faculty is allowed to counteract them publicly—not in order to overthrow their teachings but only to deny the magic power that the public superstitiously attributes to these teachings and the rites connected with them—as if, by passively surrendering themselves to such skillful guides, the people would be excused from any activity of their own and led, in ease and comfort, to achieve the ends they desire.

If the higher faculties adopt such principles (and it is certainly not their function to do this), then they are and always will be in conflict with the lower faculty. But this conflict is also *illegal*; for the higher faculties, instead of viewing transgressions of the law as hindrances, welcome them as occasions for showing their great art and skill in making everything as good as ever, and, indeed, better than it would otherwise have been.

The people want to be *led,* that is (as demagogues say), they want to be *duped.* But they want to be led not by the scholars of the faculties (whose wisdom is too high for them), but by the businessmen of the faculties—clergymen, legal officials, and doctors—who understand a botched job (*savoir faire*) and have the people's confidence. And so the government, which can work on the people only through these practitioners, will itself be *led* to obtrude on the faculties a theory that arises, not from the pure insight of their scholars, but from calculations of the influence their practitioners can exert on the people by it. For the people naturally adhere most to doctrines which demand the least self-exertion and the least use of their own reason, and which can best accommodate their duties to their inclinations—in theology, for example, the doctrine that they can be saved merely by an implicit faith, without having to examine (or even really know) what they are supposed to believe, or that their performance of certain prescribed rites will itself wash away their transgressions; or in law, the doctrine that compliance with the letter of the law exempts them from examining the legislator's intentions.

51

zwischen den obern und der untern Facultät, weil das Princip der Gesetz=
gebung für die ersteren, welches man der Regierung unterlegt, eine von
ihr autorisirte Gesetzlosigkeit selbst sein würde. — Denn da Neigung und
überhaupt das, was jemand seiner Privatabsicht zuträglich findet, sich
schlechterdings nicht zu einem Gesetze qualificirt, mithin auch nicht als ein
solches von den obern Facultäten vorgetragen werden kann, so würde eine
Regierung, welche dergleichen sanctionirte, indem sie wider die Vernunft
selbst verstößt, jene obere Facultäten mit der philosophischen in einen
Streit versetzen, der gar nicht geduldet werden kann, indem er diese gänz=
lich vernichtet, welches freilich das kürzeste, aber auch (nach dem Ausdruck
der Ärzte) ein in Todesgefahr bringendes heroisches Mittel ist, einen
Streit zu Ende zu bringen.

Vierter Abschnitt.
Vom gesetzmäßigen Streit der oberen Facultäten
mit der unteren.

Welcherlei Inhalts auch die Lehren immer sein mögen, deren öffent=
lichen Vortrag die Regierung durch ihre Sanction den obern Facultäten
aufzulegen befugt sein mag, so können sie doch nur als Statute, die von
ihrer Willkür ausgehen, und als menschliche Weisheit, die nicht unfehlbar
ist, angenommen und verehrt werden. Weil indessen die Wahrheit der=
selben ihr durchaus nicht gleichgültig sein darf, in Ansehung welcher sie
der Vernunft (deren Interesse die philosophische Facultät zu besorgen hat)
unterworfen bleiben müssen, dieses aber nur durch Verstattung völliger
Freiheit einer öffentlichen Prüfung derselben möglich ist, so wird, weil will=
kürliche, obzwar höchsten Orts sanctionirte, Satzungen mit den durch die
Vernunft als nothwendig behaupteten Lehren nicht so von selbst immer zu=
sammenstimmen dürften, erstlich zwischen den obern Facultäten und der
untern der Streit unvermeidlich, zweitens aber auch gesetzmäßig sein,
und dieses nicht blos als Befugniß, sondern auch als Pflicht der letzteren,
wenn gleich nicht die ganze Wahrheit öffentlich zu sagen, doch darauf be=
dacht zu sein, daß alles, was, so gesagt, als Grundsatz aufgestellt wird,
wahr sei.

Wenn die Quelle gewisser sanctionirter Lehren historisch ist, so
mögen diese auch noch so sehr als heilig dem unbedenklichen Gehorsam des
Glaubens anempfohlen werden: die philosophische Facultät ist berechtigt,

[If the higher faculties adopt such principles], they are involved in an essential and irreconcilable conflict with the lower faculty. And this conflict is illegal because, if the government legislated for the higher faculties according to the principle attributed to it [in the preceding paragraph], its own principle would authorize anarchy itself. *Inclination* and, in general, what someone finds useful for his *private purposes* can never qualify as a law, and so cannot be set forth as a law by the higher faculties. A government that sanctioned such principles would offend against reason itself and, by this, bring the higher faculties into conflict with the lower faculty—a conflict that cannot be tolerated because it would completely destroy the philosophy faculty. This, admittedly, is the quickest way of ending a conflict; but it is also (in medical terms) a *heroic* means—one that endangers life.

Fourth Section
On the Legal Conflict of the Higher Faculties with the Lower Faculty

Regardless of their content, any teachings that the government may be entitled to sanction for public exposition by the higher faculties can be accepted and respected only as statutes proceeding from [the government's] choice and as human wisdom, which is not infallible. But the government cannot be completely indifferent to the truth of these teachings, and in this respect they must remain subject to reason (whose interests the philosophy faculty has to safeguard). Now this is possible only if complete freedom to examine these teachings in public is permitted. So, since arbitrary propositions, though sanctioned by the supreme authority, may not always harmonize with the teachings reason maintains as necessary, there will be a conflict between the higher and lower faculties which is, first, *inevitable*, but second, *legal* as well; for the lower faculty has not only the title but also the duty, if not to state the *whole* truth in public, at least to see to it that *everything* put forward in public as a principle is true.

If the source of a sanctioned teaching is *historical,* then—no matter how highly it may be commended as sacred to the unhesitating obedience of faith—the philosophy faculty is entitled and indeed obligated to investigate its origin with critical

53

ja verbunden, diesem Ursprunge mit kritischer Bedenklichkeit nachzuspüren. Ist sie rational, ob sie gleich im Tone einer historischen Erkenntniß (als Offenbarung) aufgestellt worden, so kann ihr (der untern Facultät) nicht gewehrt werden, die Vernunftgründe der Gesetzgebung aus dem historischen Vortrage herauszusuchen und überdem, ob sie technisch= oder moralisch= praktisch sind, zu würdigen. Wäre endlich der Quell der sich als Gesetz an= kündigenden Lehre gar nur ästhetisch, d. i. auf ein mit einer Lehre ver= bundenes Gefühl gegründet (welches, da es kein objectives Princip abgiebt, nur als subjectiv gültig, ein allgemeines Gesetz daraus zu machen untaug= lich, etwa frommes Gefühl eines übernatürlichen Einflusses sein würde), so muß es der philosophischen Facultät frei stehen, den Ursprung und Ge= halt eines solchen angeblichen Belehrungsgrundes mit kalter Vernunft öffentlich zu prüfen und zu würdigen, ungeschreckt durch die Heiligkeit des Gegenstandes, den man zu fühlen vorgiebt, und entschlossen dieses ver= meinte Gefühl auf Begriffe zu bringen. — Folgendes enthält die formale Grundsätze der Führung eines solchen Streits und die sich daraus ergebende Folgen.

1) Dieser Streit kann und soll nicht durch friedliche Übereinkunft (amicabilis compositio) beigelegt werden, sondern bedarf (als Proceß) einer Sentenz, d. i. des rechtskräftigen Spruchs eines Richters (der Ver= nunft); denn es könnte nur durch Unlauterkeit, Verheimlichung der Ur= sachen des Zwistes und Beredung geschehen, daß er beigelegt würde, der= gleichen Maxime aber dem Geiste einer philosophischen Facultät, als der auf öffentliche Darstellung der Wahrheit geht, ganz zuwider ist.

2) Er kann nie aufhören, und die philosophische Facultät ist diejenige, die dazu jederzeit gerüstet sein muß. Denn statutarische Vorschriften der Regierung in Ansehung der öffentlich vorzutragenden Lehren werden immer sein müssen, weil die unbeschränkte Freiheit, alle seine Meinungen ins Publicum zu schreien, theils der Regierung, theils aber auch diesem Publi= cum selbst gefährlich werden müßte. Alle Satzungen der Regierung aber, weil sie von Menschen ausgehen, wenigstens von diesen sanctionirt werden, bleiben jederzeit der Gefahr des Irrthums oder der Zweckwidrigkeit unter= worfen; mithin sind sie es auch in Ansehung der Sanction der Regierung, womit diese die obere Facultäten versieht. Folglich kann die philosophische Facultät ihre Rüstung gegen die Gefahr, womit die Wahrheit, deren Schutz ihr aufgetragen ist, bedroht wird, nie ablegen, weil die obere Facultäten ihre Begierde zu herrschen nie ablegen werden.

scrupulosity. If the teaching, though presented in the manner of historical knowledge (as revelation), has a *rational* origin, the lower faculty cannot be prevented from investigating, in the historical narrative, the rational basis of this legislation and also evaluating it as either technically or morally practical. Finally, the source of a teaching proclaimed as law may be only *aesthetic*: in other words, the teaching may be based on a feeling connected with it (for example, a pious feeling of supernatural influence—although, since feeling yields no objective principle, it is only subjectively valid and cannot provide the basis for a universal law). In this case the philosophy faculty must be free to examine in public and to evaluate with cold reason the source and content of this alleged basis of doctrine, unintimidated by the sacredness of the object which has supposedly been experienced and determined to bring this alleged feeling to concepts. The following paragraphs contain the formal principles of procedure for such a conflict and the consequences resulting from it.

1) This conflict cannot and should not be settled by an amicable accommodation (*amicabilis compositio*), but (as a lawsuit) calls for a verdict, that is, the decision of a judge (reason) which has the force of law. For the dispute could be settled only through dishonesty, by [the lower faculty's] concealing the cause of the dissension and letting itself be persuaded; but a maxim of this kind is directly opposed to the spirit of a *philosophy* faculty, which has the public presentation of truth as its function.

2) This conflict can never end, and it is the philosophy faculty that must always be prepared to keep it going. For there must always be statutory precepts of the government regarding teachings to be set forth in public, since unlimited freedom to proclaim any sort of opinion publicly is bound to be dangerous both to the government and to the public itself. But because all the government's statutes proceed from men, or are at least sanctioned by them, there is always the danger that they may be erroneous or unsuitable; and this applies also to the statutes that the government's sanction supplies to the higher faculties. Consequently, the philosophy faculty can never lay aside its arms in the face of the danger that threatens the truth entrusted to its protection, because the higher faculties will never give up their desire to rule.

3) Dieser Streit kann dem Ansehen der Regierung nie Abbruch thun. Denn er ist nicht ein Streit der Facultäten mit der Regierung, sondern einer Facultät mit der andern, dem die Regierung ruhig zusehen kann; weil, ob sie zwar gewisse Sätze der obern in ihren besondern Schutz genommen hat, so fern sie solche der letzteren ihren Geschäftsleuten zum öffentlichen Vortrage vorschreibt, so hat sie doch nicht die Facultäten, als gelehrte Gesellschaften, wegen der Wahrheit dieser ihrer öffentlich vorzutragenden Lehren, Meinungen und Behauptungen, sondern nur wegen ihres (der Regierung) eigenen Vortheils in Schutz genommen, weil es ihrer Würde nicht gemäß sein würde, über den innern Wahrheitsgehalt derselben zu entscheiden und so selbst den Gelehrten zu spielen. — Die obere Facultäten sind nämlich der Regierung für nichts weiter verantwortlich, als für die Instruction und Belehrung, die sie ihren Geschäftsleuten zum öffentlichen Vortrage geben; denn die laufen ins Publicum als bürgerliches gemeines Wesen und sind daher, weil sie dem Einfluß der Regierung auf dieses Abbruch thun könnten, dieser ihrer Sanction unterworfen. Dagegen gehen die Lehren und Meinungen, welche die Facultäten unter dem Namen der Theoretiker unter einander abzumachen haben, in eine andere Art von Publicum, nämlich in das eines gelehrten gemeinen Wesens, welches sich mit Wissenschaften beschäftigt; wovon das Volk sich selbst bescheidet, daß es nichts davon versteht, die Regierung aber mit gelehrten Händeln sich zu befassen für sich nicht anständig findet*).

---

*) Dagegen, wenn der Streit vor dem bürgerlichen gemeinen Wesen (öffentlich, z. B. auf Kanzeln) geführt würde, wie es die Geschäftsleute (unter dem Namen der Praktiker) gern versuchen, so wird er unbefugterweise vor den Richterstuhl des Volks (dem in Sachen der Gelehrsamkeit gar kein Urtheil zusteht) gezogen und hört auf, ein gelehrter Streit zu sein; da dann jener Zustand des gesetzwidrigen Streits, wovon oben Erwähnung geschehen, eintritt, wo Lehren den Neigungen des Volks angemessen vorgetragen werden und der Same des Aufruhrs und der Factionen ausgestreut, die Regierung aber dadurch in Gefahr gebracht wird. Diese eigenmächtig sich selbst dazu aufwerfende Volkstribunen treten so fern aus dem Gelehrtenstande, greifen in die Rechte der bürgerlichen Verfassung (Welthändel) ein und sind eigentlich die Neologen, deren mit Recht verhaßter Name aber sehr mißverstanden wird, wenn er jede Urheber einer Neuigkeit in Lehren und Lehrformen trifft. (Denn warum sollte das Alte eben immer das Bessere sein?) Dagegen diejenige eigentlich damit gebrandmarkt zu werden verdienen, welche eine ganz andere Regierungsform, oder vielmehr eine Regierungslosigkeit (Anarchie) einführen, indem sie das, was eine Sache der Gelehrsamkeit ist, der Stimme des Volks zur Entscheidung übergeben, dessen Urtheil sie durch Einfluß auf seine Gewohnheiten, Gefühle und

3) This conflict can never detract from the dignity of the government. The conflict is not between the faculties and the government but between one faculty and another, and the government can look on unmoved. Though it has indeed taken certain tenets of the higher faculties under its own protection, by directing the businessmen of these faculties to expound them to the public, it is not protecting the higher faculties, as learned societies, on account of the truth of these teachings, views and opinions they are to expound publicly, but only for the sake of its (the government's) own advantage; for it would be beneath the government's dignity to decide about the intrinsic truth of these tenets and so to play the role of scholar. The higher faculties, in other words, must answer to the government only for the instruction and information they give their businessmen to expound to the public; for these circulate among the people as a *civil* community and, because they could impair the government's influence over it, are subject to its sanction. On the other hand, the teachings and views that the faculties, as theorists, have to settle with one another are directed to a different kind of public—a *learned* community devoted to the sciences; and since the people are resigned to understanding nothing about this, the government does not see fit to intervene in scholarly discussions.* The rank of the higher faculties (as the right side of the parliament of learning) supports the

---

*On the other hand, if the businessmen of the faculties (in their role of practitioners) bring the conflict before the civil community (publicly—from the pulpits, for example), as they are prone to do, they drag it illegitimately before the judgment seat of the people (who are not competent to judge in scholarly matters), and it ceases to be a scholarly debate. And then begins the state of illegal conflict mentioned above, in which doctrines in keeping with the people's inclinations are set forth, the seeds of insurrection and factions are sown, and the government is thereby endangered. These self-appointed tribunes of the people, in doing this, renounce the learned professions, encroach on the rights of the civil constitution (stir up political struggles), and really deserve to be called neologists. This justly hated name is badly misused when it is applied indiscriminately to every author of innovations in doctrine and pedagogical method (for why should the old always be better than the new?). But those who introduce a completely different form of government, or rather a lack of any government (anarchy), by handing over scholarly questions to the decision of the people, really deserve to be branded neologists; for they can steer the judgment of the people in whatever direction

Die Classe der obern Facultäten (als die rechte Seite des Parlaments der Gelahrtheit) vertheidigt die Statute der Regierung, indessen daß es in einer so freien Verfassung, als die sein muß, wo es um Wahrheit zu thun ist, auch eine Oppositionspartei (die linke Seite) geben muß, welche die Bank der philosophischen Facultät ist, weil ohne deren strenge Prüfung und Einwürfe die Regierung von dem, was ihr selbst ersprießlich oder nachtheilig sein dürfte, nicht hinreichend belehrt werden würde. — Wenn aber die Geschäftsleute der Facultäten in Ansehung der für den öffent= lichen Vortrag gegebenen Verordnung für ihren Kopf Änderungen machen wollten, so kann die Aufsicht der Regierung diese als Neuerer, welche ihr gefährlich werden könnten, in Anspruch nehmen und doch gleichwohl über sie nicht unmittelbar, sondern nur nach dem von der obern Facultät ein= gezogenen allerunterthänigsten Gutachten absprechen, weil diese Geschäfts= leute nur durch die Facultät von der Regierung zu dem Vortrage ge= wisser Lehren haben angewiesen werden können.

4) Dieser Streit kann sehr wohl mit der Eintracht des gelehrten und bürgerlichen gemeinen Wesens in Maximen zusammen bestehen, deren Be= folgung einen beständigen Fortschritt beider Classen von Facultäten zu größerer Vollkommenheit bewirken muß und endlich zur Entlassung von allen Einschränkungen der Freiheit des öffentlichen Urtheils durch die Willkür der Regierung vorbereitet.

Auf diese Weise könnte es wohl dereinst dahin kommen, daß die Letzten die Ersten (die untere Facultät die obere) würden, zwar nicht in der Macht= habung, aber doch in Berathung des Machthabenden (der Regierung), als welche in der Freiheit der philosophischen Facultät und der ihr daraus erwachsenden Einsicht besser als in ihrer eigenen absoluten Autorität Mittel zu Erreichung ihrer Zwecke antreffen würde.

Resultat.

Dieser Antagonism, d. i. Streit zweier mit einander zu einem ge= meinschaftlichen Endzweck vereinigten Parteien, (concordia discors, dis= cordia concors) ist also kein Krieg, d. i. keine Zwietracht aus der Ent= gegensetzung der Endabsichten in Ansehung des gelehrten Mein und Dein,

---

Neigungen nach Belieben lenken und so einer gesetzmäßigen Regierung den Einfluß abgewinnen können.

3*

government's statutes; but in as free a system of government as must exist when it is a question of truth, there must also be an opposition party (the left side), and this is the philosophy faculty's bench. For without its rigorous examinations and objections, the government would not be adequately informed about what could be to its own advantage or detriment. But if the businessmen of the faculties should want, on their own initiative, to make changes in the decrees given for them to expound publicly, then the government in its vigilance could lay claim to [jurisdiction over] them as *innovators* who could be dangerous to it. It could not, however, pass judgment on them directly, but only in accordance with the most loyal verdict drawn from the higher faculties, since it is only *through the faculty* that the government can direct these businessmen to expound certain teachings.

4) This conflict is quite compatible with an agreement of the learned and civil community in maxims which, if observed, must bring about a constant progress of both ranks of the faculties toward greater perfection, and finally prepare the way for the government to remove all restrictions that its choice has put on freedom of public judgment.

In this way, it could well happen that the last would some day be first (the lower faculty would be the higher)—not, indeed, in authority, but in counseling the authority (the government). For the government may find the freedom of the philosophy faculty, and the increased insight gained from this freedom, a better means for achieving its ends than its own absolute authority.

Outcome

So this antagonism, that is, this *conflict* of two parties united in [their striving toward] one and the same final end (*concordia discors, discordia concors*), is not a *war*, that is, not a dispute arising from conflicting final aims regarding the *Mine* and *Thine* of learning. And since, like the political Mine and

they please, by working on their habits, feelings, and inclinations, and so win them away from the influence of a legitimate government.

welches so wie das politische aus Freiheit und Eigenthum besteht, wo jene als Bedingung nothwendig vor diesem vorhergehen muß; folglich den oberen Facultäten kein Recht verstattet werden kann, ohne daß es der unteren zugleich erlaubt bleibe, ihre Bedenklichkeit über dasselbe an das gelehrte Publicum zu bringen.

Anhang

einer Erläuterung des Streits der Facultäten durch das Bei= spiel desjenigen zwischen der theologischen und philosophischen.

I.

Materie des Streits.

Der biblische Theolog ist eigentlich der Schriftgelehrte für den Kirchenglauben, der auf Statuten, d. i. auf Gesetzen beruht, die aus der Willkür eines andern ausfließen; dagegen ist der rationale der Ver= nunftgelehrte für den Religionsglauben, folglich denjenigen, der auf innern Gesetzen beruht, die sich aus jedes Menschen eigener Vernunft entwickeln lassen. Daß dieses so sei, d. i. daß Religion nie auf Satzungen (so hohen Ursprungs sie immer sein mögen) gegründet werden könne, er= hellt selbst aus dem Begriffe der Religion. Nicht der Inbegriff gewisser Lehren als göttlicher Offenbarungen (denn der heißt Theologie), sondern der aller unserer Pflichten überhaupt als göttlicher Gebote (und subjectiv der Maxime sie als solche zu befolgen) ist Religion. Religion unterscheidet sich nicht der Materie, d. i. dem Object, nach in irgend einem Stücke von der Moral, denn sie geht auf Pflichten überhaupt, sondern ihr Unterschied von dieser ist blos formal, d. i. eine Gesetzgebung der Vernunft, um der Moral durch die aus dieser selbst erzeugte Idee von Gott auf den mensch= lichen Willen zu Erfüllung aller seiner Pflichten Einfluß zu geben. Darum ist sie aber auch nur eine einzige, und es giebt nicht verschiedene Religio= nen, aber wohl verschiedene Glaubensarten an göttliche Offenbarung und deren statutarische Lehren, die nicht aus der Vernunft entspringen können, d. i. verschiedene Formen der sinnlichen Vorstellungsart des göttlichen Willens, um ihm Einfluß auf die Gemüther zu verschaffen, unter denen das Christenthum, so viel wir wissen, die schicklichste Form ist. Dies findet sich nun in der Bibel aus zwei ungleichartigen Stücken zusammengesetzt, dem

Thine, this consists in *freedom* and *property,* with freedom necessarily preceding property as its condition, any right granted to the higher faculty entails permission for the lower faculty to bring its scruples about this right before the learned public.

Appendix

The Conflict between the Theology and Philosophy Faculties, as an Example to Clarify the Conflict of the Faculties

I.

Subject Matter of the Conflict

A biblical theologian is, properly speaking, one *versed in the Scriptures* with regard to *ecclesiastical faith,* which is based on statutes—that is, on laws proceeding from another person's act of choice. A rational theologian, on the other hand, is one *versed in reason* with regard to *religious* faith, which is based on inner laws that can be developed from every man's own reason. The very concept of religion shows that it can never be based on decrees (no matter how high their source); for religion is not the sum of certain teachings regarded as divine revelations (that is called theology), but the sum of all our duties regarded as divine *commands* (and, on the subject's part, the maxim of fulfilling them as such). As far as its matter or object is concerned, religion does not differ in any point from morality, for it is concerned with duties as such. Its distinction from morality is a merely formal one: that reason in its legislation uses the Idea of God, which is derived from morality itself, to give morality influence on man's will to fulfill all his duties. This is why there is only one religion. Although there are indeed different varieties of belief in divine revelation and its statutory teachings, which cannot spring from reason—that is, different forms in which the divine will is represented sensibly so as to give it influence on our minds—there are not different religions. Of these forms Christianity, as far as we know, is the most adequate. Now Christianity, as found in the Bible, is composed of two heterogeneous elements, one of which comprises the canon of

einen, welches den Kanon, dem andern, was das Organon oder Vehikel der Religion enthält, wovon der erste der reine Religionsglaube (ohne Statuten auf bloßer Vernunft gegründet), der andere der Kirchenglaube, der ganz auf Statuten beruht, genannt werden kann, die einer Offenbarung bedurften, wenn sie für heilige Lehre und Lebensvorschriften gelten sollten. — Da aber auch dieses Leitzeug zu jenem Zweck zu gebrauchen Pflicht ist, wenn es für göttliche Offenbarung angenommen werden darf, so läßt sich daraus erklären, warum der sich auf Schrift gründende Kirchenglaube bei Nennung des Religionsglaubens gemeiniglich mit verstanden wird.

Der biblische Theolog sagt: suchet in der Schrift, wo ihr meinet das ewige Leben zu finden. Dieses aber, weil die Bedingung desselben keine andere als die moralische Besserung des Menschen ist, kann kein Mensch in irgend einer Schrift finden, als wenn er sie hineinlegt, weil die dazu erforderlichen Begriffe und Grundsätze eigentlich nicht von irgend einem andern gelernt, sondern nur bei Veranlassung eines Vortrages aus der eigenen Vernunft des Lehrers entwickelt werden müssen. Die Schrift aber enthält noch mehr, als was an sich selbst zum ewigen Leben erforderlich ist, was nämlich zum Geschichtsglauben gehört und in Ansehung des Religionsglaubens als bloßes sinnliches Vehikel zwar (für diese oder jene Person, für dieses oder jenes Zeitalter) zuträglich sein kann, aber nicht nothwendig dazu gehört. Die biblisch-theologische Facultät dringt nun darauf als göttliche Offenbarung in gleichem Maße, als wenn der Glaube desselben zur Religion gehörte. Die philosophische aber widerstreitet jener in Ansehung dieser Vermengung und dessen, was jene über die eigentliche Religion Wahres in sich enthält.

Zu diesem Vehikel (d. i. dem, was über die Religionslehre noch hin= zukommt) gehört auch noch die Lehrmethode, die man als den Aposteln selbst überlassen und nicht als göttliche Offenbarung betrachten darf, son= dern beziehungsweise auf die Denkungsart der damaligen Zeiten (κατ' ανθρωπον) und nicht als Lehrstücke an sich selbst (κατ' αληθειαν) geltend an= nehmen kann, und zwar entweder negativ als bloße Zulassung gewisser damals herrschender, an sich irriger Meinungen, um nicht gegen einen herrschenden, doch im Wesentlichen gegen die Religion nicht streitenden damaligen Wahn zu verstoßen (z. B. das von den Besessenen), oder auch positiv, um sich der Vorliebe eines Volks für ihren alten Kirchenglauben, der jetzt ein Ende haben sollte, zu bedienen, um den neuen zu introduciren. (Z. B. die Deutung der Geschichte des alten Bundes als Vorbilder von

religion and the other its organon or vehicle. The canon of religion can be called *pure religious faith* (which has no statutes and is based on mere reason); its vehicle can be callled *ecclesiastical faith,* which is based entirely on statutes that need to be revealed in order to hold as sacred doctrines and precepts for conduct. But since we have a duty to use ecclesiastical faith too (provided we can adopt it as divine revelation) as a guide to our end of pure religious faith, we can see why the term "religious faith" commonly includes dogma based on Scripture as well.

The biblical theologian says: "Search the Scriptures, where you think you find eternal life." [11] But since our moral improvement is the sole condition of eternal life, the only way we can find eternal life in any Scripture whatsoever is by putting it there. For the concepts and principles required for eternal life cannot really be learned from anyone else: the teacher's exposition is only the occasion for him to develop them out of his own reason. But the Scriptures contain more than what is in itself required for eternal life; part of their content is a matter of historical belief, and while this can indeed be useful to religious faith as its mere sensible vehicle (for certain people and certain eras), it is not an essential part of religious faith. Now the faculty of biblical theologians insists on this historical content as divine revelation as strongly as if belief in it belonged to religion. The philosophy faculty, however, opposes the theology faculty regarding this confusion, and what divine revelation contains that is true of religion proper.

A *method of teaching,* too, is connected with this vehicle (that is, with what is added on to the teachings of religion). This method is not to be taken as divine revelation but as something left to the apostles' discretion. However, we can accept it as valid in relation to the way of thinking in the apostles' times (χατ' ανθρωπον), not as a part of doctrine itself (χατ' αληθειαν): having value either in a negative way, as a mere concession to certain erroneous but widely held views, so that the apostles need not offend against a prevalent illusion that was not essentially opposed to religion (for example, belief in diabolical possession), or also in a positive way, as taking advantage of a people's partiality to its old ecclesiastical faith, which was now to end, in

dem, was im neuen geschah, welche als Judaism, wenn sie irrigerweise in die Glaubenslehre als ein Stück derselben aufgenommen wird, uns wohl den Seufzer ablocken kann: nunc istae reliquiae nos exercent. *Cicero*.)

Um deswillen ist eine Schriftgelehrsamkeit des Christenthums manchen Schwierigkeiten der Auslegungskunst unterworfen, über die und deren Princip die obere Facultät (der biblische Theolog) mit der unteren in Streit gerathen muß, indem die erstere als für die theoretische biblische Erkenntniß vorzüglich besorgt die letztere in Verdacht zieht, alle Lehren, die als eigentliche Offenbarungslehren und also buchstäblich angenommen werden müßten, wegzuphilosophiren und ihnen einen beliebigen Sinn unterzuschieben, diese aber als mehr aufs Praktische, d. i. mehr auf Religion als auf Kirchenglauben, sehend umgekehrt jene beschuldigt durch solche Mittel den Endzweck, der als innere Religion moralisch sein muß und auf der Vernunft beruht, ganz aus den Augen zu bringen. Daher die letztere, welche die Wahrheit zum Zweck hat, mithin die Philosophie im Falle des Streits über den Sinn einer Schriftstelle sich das Vorrecht anmaßt, ihn zu bestimmen. Folgendes sind die philosophischen Grundsätze der Schriftauslegerei, wodurch nicht verstanden werden will, daß die Auslegung philosophisch (zur Erweiterung der Philosophie abzielt), sondern daß blos die Grundsätze der Auslegung so beschaffen sein müssen: weil alle Grundsätze, sie mögen nun eine historisch= oder grammatisch=kritische Auslegung betreffen, jederzeit, hier aber besonders, weil, was aus Schriftstellen für die Religion (die blos ein Gegenstand der Vernunft sein kann) auszumitteln sei, auch von der Vernunft dictirt werden müssen.

II.
Philosophische Grundsätze der Schriftauslegung zu Beilegung des Streits.

I. Schriftstellen, welche gewisse theoretische, für heilig angekündigte, aber allen (selbst den moralischen) Vernunftbegriff übersteigende Lehren enthalten, dürfen, diejenige aber, welche der praktischen Vernunft widersprechende Sätze enthalten, müssen zum Vortheil der letzteren ausgelegt werden. — Folgendes enthält hiezu einige Beispiele.

a) Aus der Dreieinigkeitslehre, nach dem Buchstaben genommen, läßt sich schlechterdings nichts fürs Praktische machen, wenn man sie gleich zu verstehen glaubte, noch weniger aber wenn man inne wird, daß

introducing the new (for example, interpreting the history of the old covenant as a prototype for the events of the new—though if we make the mistake of including [these remnants of] Judaism in the tenets of faith, they can well make us moan: *nunc istae reliquias nos exercent* ["those remains now weary us"]—*Cicero*).

For this reason scriptural erudition in Christianity is subject to many difficulties in the art of exegesis, and the higher faculty (of biblical theologians) is bound to come into conflict with the lower faculty over it and its principle. For the higher faculty, being concerned primarily for theoretical biblical knowledge, suspects the lower faculty of philosophizing away all the teachings that must be considered real revelation and so taken literally, and of ascribing to them whatever sense suits it. On the other hand the lower faculty, looking more to the practical—that is, more to religion than to dogma—accuses the higher of so concentrating on the means, dogma, that it completely loses sight of the final end, inner religion, which must be moral and based on reason. And so, when conflict arises about the sense of a scriptural text, philosophy—that is, the lower faculty, which has truth as its end—claims the prerogative of deciding its meaning. The following section contains the philosophical principles of scriptural exegesis. By this I do not mean that the interpretation must be philosophical (aimed at contributing to philosophy), but only that the *principles* of interpretation must be philosophical. For any principle—even those exegetical principles having to do with historical or grammatical criticism—must always be dictated by reason; and this is especially true here, since what the text yields for religion can be only an object of reason. [12]

II.

Philosophical Principles of Scriptural Exegesis for Settling the Conflict

I. If a scriptural text contains certain *theoretical* teachings which are proclaimed sacred but which *transcend* all rational concepts (even moral ones), it *may be* interpreted in the interests of practical reason; but if it contains statements that contradict practical reason, it *must be* interpreted in the interests of practical reason. Here are some pertinent examples.

a) The doctrine of the Trinity, taken literally, has *no practical relevance at all*, even if we think we understand it; and it

fie gar alle unsere Begriffe übersteigt. — Ob wir in der Gottheit drei oder zehn Personen zu verehren haben, wird der Lehrling mit gleicher Leichtigkeit aufs Wort annehmen, weil er von einem Gott in mehreren Personen (Hypostasen) gar keinen Begriff hat, noch mehr aber weil er aus dieser Verschiedenheit für seinen Lebenswandel gar keine verschiedene Regeln ziehen kann. Dagegen wenn man in Glaubenssätzen einen mo= ralischen Sinn hereinträgt (wie ich es: Religion innerhalb den Gränzen ꝛc. versucht habe), er nicht einen folgeleeren, sondern auf unsere moralische Bestimmung bezogenen verständlichen Glauben enthalten würde. Eben so ist es mit der Lehre der Menschwerdung einer Person der Gottheit bewandt. Denn wenn dieser Gottmensch nicht als die in Gott von Ewigkeit her liegende Idee der Menschheit in ihrer ganzen ihm wohlgefälligen moralischen Vollkommenheit*) (ebendaselbst S. 73 f.)¹), son= dern als die in einem wirklichen Menschen „leibhaftig wohnende" und als zweite Natur in ihm wirkende Gottheit vorgestellt wird: so ist aus diesem Geheimnisse gar nichts Praktisches für uns zu machen, weil wir doch von uns nicht verlangen können, daß wir es einem Gotte gleich thun sollen, er also in so fern kein Beispiel für uns werden kann, ohne noch die Schwie= rigkeit in Anregung zu bringen, warum, wenn solche Vereinigung einmal möglich ist, die Gottheit nicht alle Menschen derselben hat theilhaftig wer= den lassen, welche alsdann unausbleiblich ihm alle wohlgefällig geworden wären. — Ein Ähnliches kann von der Auferstehungs= und Himmelfahrts= geschichte eben desselben gesagt werden.

---

*) Die Schwärmerei des Postellus in Venedig über diesen Punkt im 16ten Jahrhundert ist von so originaler Art und dient so gut zum Beispiel, in welche Verirrungen, und zwar mit Vernunft zu rasen, man gerathen kann, wenn man die Versinnlichung einer reinen Vernunftidee in die Vorstellung eines Gegen= standes der Sinne verwandelt. Denn wenn unter jener Idee nicht das Abstrac= tum der Menschheit, sondern ein Mensch verstanden wird, so muß dieser von irgend einem Geschlecht sein. Ist dieser von Gott Gezeugte männlichen Geschlechts (ein Sohn), hat die Schwachheit der Menschen getragen und ihre Schuld auf sich ge= nommen, so sind die Schwachheiten sowohl als die Übertretungen des anderen Ge= schlechts doch von denen des männlichen specifisch unterschieden, und man wird nicht ohne Grund versucht anzunehmen, daß dieses auch seine besondere Stellver= treterin (gleichsam eine göttliche Tochter) als Versöhnerin werde bekommen haben; und diese glaubte Postell in der Person einer frommen Jungfrau in Venedig ge= funden zu haben.

¹) VI 60 f.

is even more clearly irrelevant if we realize that it transcends all our concepts. Whether we are to worship three or ten persons in the Divinity makes no difference: the pupil will implicitly accept one as readily as the other because he has no concept at all of a number of persons in one God (hypostases), and still more so because this distinction can make no difference in his rules of conduct. On the other hand, if we read a moral meaning into this article of faith (as I have tried to do in *Religion within the Limits* etc.), it would no longer contain an inconsequential belief but an intelligible one that refers to our moral vocation. The same holds true of the doctrine that one person of the Godhead became man. For if we think of this God-man, not as the Idea of humanity in its full moral perfection, present in God from eternity and beloved by Him* (cf. *Religion,* p. 73 ff), but as the Divinity "dwelling incarnate" in a real man and working as a second nature in him, then we can draw nothing practical from this mystery: since we cannot require ourselves to rival a God, we cannot take him as an example. And I shall not insist on the further difficulty—why, if such a union is possible in one case, God has not let all men participate in it, so that everyone would necessarily be pleasing to Him. Similar considerations can be raised about the stories of the Resurrection and Ascension of this God-man.

---

*The fanaticism of *Postellus,*[13] a sixteenth-century Venetian, on this point is of a highly original kind and serves as an excellent example of the sort of aberration, and indeed *logical* raving people can fall into if they transform the perceptible rendering of a pure idea of reason into the representation of an object of the senses. For if we understand by that Idea not humanity in the abstract but a real human being, this person must be of one or the other sex. And if this divine offspring is of the male sex (a son), he has masculine frailties and has taken on himself the guilt of men. But since the frailties as well as the transgressions of the other sex are specifically different from those of the male, we are, not without reason, tempted to suppose that the female sex will also have its special representative (a divine daughter, as it were) as its expiatress. And Postellus thought he had found her, in the person of a pious Venetian maiden.

Ob wir künftig blos der Seele nach leben, oder ob dieselbe Materie, daraus unser Körper hier bestand, zur Identität unserer Person in der andern Welt erforderlich, die Seele also keine besondere Substanz sei, unser Körper selbst müsse auferweckt werden, das kann uns in praktischer Absicht ganz gleichgültig sein; denn wem ist wohl sein Körper so lieb, daß er ihn gern in Ewigkeit mit sich schleppen möchte, wenn er seiner entübrigt sein kann? Des Apostels Schluß also: „Ist Christus nicht auferstanden (dem Körper nach lebendig geworden), so werden wir auch nicht auferstehen (nach dem Tode gar nicht mehr leben)" ist nicht bündig. Er mag es aber auch nicht sein (denn dem Argumentiren wird man doch nicht auch eine Inspiration zum Grunde legen), so hat er doch hiemit nur sagen wollen, daß wir Ursache haben zu glauben, Christus lebe noch, und unser Glaube sei eitel, wenn selbst ein so vollkommner Mensch nicht nach dem (leiblichen) Tode leben sollte, welcher Glaube, den ihm (wie allen Menschen) die Vernunft eingab, ihn zum historischen Glauben an eine öffentliche Sache bewog, die er treuherzig für wahr annahm und sie zum Beweisgrunde eines moralischen Glaubens des künftigen Lebens brauchte, ohne inne zu werden, daß er selbst dieser Sage ohne den letzteren schwerlich würde Glauben beigemessen haben. Die moralische Absicht wurde hiebei erreicht, wenn gleich die Vorstellungsart das Merkmal der Schulbegriffe an sich trug, in denen er war erzogen worden. — Übrigens stehen jener Sache wichtige Einwürfe entgegen: die Einsetzung des Abendmahls (einer traurigen Unterhaltung) zum Andenken an ihn sieht einem förmlichen Abschied (nicht blos aufs baldige Wiedersehen) ähnlich. Die klagende Worte am Kreuz drücken eine fehlgeschlagene Absicht aus (die Juden noch bei seinem Leben zur wahren Religion zu bringen), da doch eher das Frohsein über eine vollzogne Absicht hätte erwartet werden sollen. Endlich der Ausdruck der Jünger bei dem Lucas: „Wir dachten, er solle Israel erlösen" läßt auch nicht abnehmen, daß sie auf ein in drei Tagen erwartetes Wiedersehen vorbereitet waren, noch weniger, daß ihnen von seiner Auferstehung etwas zu Ohren gekommen sei. — Aber warum sollten wir wegen einer Geschichtserzählung, die wir immer an ihren Ort (unter die Adiaphora) gestellt sein lassen sollen, uns in so viel gelehrte Untersuchungen und Streitigkeiten verflechten, wenn es um Religion zu thun ist, zu welcher der Glaube in praktischer Beziehung, den die Vernunft uns einflößt, schon für sich hinreichend ist.

b) In der Auslegung der Schriftstellen, in welchen der Ausdruck un-

For practical purposes we can be quite indifferent as to whether we shall live as pure spirits after death or whether our personal identity in the next world requires the same matter that now forms our body, so that our soul is not a distinct substance and our body must be restored to life. For who is so fond of his body that he would want to drag it around with him for eternity, if he can get along without it? So the apostle's conclusion: "If Christ had not risen" (if his body had not come to life), "neither would we rise again" (we would not continue to live after death) is not valid. But it may not be a conclusion (for one does not argue on the basis of an inspiration); he may have meant only that we have reason to believe Christ is still alive and that our faith would be in vain if even so perfect a man did not continue to live after (bodily) death. This belief, which reason suggested to him (as to all men), moved him to historical belief in a public event, which he accepted in good faith as true and used as a basis of proof for moral belief in the future life, failing to realize that, apart from his moral belief, he himself would have found it hard to credit this tale. In this way the moral purpose would be achieved, though the apostle's way of representing it bears the mark of the school of thought in which he was trained. Moreover, there are serious objections to that event. By establishing the Lord's Supper (a sad colloquy) as a commemoration of himself, Christ seems to be taking formal leave of his disciples (not looking forward to a speedy reunion with them). His complaints on the cross express failure in his purpose (to lead the Jews to the true religion in his lifetime), whereas we should rather have expected satisfaction in an aim accomplished. Finally, the disciples' words according to Luke: "We had thought he would deliver Israel," do not imply that they were expecting a reunion with him in three days, still less that any word of his resurrection had reached them. But when we are dealing with religion, where the faith instilled by reason with regard to the practical is sufficient to itself, why should we get entangled in all these learned investigations and disputes because of a historical narrative that should always be left in its proper place (among matters that are indifferent)?

b) It seems to violate outright the highest rule of exegesis that reason feels entitled to interpret the text in a way it finds

serm Vernunftbegriff von der göttlichen Natur und seinem Willen widerstreitet, haben biblische Theologen sich längst zur Regel gemacht, daß, was
menschlicherweise (ανθρωποπαθως) ausgedrückt ist, nach einem gottwürdi-
gen Sinne (θεοπρεπως) müsse ausgelegt werden; wodurch sie dann
ganz deutlich das Bekenntniß ablegten, die Vernunft sei in Religions-
sachen die oberste Auslegerin der Schrift. — Daß aber selbst, wenn man
dem heil. Schriftsteller keinen andern Sinn, den er wirklich mit seinen Aus-
drücken verband, unterlegen kann, als einen solchen, der mit unserer Vernunft gar in Widerspruche steht, die Vernunft sich doch berechtigt fühle,
seine Schriftstelle so auszulegen, wie sie es ihren Grundsätzen gemäß
findet, und nicht dem Buchstaben nach auslegen solle, wenn sie jenen nicht
gar eines Irrthums beschuldigen will, das scheint ganz und gar wider die
oberste Regeln der Interpretation zu verstoßen, und gleichwohl ist es noch
immer mit Beifall von den belobtesten Gottesgelehrten geschehen. — So
ist es mit St. Paulus' Lehre von der Gnadenwahl gegangen, aus welcher
aufs deutlichste erhellt, daß seine Privatmeinung die Prädestination im
strengsten Sinne des Worts gewesen sein muß, welche darum auch von
einer großen protestantischen Kirche in ihren Glauben aufgenommen worden, in der Folge aber von einem großen Theil derselben wieder verlaßen,
oder, so gut wie man konnte, anders gedeutet worden ist, weil die Vernunft sie mit der Lehre von der Freiheit, der Zurechnung der Handlungen
und so mit der ganzen Moral unvereinbar findet. — Auch wo der Schrift-
glaube in keinen Verstoß gewisser Lehren wider sittliche Grundsätze, sondern nur wider die Vernunftmaxime in Beurtheilung physischer Erscheinungen geräth, haben Schriftausleger mit fast allgemeinem Beifall manche
biblische Geschichtserzählungen, z. B. von den Besessenen (dämonischen
Leuten), ob sie zwar in demselben historischen Tone wie die übrige heil.
Geschichte in der Schrift vorgetragen worden und fast nicht zu zweifeln
ist, daß ihre Schriftsteller sie buchstäblich für wahr gehalten haben, doch
so ausgelegt, daß die Vernunft dabei bestehen könnte (um nicht allem
Aberglauben und Betrug freien Eingang zu verschaffen), ohne daß man
ihnen diese Befugniß bestritten hat.

II. Der Glaube an Schriftlehren, die eigentlich haben offenbart
werden müssen, wenn sie haben gekannt werden sollen, hat an sich kein
Verdienst, und der Mangel desselben, ja sogar der ihm entgegen-
stehende Zweifel ist an sich keine Verschuldung, sondern alles kommt
in der Religion aufs Thun an, und diese Endabsicht, mithin auch ein

consistent with its own principles, even when it is confronted with a text where no other meaning can be ascribed to the sacred author, as what he actually intended by his words, than one which contradicts reason: [in other words], that we should not interpret the text literally, unless we are willing to charge it with error. Yet this is what has always happened, with the approval of the most eminent theologians. In their interpretation of scriptural texts which literally contradict our rational concept of God's nature and will, biblical theologians have long made it their rule that what is expressed in human terms ($\jmath\rho\omega\pi o\pi a\theta\omega\varsigma$) must be *interpreted* in a sense worthy of God ($\theta\epsilon o\pi\rho\epsilon\pi\omega\varsigma$). By this they quite clearly confess that in matters of religion reason is the highest interpreter of the scriptures. They followed this rule with regard to St. Paul's teaching on predestination, which clearly shows that his personal view must have been that men are predestined in the strictest sense of the term. Although a major Protestant church, following him, adopted this teaching into its creed, a great part of that church later abandoned the doctrine or, as far as possible, changed its meaning, because reason finds that predestination cannot be reconciled with its own teachings on freedom and the imputation of action, and so with the whole of morality. Even when belief in scriptural teachings would involve no offense against moral principles but only against rational maxims for judging natural phenomena, scriptural exegetes, with almost unanimous approval, have proceeded in the same way. Many biblical stories—about diabolical possession (demoniacs), for example—have been interpreted in such a way that reason can hold its own with them (so as not to open the door to every kind of superstition and imposture); and the right to do this has not been challenged, even though the scriptures relate these tales in the same historical style as the rest of sacred history and it is almost certain that their author thought they were literally true.

II. With regard to scriptural teachings that we can know only by revelation, faith is not in itself *meritorious*, and lack of such faith, and even doubt opposed to it, in itself involves no *guilt*. The only thing that matters in religion is *deeds*, and this

dieser gemäßer Sinn muß allen biblischen Glaubenslehren untergelegt werden.

Unter Glaubenssätzen versteht man nicht, was geglaubt werden soll (denn das Glauben verstattet keinen Imperativ), sondern das, was in praktischer (moralischer) Absicht anzunehmen möglich und zweckmäßig, obgleich nicht eben erweislich ist, mithin nur geglaubt werden kann. Nehme ich das Glauben ohne diese moralische Rücksicht blos in der Bedeutung eines theoretischen Fürwahrhaltens, z. B. dessen, was sich auf dem Zeugniß anderer geschichtmäßig gründet, oder auch, weil ich mir gewisse gegebene Erscheinungen nicht anders als unter dieser oder jener Voraussetzung erklären kann, zu einem Princip an, so ist ein solcher Glaube, weil er weder einen besseren Menschen macht noch einen solchen beweiset, gar kein Stück der Religion; ward er aber nur als durch Furcht und Hoffnung aufgedrungen in der Seele erkünstelt, so ist er der Aufrichtigkeit, mithin auch der Religion zuwider. — Lauten also Spruchstellen so, als ob sie das Glauben einer Offenbarungslehre nicht allein als an sich verdienstlich ansähen, sondern wohl gar über moralisch-gute Werke erhöben, so müssen sie so ausgelegt werden, als ob nur der moralische, die Seele durch Vernunft bessernde und erhebende Glaube dadurch gemeint sei; gesetzt auch, der buchstäbliche Sinn, z. B. wer da glaubet und getauft wird, wird selig zc., lautete dieser Auslegung zuwider. Der Zweifel über jene statutarische Dogmen und ihre Authenticität kann also eine moralische, wohlgesinnte Seele nicht beunruhigen. — Eben dieselben Sätze können gleichwohl als wesentliche Erfordernisse zum Vortrag eines gewissen Kirchenglaubens angesehen werden, der aber, weil er nur Vehikel des Religionsglaubens, mithin an sich veränderlich ist und einer allmähligen Reinigung bis zur Congruenz mit dem letzteren fähig bleiben muß, nicht zum Glaubensartikel selbst gemacht, obzwar doch auch in Kirchen nicht öffentlich angegriffen oder auch mit trockenem Fuß übergangen werden darf, weil er unter der Gewahrsame der Regierung steht, die für öffentliche Eintracht und Frieden Sorge trägt, indessen daß es des Lehrers Sache ist davor zu warnen, ihm nicht eine für sich bestehende Heiligkeit beizulegen, sondern ohne Verzug zu dem dadurch eingeleiteten Religionsglauben überzugehen.

III. Das Thun muß als aus des Menschen eigenem Gebrauch seiner moralischen Kräfte entspringend und nicht als Wirkung vom Einfluß einer äußeren höheren wirkenden Ursache, in Ansehung deren der Mensch

ultimate aim and, accordingly, a meaning appropriate to it, must be attributed to every biblical dogma.

Dogma is not what we ought to believe (for faith admits of no imperative), but what we find it possible and useful to admit for practical (moral) purposes, although we cannot demonstrate it and so can only believe it. If we ignore this moral consideration and admit as a principle faith merely in the sense of theoretical assent—assent, for example, to what is based historically on the testimony of others, or to some assumption or other without which I cannot explain certain given phenomena—such faith is no part of religion because it neither makes nor gives proof of a better man; and if such belief is feigned in the soul, thrust upon it only by fear and hope, then it is opposed to sincerity and so to religion as well. And so, if certain texts seem to regard faith in revealed doctrine as not only meritorious in itself but even superior to morally good works, we must interpret them as referring only to moral faith, which improves and elevates the soul by reason—although, admittedly, the literal meaning of such texts as "he who believes and is baptized will be saved" etc. goes against this interpretation. Doubt concerning these statutory dogmas and their authenticity, therefore, cannot disturb a morally well-disposed soul. Yet these same propositions can be considered essential requirements for *expounding* a certain *ecclesiastical faith*. But since ecclesiastical faith, as the mere vehicle of religious faith, is mutable and must remain open to gradual purification until it coincides with religious faith, it cannot be made an article of faith itself. This does not mean that it may be attacked publicly in the churches or even passed over dry-shod; for it comes under the protection of the government, which watches over public unity and peace. However, the teacher should warn [the people] not to ascribe holiness to dogma itself but to pass over, without delay, to the religious faith it has introduced.

III. Action must be represented as issuing from man's own use of his moral powers, not as an effect [resulting] from the influence of an external, higher cause by whose activity man is passively healed. The interpretation of scriptural texts which,

sich leidend verhielte, vorgestellt werden; die Auslegung der Schriftstellen, welche buchstäblich das letztere zu enthalten scheinen, muß also auf die Übereinstimmung mit dem ersteren Grundsatze absichtlich gerichtet werden.

Wenn unter Natur das im Menschen herrschende Princip der Beförderung seiner Glückseligkeit, unter Gnade aber die in uns liegende unbegreifliche moralische Anlage, d. i. das Princip der reinen Sittlichkeit, verstanden wird, so sind Natur und Gnade nicht allein von einander unterschieden, sondern auch oft gegen einander in Widerstreit. Wird aber unter Natur (in praktischer Bedeutung) das Vermögen aus eigenen Kräften überhaupt gewisse Zwecke auszurichten verstanden, so ist Gnade nichts anders als Natur des Menschen, so fern er durch sein eigenes inneres, aber übersinnliches Princip (die Vorstellung seiner Pflicht) zu Handlungen bestimmt wird, welches, weil wir uns es erklären wollen, gleichwohl aber weiter keinen Grund davon wissen, von uns als von der Gottheit in uns gewirkter Antrieb zum Guten, dazu wir die Anlage in uns nicht selbst gegründet haben, mithin als Gnade vorgestellt wird. — Die Sünde nämlich (die Bösartigkeit in der menschlichen Natur) hat das Strafgesetz (gleich als für Knechte) nothwendig gemacht, die Gnade aber (d. i. die durch den Glauben an die ursprüngliche Anlage zum Guten in uns und die durch das Beispiel der Gott wohlgefälligen Menschheit an dem Sohne Gottes lebendig werdende Hoffnung der Entwickelung dieses Guten) kann und soll in uns (als Freien) noch mächtiger werden, wenn wir sie nur in uns wirken, d. h. die Gesinnungen eines jenem heil. Beispiel ähnlichen Lebenswandels thätig werden lassen. — Die Schriftstellen also, die eine blos passive Ergebung an eine äußere in uns Heiligkeit wirkende Macht zu enthalten scheinen, müssen so ausgelegt werden, daß daraus erhelle, wir müssen an der Entwickelung jener moralischen Anlage in uns selbst arbeiten, ob sie zwar selber eine Göttlichkeit eines Ursprungs beweiset, der höher ist als alle Vernunft (in der theoretischen Nachforschung der Ursache), und daher, sie besitzen, nicht Verdienst, sondern Gnade ist.

IV. Wo das eigene Thun zur Rechtfertigung des Menschen vor seinem eigenen (strenge richtenden) Gewissen nicht zulangt, da ist die Vernunft befugt allenfalls eine übernatürliche Ergänzung seiner mangelhaften Gerechtigkeit (auch ohne daß sie bestimmen darf, worin sie bestehe) gläubig anzunehmen.

Diese Befugniß ist für sich selbst klar; denn was der Mensch nach seiner Bestimmung sein soll (nämlich dem heil. Gesetz angemessen), das

taken literally, seem to contain the latter view must therefore be deliberately directed toward making them consistent with the former view.

If by nature we mean the principle that impels us to promote our *happiness,* and by grace the incomprehensible moral disposition in us—that is, the principle of *pure morality*—then nature and grace not only differ from each other but often come into conflict. But if by nature (in the practical sense) we mean our ability to achieve certain ends by our own powers in general, then grace is none other than the nature of man in so far as he is determined to actions by a principle which is intrinsic to his own being, but supersensible (the thought of his duty). Since we want to explain this principle, although we know no further ground for it, we represent it as a stimulus to good produced in us by God, the predisposition to which we did not establish in outselves, and so, as grace. That is to say, sin (evil in human nature) has made penal law necessary (as if for slaves); grace, however, is the hope that good will develop in us—a hope awakened by belief in our original moral predisposition to good and by the example of humanity as pleasing to God in His Son. And grace can and should become more powerful than sin in us (as free beings), if only we let it act in us or let our disposition to the kind of conduct shown in that holy example become active. Scriptural texts which seem to enjoin a merely passive surrender to an external power that produces holiness in us must, then, be interpreted differently. It has to be made clear from them that *we ourselves must work* at developing that moral predisposition, although this predisposition does point to a divine source that reason can never reach (in its theoretical search for causes), so that our possession of it is not meritorious, but rather the work of grace.

IV. If man's own deeds are not sufficient to justify him before his conscience (as it judges him strictly), reason is entitled to adopt on faith a supernatural supplement to fill what is lacking to his justification (though not to specify in what this consists).

That reason has this title is self-evident. For man must be able to become what his vocation requires him to be (adequate to the holy law); and if he cannot do this naturally by his own

muß er auch werden können, und ist es nicht durch eigene Kräfte natür=
licherweise möglich, so darf er hoffen, daß es durch äußere göttliche Mit=
wirkung (auf welche Art es auch sei) geschehen werde. — Man kann noch
hinzusetzen, daß der Glaube an diese Ergänzung seligmachend sei, weil er
dadurch allein zum gottwohlgefälligen Lebenswandel (als der einzigen
Bedingung der Hoffnung der Seligkeit) Muth und feste Gesinnung fassen
kann, daß er am Gelingen seiner Endabsicht (Gott wohlgefällig zu wer=
den) nicht verzweifelt. — Daß er aber wissen und bestimmt müsse ange=
ben können, worin das Mittel dieses Ersatzes (welches am Ende doch
überschwenglich und bei allem, was uns Gott darüber selbst sagen möchte,
für uns unbegreiflich ist) bestehe, das ist eben nicht nothwendig, ja, auf
diese Kenntniß auch nur Anspruch zu machen, Vermessenheit. — Die
Schriftstellen also, die eine solche specifische Offenbarung zu enthalten
scheinen, müssen so ausgelegt werden, daß sie nur das Vehikel jenes mo=
ralischen Glaubens für ein Volk nach dessen bisher bei ihm im Schwang
gewesenen Glaubenslehren betreffen und nicht Religionsglauben (für alle
Menschen), mithin blos den Kirchenglauben (z. B. für Judenchristen) an=
gehen, welcher historischer Beweise bedarf, deren nicht jedermann theil=
haftig werden kann; statt dessen Religion (als auf moralische Begriffe
gegründet) für sich vollständig und zweifelsfrei sein muß.

*   *
*

Aber selbst wider die Idee einer philosophischen Schriftauslegung
höre ich die vereinigte Stimme der biblischen Theologen sich erheben: sie
hat, sagt man, erstlich eine naturalistische Religion und nicht Christen=
thum zur Absicht. Antwort: das Christenthum ist die Idee von der Re=
ligion, die überhaupt auf Vernunft gegründet und so fern natürlich sein
muß. Es enthält aber ein Mittel der Einführung derselben unter Men=
schen, die Bibel, deren Ursprung für übernatürlich gehalten wird, die (ihr
Ursprung mag sein, welcher er wolle), so fern sie den moralischen Vor=
schriften der Vernunft in Ansehung ihrer öffentlichen Ausbreitung und
inniglicher Belebung beförderlich ist, als Vehikel zur Religion gezählt
werden kann und als ein solches auch für übernatürliche Offenbarung an=
genommen werden mag. Nun kann man eine Religion nur natura=
listisch nennen, wenn sie es zum Grundsatze macht, keine solche Offen=
barung einzuräumen. Also ist das Christenthum darum nicht eine natu=

76

powers, he may hope to achieve it by God's cooperation from without (whatever form this may take). We can add, further, that faith in this supplement for his deficiency is sanctifying, for only by it can man cease to doubt that he can reach his final end (to become pleasing to God) and so lay hold of the courage and firmness of attitude he needs to lead a life pleasing to God (the sole condition of his hope for eternal life). But we need not be able to understand and state exactly what the means of this replenishment is (for the final analysis this is transcendent and, despite all that God Himself might tell us about it, inconceivable to us); even to lay claim to this knowledge would, in fact, be presumptuous. Accordingly, scriptural texts that seem to contain such a specific revelation must be interpreted as concerning, not moral faith (for all men), but only the vehicle of that moral faith, designed to fit in with the creed which a certain people already held about it. And so they have to do with mere ecclesiastical faith (for Jewish Christians, for example), which requires historical evidence that not everyone can share, whereas religion (because it is based on moral concepts) must be complete in itself and free from doubt.

*   *

*

But I hear biblical theologians cry out in unison against the very idea of a philosophical interpretation of Scripture. Philosophical exegesis, they say, aims primarily at a natural religion, not Christianity. I *reply* that Christianity is the Idea of religion, which must as such be based on reason and to this extent be natural. But it contains a means for introducing this religion to men, the Bible, which is thought to have a supernatural source; and in so far as the Bible (whatever its source may be) promotes moral precepts of reason by propagating them publicly and strengthening them within men's souls, we can consider it the vehicle of religion and accept it, in this respect, as supernatural revelation. Now only a religion that makes it a principle not to admit supernatural revelation can be called *naturalistic*. So Christianity is not a naturalistic religion—though it is a merely

ralistische Religion, obgleich es blos eine natürliche ist, weil es nicht in
Abrede ist, daß die Bibel nicht ein übernatürliches Mittel der Introduction der letzteren und der Stiftung einer sie öffentlich lehrenden und be-
kennenden Kirche sein möge, sondern nur auf diesen Ursprung, wenn es
auf Religionslehre ankommt, nicht Rücksicht nimmt.

III.
Einwürfe und Beantwortung derselben, die Grundsätze der Schriftauslegung betreffend.

Wider diese Auslegungsregeln höre ich ausrufen: erstlich: das sind
ja insgesammt Urtheile der philosophischen Facultät, welche sich also in
das Geschäft des biblischen Theologen Eingriffe erlaubt. — Antwort:
zum Kirchenglauben wird historische Gelehrsamkeit, zum Religionsglauben blos Vernunft erfordert. Jenen als Vehikel des letzteren auszulegen
ist freilich eine Forderung der Vernunft, aber wo ist eine solche rechtmäßi-
ger, als wo etwas nur als Mittel zu etwas Anderem als Endzweck (dergleichen die Religion ist) einen Werth hat, und giebt es überall wohl ein
höheres Princip der Entscheidung, wenn über Wahrheit gestritten wird,
als die Vernunft? Es thut auch der theologischen Facultät keinesweges
Abbruch, wenn die philosophische sich der Statuten derselben bedient, ihre
eigene Lehre durch Einstimmung mit derselben zu bestärken; man sollte
vielmehr denken, daß jener dadurch eine Ehre widerfahre. Soll aber
doch, was die Schriftauslegung betrifft, durchaus Streit zwischen beiden
sein, so weiß ich keinen andern Vergleich als diesen: wenn der biblische Theolog aufhören wird sich der Vernunft zu seinem Behuf zu bedienen, so wird der philosophische auch aufhören zu
Bestätigung seiner Sätze die Bibel zu gebrauchen. Ich zweifle
aber sehr, daß der erstere sich auf diesen Vertrag einlassen dürfte. —
Zweitens: jene Auslegungen sind allegorisch=mystisch, mithin weder bib-
lisch noch philosophisch. Antwort: Es ist gerade das Gegentheil, nämlich daß, wenn der biblische Theolog die Hülle der Religion für die Religion selbst nimmt, er z. B. das ganze alte Testament für eine fortgehende
Allegorie (von Vorbildern und symbolischen Vorstellungen) des noch
kommenden Religionszustandes erklären muß, wenn er nicht annehmen
will, das wäre damals schon wahre Religion gewesen (die doch nicht noch
wahrer als wahr sein kann), wodurch dann das neue entbehrlich gemacht

natural one—because it does not deny that the Bible may be a supernatural means for introducing religion and that a church may be established to teach and profess it publicly: it simply takes no notice of this source where religious doctrine is concerned.

III.

Objections concerning the Principles of Scriptural Exegesis, along with Replies to Them

Against these rules of exegesis I hear the outcry, *first,* that they are all judgments of the philosophy faculty, which, by giving them, presumes to interfere in the biblical theologian's business. I *reply* that whereas dogma requires historical scholarship, reason alone is sufficient for religious faith. Reason does, it is true, claim to interpret dogma, in so far as it is the vehicle of religious faith. But since the value of dogma is only that of a means to religion as its final end, could such a claim be more legitimate? And can there be any principle higher than reason for settling arguments about truth? Moreover, the philosophy faculty does theologians no harm if it uses their statutes to corroborate its own teachings by showing that they are consistent with these statutes; one would rather expect the theology faculty to feel honored by this. But if the two faculties still find themselves in thoroughgoing conflict about interpreting the Bible, I can suggest only this compromise: *If biblical theologians will stop using reason for their purposes, philosophical theologians will stop using the Bible to confirm their propositions.* But I seriously doubt that biblical theologians would agree to this settlement. The *second* objection is that these interpretations are allegorical and mystical, and so neither biblical nor philosophical. My *reply* is that the exact opposite is true. If the biblical theologian mistakes the husk of religion for religion itself, [it is he who must interpret the scriptures allegorically:] he must explain the entire Old Testament, for example, as a continuous *allegory* (of prototypes and symbols) of the religious state still to come—or else admit that true religion (which cannot be truer than true) had already appeared then, making the New Testament superfluous. As for the charge that rational

würde. Was aber die vorgebliche Mystik der Vernunftauslegungen be=
trifft, wenn die Philosophie in Schriftstellen einen moralischen Sinn auf=
gespäht, ja gar ihn dem Texte aufdringt, so ist diese gerade das einzige
Mittel, die Mystik (z. B. eines Swedenborgs) abzuhalten. Denn die
Phantasie verläuft sich bei Religionsdingen unvermeidlich ins Über=
schwengliche, wenn sie das Übersinnliche (was in allem, was Religion
heißt, gedacht werden muß) nicht an bestimmte Begriffe der Vernunft,
dergleichen die moralische sind, knüpft, und führt zu einem Illuminatism
innerer Offenbarungen, deren ein jeder alsdann seine eigene hat und kein
öffentlicher Probirstein der Wahrheit mehr Statt findet.

Es giebt aber noch Einwürfe, die die Vernunft ihr selbst gegen die
Vernunftauslegung der Bibel macht, die wir nach der Reihe oben ange=
führter Auslegungsregeln kürzlich bemerken und zu heben suchen wollen.
a) Einwurf: Als Offenbarung muß die Bibel aus sich selbst und nicht
durch die Vernunft gedeutet werden; denn der Erkenntnißquell selbst liegt
anderswo als in der Vernunft. Antwort: Eben darum, weil jenes Buch
als göttliche Offenbarung angenommen wird, muß sie nicht blos nach
Grundsätzen der Geschichtslehren (mit sich selbst zusammen zu stimmen)
theoretisch, sondern nach Vernunftbegriffen praktisch ausgelegt werden;
denn daß eine Offenbarung göttlich sei, kann nie durch Kennzeichen,
welche die Erfahrung an die Hand giebt, eingesehen werden. Ihr Cha=
rakter (wenigstens als conditio sine qua non) ist immer die Übereinstim=
mung mit dem, was die Vernunft für Gott anständig erklärt. — b) Ein=
wurf: Vor allem Praktischen muß doch immer eine Theorie vorhergehen,
und da diese als Offenbarungslehre vielleicht Absichten des Willens Got=
tes, die wir nicht durchdringen können, für uns aber verbindend sein dürf=
ten, sie zu befördern, enthalten könnten, so scheint das Glauben an derglei=
chen theoretische Sätze für sich selbst eine Verbindlichkeit, mithin das Be=
zweifeln derselben eine Schuld zu enthalten. Antwort: Man kann dieses
einräumen, wenn vom Kirchenglauben die Rede ist, bei dem es auf keine
andere Praxis als die der angeordneten Gebräuche angesehen ist, wo die,
so sich zu einer Kirche bekennen, zum Fürwahrnehmen nichts mehr, als
daß die Lehre nicht unmöglich sei, bedürfen; dagegen zum Religionsglau=
ben Überzeugung von der Wahrheit erforderlich ist, welche aber durch
Statute (daß sie göttliche Sprüche sind) nicht beurkundigt werden kann,
weil, daß sie es sind, nur immer wiederum durch Geschichte bewiesen
werden müßte, die sich selbst für göttliche Offenbarung auszugeben nicht

interpretation of the Scriptures is mystical, the sole means of avoiding mysticism (such as Swedenborg's [14]) is for philosophy to be on the lookout for a moral meaning in scriptural texts and even to impose it on them. For unless the supersensible (the thought of which is essential to anything called religion) is anchored to determinate concepts of reason, such as those of morality, fantasy inevitably gets lost in the transcendent, where religious matters are concerned, and leads to an Illuminism in which everyone has his private, inner revelations, and there is no longer any public touchstone of truth.

But reason has its own objections to a rational interpretation of the Bible, which we shall note briefly and try to resolve according to the list of interpretive rules cited above. a) *Objection*: As *revelation*, the Bible must be interpreted in its own terms, not by reason; for the source of the knowledge it contains lies elsewhere than in reason. *Reply*: Precisely because we accept this book as divine revelation, we cannot give a merely theoretical interpretation of it by applying the principles proper to the study of history (that it must be consistent with itself); we must interpret this book in a practical way, according to rational concepts. For the kind of characteristics that experience provides can never show us that a revelation is divine: the mark of its divinity (at least as the *conditio sine qua non*) is its harmony with what reason pronounces worthy of God. b) *Objection*: A theory must always precede anything practical; and if the theory in question is a revealed doctrine, it could contain purposes of the divine will which we might be obligated to promote even though we cannot penetrate them. So it seems that faith in these theoretical propositions is obligatory in itself and that doubt concerning them involves guilt. *Reply*: This can be granted in the case of ecclesiastical faith, whose concern with practice goes no further than the formalities it enjoins, where the fact that the dogma of a church is not impossible is all that its members need in order to accept it as true. But we cannot have religious faith unless we are *convinced* of its truth, and its truth cannot be certified by statutes (declaring themselves divine pronounce-ments); for, again, only history could be used to prove that these statutes are divine, and history is not entitled to pass *itself* off as divine revelation. And so for religious faith, which is directed

befugt ist. Daher bei diesem, der gänzlich auf Moralität des Lebenswan=
dels, aufs Thun, gerichtet ist, das Fürwahrhalten historischer, obschon
biblischer Lehren an sich keinen moralischen Werth oder Unwerth hat und
unter die Adiaphora gehört. — c) Einwurf: Wie kann man einem
Geistlichtodten das „Stehe auf und wandle!" zurufen, wenn diesen Zuruf
nicht zugleich eine übernatürliche Macht begleitet, die Leben in ihn hin=
einbringt? Antwort: Der Zuruf geschieht an den Menschen durch seine
eigene Vernunft, sofern sie das übersinnliche Princip des moralischen
Lebens in sich selbst hat. Durch dieses kann der Mensch zwar vielleicht
nicht sofort zum Leben und um von selbst aufzustehen, aber doch sich zu
regen und zur Bestrebung eines guten Lebenswandels erweckt werden (wie
einer, bei dem die Kräfte nur schlafen, aber darum nicht erloschen sind),
und das ist schon ein Thun, welches keines äußeren Einflusses bedarf und,
fortgesetzt, den beabsichtigten Wandel bewirken kann. — d) Einwurf:
Der Glaube an eine uns unbekannte Ergänzungsart des Mangels unse=
rer eigenen Gerechtigkeit, mithin als Wohlthat eines Anderen ist eine
umsonst angenommene Ursache (petitio principii) zu Befriedigung des
von uns gefühlten Bedürfnisses. Denn was wir von der Gnade eines
Oberen erwarten, davon können wir nicht, als ob es sich von selbst ver=
stände, annehmen, daß es uns zu Theil werden müsse, sondern nur, wenn
es uns wirklich versprochen worden, und daher nur durch Acceptation eines
uns geschehenen bestimmten Versprechens, wie durch einen förmlichen Ver=
trag. Also können wir, wie es scheint, jene Ergänzung nur, sofern sie durch
göttliche Offenbarung wirklich zugesagt worden, und nicht auf gut
Glück hin hoffen und voraussetzen. Antwort: Eine unmittelbare göttliche
Offenbarung in dem tröstenden Ausspruch: „Dir sind deine Sünden ver=
geben," wäre eine übersinnliche Erfahrung, welche unmöglich ist. Aber
diese ist auch in Ansehung dessen, was (wie die Religion) auf moralischen
Vernunftgründen beruht und dadurch a priori, wenigstens in praktischer
Absicht, gewiß ist, nicht nöthig. Von einem heiligen und gütigen Gesetz=
geber kann man sich die Decrete in Ansehung gebrechlicher, aber Alles,
was sie für Pflicht erkennen, nach ihrem ganzen Vermögen zu befolgen
strebender Geschöpfe nicht anders denken, und selbst der Vernunftglaube
und das Vertrauen auf eine solche Ergänzung, ohne daß eine bestimmte
empirisch ertheilte Zusage dazu kommen darf, beweiset mehr die ächte mo=
ralische Gesinnung und hiemit die Empfänglichkeit für jene gehoffte Gna=
denbezeigung, als es ein empirischer Glaube thun kann.

solely to the morality of conduct, to deeds, acceptance of historical—even biblical—teachings has in itself no positive or negative moral value and comes under the heading of what is indifferent. c) *Objection*: How can the call "Arise and walk" come to someone spiritually dead unless it is accompanied by a supernatural power to restore him to life? *Reply*: This call comes to man through his own reason, in so far as it contains the supersensible principle of moral life. It is true that this may not immediately restore him to life so that he can arise by himself: [at first] perhaps it awakens him only to stir himself and strive toward a good life (like one whose powers are merely dormant and not extinct). But this striving is already a deed, which requires no external influence and, if it continues, can produce the kind of conduct intended. d) *Objection*: To believe that God, by an act of kindness, will in some unknown way fill what is lacking to our justification is to assume gratuitously a cause that will satisfy the need we feel (it is to commit a *petitio principii*); for when we expect something by the grace of a superior, we cannot assume that we must get it as a matter of course; we can expect it only if it was actually promised to us, and hence only by acceptance of a definite promise made to us, as in a formal contract. So it seems that we can hope for that supplement and assume that we shall get it only in so far as it has been actually pledged through divine *revelation*, not as a stroke of luck. *Reply*: A direct revelation from God embodied in the comforting statement "Your sins are forgiven you" would be a supersensible experience, and this is impossible. But it is also unnecessary with regard to what (like religion) is based on moral principles of reason and is therefore certain a priori, at least for practical purposes. There is no other way we can conceive the decrees of a holy and benevolent law-giver with regard to frail creatures who are yet striving with all their might to fulfill whatever they recognize as their duty; and if, without the aid of a definite, empirically given promise, we have a rational faith and trust in His help, we show better evidence of a pure moral attitude and so of our receptivity to the manifestation of grace we hope for than we could by empirical belief.

*   *   *

Auf solche Weise müssen alle Schriftauslegungen, so fern sie die Religion betreffen, nach dem Princip der in der Offenbarung abgezweckten Sittlichkeit gemacht werden und sind ohne das entweder praktisch leer oder gar Hindernisse des Guten. — Auch sind sie alsdann nur eigentlich authentisch, d. i. der Gott in uns ist selbst der Ausleger, weil wir niemand verstehen als den, der durch unsern eigenen Verstand und unsere eigene Vernunft mit uns redet, die Göttlichkeit einer an uns ergangenen Lehre also durch nichts, als durch Begriffe unserer Vernunft, so fern sie rein-moralisch und hiemit untrüglich sind, erkannt werden kann.

Allgemeine Anmerkung.

Von Religionssecten.

In dem, was eigentlich Religion genannt zu werden verdient, kann es keine Sectenverschiedenheit geben (denn sie ist einig, allgemein und nothwendig, mithin unveränderlich), wohl aber in dem, was den Kirchenglauben betrifft, er mag nun blos auf die Bibel, oder auch auf Tradition gegründet sein: so fern der Glaube an das, was blos Vehikel der Religion ist, für Artikel derselben gehalten wird.

Es wäre Herculische und dabei undankbare Arbeit, nur blos die Secten des Christenthums, wenn man unter ihm den messianischen Glauben versteht, alle aufzuzählen; denn da ist jenes blos eine Secte*) des letztern, so daß es dem Judenthum in engerer Bedeutung (in dem letzten Zeitpunkt seiner ungetheilten Herrschaft über das Volk) entgegengesetzt wird, wo die Frage ist: „Bist du es, der da kommen soll, oder sollen

---

*) Es ist eine Sonderbarkeit des deutschen Sprachgebrauchs (oder Mißbrauchs), daß sich die Anhänger unserer Religion Christen nennen; gleich als ob es mehr als einen Christus gebe und jeder Gläubige ein Christus wäre. Sie müßten sich Christianer nennen. — Aber dieser Name würde sofort wie ein Sectenname angesehen werden von Leuten, denen man (wie im Peregrinus Proteus geschieht) viel Übels nachsagen kann: welches in Ansehung des Christen nicht Statt findet. — So verlangte ein Recensent in der Hallischen gel. Zeitung, daß der Name Jehovah durch Jahwoh ausgesprochen werden sollte. Aber diese Veränderung würde eine bloße Nationalgottheit, nicht den Herrn der Welt zu bezeichnen scheinen.

*   *

*

It is in this way, according to the principle of the morality which revelation has in view, that we must interpret the Scriptures *in so far as they have to do with religion;* otherwise our interpretations are either empty of practical content or even obstacles to the good. Only a moral interpretation, moreover, is really an authentic one—that is, one given by the God within us; for since we cannot understand anyone unless he speaks to us through our own understanding and reason, it is only by concepts of *our* reason, in so far as they are pure moral concepts and hence infallible, that we can recognize the divinity of a teaching promulgated to us.

On Religious Sects

In what really deserves to be called religion, there can be no division into sects (for since religion is one, universal and necessary, it cannot vary). But there can well be division into sects with regard to ecclesiastical faith, whether it is based merely on the Bible or on tradition as well, to the extent that belief in what is merely the vehicle of religion is taken as an article of religion.

If Christianity is understood as belief in a *messiah,* merely to enumerate its sects would be a Herculean task, and a thankless one as well; for Christianity so understood is itself merely a sect* of messianic faith, as distinguished from *Judaism* in the narrower sense (in the final period of its undivided dominion over the people), when the question was raised: "Are you he who was to come, or shall we look for another?" And this is how the

---

*It is a peculiarity of the German use (or abuse) of language that the followers of our religion call themselves *Christen,* as if there were more than one Christ and each believer were a Christ. They should rather call themselves *Christianer.* But "Christian" would immediately be regarded as the name of a sect, people of whom one could say many evil things (as happens in *Peregrinus Proteus*). [15] So a critic in the *Halle Scientific Journal* maintains that the name Jehovah should be pronounced Jahweh. But if the name were altered in this way, it would seem to designate a merely national deity, not the Lord of the World.

wir eines Anderen warten?", wofür es auch anfänglich die Römer nahmen. In dieser Bedeutung aber würde das Christenthum ein gewisser auf Satzungen und Schrift gegründeter Volksglaube sein, von dem man nicht wissen könnte, ob er gerade für alle Menschen gültig oder der letzte Offen=barungsglaube sein dürfte, bei dem es forthin bleiben müßte, oder ob nicht künftig andere göttliche Statuten, die dem Zweck noch näher träten, zu erwarten wären.

Um also ein bestimmtes Schema der Eintheilung einer Glaubenslehre in Secten zu haben, können wir nicht von empirischen Datis, sondern wir müssen von Verschiedenheiten anfangen, die sich a priori durch die Ver=nunft denken lassen, um in der Stufenreihe der Unterschiede der Denkungs=art in Glaubenssachen die Stufe auszumachen, in der die Verschiedenheit zuerst einen Sectenunterschied begründen würde.

In Glaubenssachen ist das Princip der Eintheilung nach der ange=nommenen Denkungsart entweder Religion oder Heidenthum (die einander wie A und non A entgegen sind). Die Bekenner der ersteren werden gewöhnlich Gläubige, die des zweiten Ungläubige genannt. Religion ist derjenige Glaube, der das Wesentliche aller Verehrung Gottes in der Moralität des Menschen setzt: Heidenthum, der es nicht darin setzt; entweder weil es ihm gar an dem Begriffe eines übernatür=lichen und moralischen Wesens mangelt (Ethnicismus brutus), oder weil er etwas Anderes als die Gesinnung eines sittlich wohlgeführten Lebens=wandels, also das Nichtwesentliche der Religion, zum Religionsstück macht (Ethnicismus speciosus).

Glaubenssätze, welche zugleich als göttliche Gebote gedacht werden sollen, sind nun entweder blos statutarisch, mithin für uns zufällig und Offenbarungslehren, oder moralisch, mithin mit dem Bewußtsein ihrer Nothwendigkeit verbunden und a priori erkennbar, d. i. Vernunftlehren des Glaubens. Der Inbegriff der ersteren Lehren macht den Kirchen=, der anderen aber den reinen Religionsglauben aus.*)

Allgemeinheit für einen Kirchenglauben zu fordern (catholicismus hierarchicus) ist ein Widerspruch, weil unbedingte Allgemeinheit Noth=wendigkeit voraus setzt, die nur da Statt findet, wo die Vernunft selbst die Glaubenssätze hinreichend begründet, mithin diese nicht bloße Statute

---

*) Diese Eintheilung, welche ich nicht für präcis und dem gewöhnlichen Rede=gebrauch angemessen ausgebe, mag einstweilen hier gelten.

Kant's Schriften. Werke. VII. 4

Romans at first took Christianity. But Christianity in this sense would be the faith of a certain people, based on dogmas and Scriptures, and we could not know whether it is directly valid for all men, the final revelation by which we must henceforth abide, or whether we can expect the future to bring other divine statutes that will approximate still more closely to the end.

So if we are to divide ecclesiastical faith into sects according to a determinate plan, we cannot begin with what is given empirically. We must rather begin with distinctions that reason can think a priori, in order to determine the step, in the series formed by different opinions in matters of faith, at which a distinction would give rise to different sects.

According to the *accepted* view, the principle of division in matters of faith is either *religion* or *paganism* (which are opposed to each other as A to non-A). Those who profess religion are commonly called *believers*; those who profess paganism, *infidels*. Religion is the kind of faith that locates the *essence* of all divine worship in man's morality; paganism is the kind that does not, either because it lacks the concept of a supernatural moral being (*Ethnicismus brutus*), or because it makes something other than the attitude of living a morally good life, hence something non-essential to religion, a part of religion (*Ethnicismus speciosus*).

Now tenets of faith which are also to be conceived as divine commands are either merely *statutory* doctrines, which are contingent for us and [must be] revealed [if we are to know them], or *moral* doctrines, which involve consciousness of their necessity and can be recognized a priori—that is, *rational* doctrines. The sum of statutory teachings comprises *ecclesiastical faith* [or dogma]; that of moral teachings, pure *religious* faith.*

To claim *universal validity* for a dogma (*catholicismus hierarchius*) involves a contradiction: for unconditioned universality presupposes necessity, and since this occurs only where reason itself provides sufficient grounds for the tenets of faith, no mere statute can be universally valid. Pure religious

---

*I do not say that this division is either precise or in keeping with ordinary usage; but it may stand for the time being.

sind. Dagegen hat der reine Religionsglaube rechtmäßigen Anspruch auf Allgemeingültigkeit (catholicismus rationalis). Die Sectirerei in Glaubenssachen wird also bei dem letztern nie Statt finden, und wo sie angetroffen wird, da entspringt sie immer aus einem Fehler des Kirchenglaubens: seine Statute (selbst göttliche Offenbarungen) für wesentliche Stücke der Religion zu halten, mithin den Empirism in Glaubenssachen dem Rationalism unterzuschieben und so das blos Zufällige für an sich nothwendig auszugeben. Da nun in zufälligen Lehren es vielerlei einander widerstreitende, theils Satzungen, theils Auslegung von Satzungen, geben kann: so ist leicht einzusehen, daß der bloße Kirchenglaube, ohne durch den reinen Religionsglauben geläutert zu sein, eine reiche Quelle unendlich vieler Secten in Glaubenssachen sein werde.

Um diese Läuterung, worin sie bestehe, bestimmt anzugeben, scheint mir der zum Gebrauch schicklichste Probirstein der Satz zu sein: ein jeder Kirchenglaube, so fern er blos statutarische Glaubenslehren für wesentliche Religionslehren ausgiebt, hat eine gewisse Beimischung von Heidenthum; denn dieses besteht darin, das Äußerliche (Außerwesentliche) der Religion für wesentlich auszugeben. Diese Beimischung kann gradweise so weit gehen, daß die ganze Religion darüber in einen bloßen Kirchenglauben, Gebräuche für Gesetze auszugeben, übergeht und alsdann baares Heidenthum wird,*) wider welchen Schimpfnamen es nichts verschlägt zu sagen, daß jene Lehren doch göttliche Offenbarungen seien; denn nicht jene statutarische Lehren und Kirchenpflichten selbst, sondern der unbedingte ihnen beigelegte Werth (nicht etwa blos Vehikel, sondern selbst Religionsstücke zu sein, ob sie zwar keinen inneren moralischen Gehalt bei sich führen, also nicht die Materie der Offenbarung, sondern die Form ihrer Aufnahme in seine praktische Gesinnung) ist das, was auf eine solche Glaubensweise den Namen des Heidenthums mit Recht fallen läßt. Die kirchliche Autorität, nach einem solchen Glauben selig zu sprechen oder zu verdammen, würde das Pfaffenthum genannt werden, von welchem Ehrennamen sich so nennende Protestanten nicht auszuschließen sind, wenn sie das Wesent-

---

*) Heidenthum (Paganismus) ist der Worterklärung nach der religiöse Aberglaube des Volks in Wäldern (Heiden), d. i. einer Menge, deren Religionsglaube noch ohne alle kirchliche Verfassung, mithin ohne öffentliches Gesetz ist. Juden aber, Mohammedaner und Indier halten das für kein Gesetz, was nicht das ihrige ist, und benennen andere Völker, die nicht eben dieselbe kirchliche Observanzen haben, mit dem Titel der Verwerfung (Goj, Dschaur u. s. w.), nämlich der Ungläubigen.

faith, on the other hand, can justly claim universal validity (*catholicismus rationalis*). So a division into sects can never occur in matters of pure religious belief. Wherever sectarianism is to be found, it arises from a mistake on the part of ecclesiastical faith: the mistake of regarding its statutes (even if they are divine revelations) for essential parts of religion, and so substituting empiricism in matters of faith for rationalism and passing off what is merely contingent as necessary in itself. But since, in contingent doctrines, there can be all sorts of conflicting articles or interpretations of articles, we can readily see that mere dogma will be a prolific source of innumerable sects in matters of faith, unless it is rectified by pure religious faith.

To indicate precisely how religious belief purifies dogma, I think the following proposition is the most convenient touchstone we can use: to the extent that any dogma gives out merely statutory teachings of faith as essential religious teachings, it contains a certain *admixture of paganism*; for paganism consists in passing off the externals (non-essentials) of religion as essential. This admixture can be present to such a degree that it turns the entire religion into a mere dogma, which raises practices to the status of laws, and so becomes sheer paganism.* And [a church] cannot escape this rude name by saying that its doctrines are, nevertheless, divine revelations. For it is not because of such statutory doctrines and ecclesiastical duties themselves that this sort of faith deserves to be called pagan, but rather because of the unconditioned value it attributes to them (as parts of religion itself and not its mere vehicle, although they have no intrinsic moral content; and so what counts, here, is not the matter of revelation but the way in which this is adopted [by a church] in its practical attitude). Ecclesiastical authority to pronounce salvation or damnation according to this sort of faith would be called clericalism. And

---

Paganism, according to its etymology, is the religious superstition of people in the woods—that is, of a group whose religious belief has no ecclesiastical system of government and hence no public law. The Jews, Mohammedans, and Hindus, however, refuse to recognize as a law anything that differs from theirs, and give other peoples, who do not have exactly the same ecclesiastical rites as theirs, the title of reprobation (Goj, Dschaur, etc.)—that is, of infidels.

liche ihrer Glaubenslehre in Glauben an Sätze und Obfervanzen, von
denen ihnen die Vernunft nichts sagt, und welche zu bekennen und zu
beobachten der schlechteste, nichtswürdigste Mensch in eben demselben Grade
tauglich ist als der beste, zu setzen bedacht sind: sie mögen auch einen noch
so großen Nachtrapp von Tugenden, als die aus der wundervollen Kraft
der ersteren entsprängen (mithin ihre eigene Wurzel nicht haben), an=
hängen, als sie immer wollen.

Von dem Punkte also, wo der Kirchenglaube anfängt, für sich selbst
mit Autorität zu sprechen, ohne auf seine Rectification durch den reinen
Religionsglauben zu achten, hebt auch die Sectirerei an; denn da dieser
(als praktischer Vernunftglaube) seinen Einfluß auf die menschliche Seele
nicht verlieren kann, der mit dem Bewußtsein der Freiheit verbunden ist,
indessen daß der Kirchenglaube über die Gewissen Gewalt ausübt: so sucht
ein jeder etwas für seine eigene Meinung in den Kirchenglauben hinein
oder aus ihm heraus zu bringen.

Diese Gewalt veranlaßt entweder bloße Absonderung von der Kirche
(Separatism), d. i. Enthaltung von der öffentlichen Gemeinschaft mit ihr,
oder öffentliche Spaltung der in Ansehung der kirchlichen Form Anders=
denkenden, ob sie zwar der Materie nach sich zu eben derselben bekennen
(Schismatiker), oder Zusammentretung der Dissidenten in Ansehung ge=
wisser Glaubenslehren in besondere, nicht immer geheime, aber doch vom
Staat nicht sanctionirte Gesellschaften (Sectirer), deren einige noch be=
sondere, nicht fürs große Publicum gehörende, geheime Lehren aus eben
demselben Schatz her holen (gleichsam Clubbisten der Frömmigkeit), endlich
auch falsche Friedensstifter, die durch die Zusammenschmelzung verschie=
dener Glaubensarten allen genug zu thun meinen (Synkretisten); die dann
noch schlimmer sind als Sectirer, weil Gleichgültigkeit in Ansehung der
Religion überhaupt zum Grunde liegt und, weil einmal doch ein Kirchen=
glaube im Volk sein müsse, einer so gut wie der andere sei, wenn er sich nur
durch die Regierung zu ihren Zwecken gut handhaben läßt; ein Grundsatz,
der im Munde des Regenten, als eines solchen, zwar ganz richtig, auch
sogar weise ist, im Urtheile des Unterthanen selbst aber, der diese Sache
aus seinem eigenen und zwar moralischen Interesse zu erwägen hat, die
äußerste Geringschätzung der Religion verrathen würde; indem, wie selbst
das Vehikel der Religion beschaffen sei, was jemand in seinen Kirchen=
glauben aufnimmt, für die Religion keine gleichgültige Sache ist.

In Ansehung der Sectirerei (welche auch wohl ihr Haupt bis zur

4*

self-styled Protestants should not be deprived of this honorific title if they insist on making the essence of their creed belief in tenets and rites which reason says nothing about, and which the most evil and worthless man can profess and observe as well as the best—even if they add on an imposing rear guard of virtues that spring from the wondrous power of these tenets and rites (and so have no roots of their own).

As soon, then, as ecclesiastical faith begins to speak with authority on its own and forgets that it must be rectified by pure *religious faith,* sectarianism sets in. For, since pure religious faith (as practical rational faith) cannot lose its influence on the human soul—an influence that involves consciousness of our freedom—while ecclesiastical faith uses force on our conscience, everyone tries to put into or get out of dogma something in keeping with his own view.

The force that dogma uses on man's conscience gives rise to three types of movement: a mere separation from the church, that is, abstention from public association with it (by separatists); a public rift regarding the form of the church, although the dissidents accept the content of its doctrines (by schismatics); or a union of dissenters from certain doctrines of faith into particular societies which, though not always secret, are not sanctioned by the state (sectarians). And some of these sects (cliques of the pious, so to speak) fetch from the same treasury still more particular, secret doctrines not intended for the great audience of the public. Finally, false peacemakers (syncretists) arise, who want to satisfy everyone by melting down the different creeds. These syncretists are even worse than sectarians, because they are basically indifferent to religion in general and take the attitude that, if the people must have dogma, one is as good as another so long as it lends itself readily to the government's aims. This principle is quite correct and even wise when the ruler states it in his capacity as ruler. But as the judgment of the subject himself, who must ponder this matter in his own—and indeed his moral—interest, it would betray the utmost contempt for religion; for religion cannot be indifferent to the character of its vehicle which we adopt in our dogma.

On the subject of sectarianism (which, as in Protestantism, goes so far as to multiply churches), we are accustomed to say that

Vermannigfaltigung der Kirchen erhebt, wie es bei den Protestanten ge=
schehen ist) pflegt man zwar zu sagen: es ist gut, daß es vielerlei Religio=
nen (eigentlich kirchliche Glaubensarten in einem Staate) giebt, und so
fern ist dieses auch richtig, als es ein gutes Zeichen ist: nämlich daß Glau=
bensfreiheit dem Volke gelassen worden; aber das ist eigentlich nur ein
Lob für die Regierung. An sich aber ist ein solcher öffentlicher Religions=
zustand doch nicht gut, dessen Princip so beschaffen ist, daß es nicht, wie
es doch der Begriff einer Religion erfordert, Allgemeinheit und Einheit
der wesentlichen Glaubensmaximen bei sich führt und den Streit, der von
dem Außerwesentlichen herrührt, nicht von jenem unterscheidet. Der Unter=
schied der Meinungen in Ansehung der größeren oder minderen Schicklich=
keit oder Unschicklichkeit des Vehikels der Religion zu dieser als Endabsicht
selbst (nämlich die Menschen moralisch zu bessern) mag also allenfalls Ver=
schiedenheit der Kirchensecten, darf aber darum nicht Verschiedenheit der
Religionssecten bewirken, welche der Einheit und Allgemeinheit der Reli=
gion (also der unsichtbaren Kirche) gerade zuwider ist. Aufgeklärte Katho=
liken und Protestanten werden also einander als Glaubensbrüder ansehen
können, ohne sich doch zu vermengen, beide in der Erwartung (und Bear=
beitung zu diesem Zweck): daß die Zeit unter Begünstigung der Regierung
nach und nach die Förmlichkeiten des Glaubens (der freilich alsdann nicht
ein Glaube sein muß, Gott sich durch etwas anders, als durch reine mo=
ralische Gesinnung günstig zu machen oder zu versöhnen) der Würde ihres
Zwecks, nämlich der Religion selbst, näher bringen werde. — Selbst in
Ansehung der Juden ist dieses ohne die Träumerei einer allgemeinen
Judenbekehrung*) (zum Christenthum als einem messianischen Glauben)
möglich, wenn unter ihnen, wie jetzt geschieht, geläuterte Religionsbegriffe
erwachen und das Kleid des nunmehr zu nichts dienenden, vielmehr alle

---

*) Moses Mendelssohn wies dieses Ansinnen auf eine Art ab, die seiner Klug=
heit Ehre macht (durch eine argumentatio ad hominem). So lange (sagt er) als
nicht Gott vom Berge Sinai eben so feierlich unser Gesetz aufhebt, als er es (unter
Donner und Blitz) gegeben, d. i. bis zum Nimmertag, sind wir daran gebunden;
womit er wahrscheinlicher Weise sagen wollte: Christen, schafft ihr erst das Juden=
thum aus Eurem eigenen Glauben weg: so werden wir auch das unsrige verlassen.
— Daß er aber seinen eignen Glaubensgenossen durch diese harte Forderung die
Hoffnung zur mindesten Erleichterung der sie drückenden Lasten abschnitt, ob er zwar
wahrscheinlich die wenigsten derselben für wesentlich seinem Glauben angehörig hielt,
ob das seinem guten Willen Ehre mache, mögen diese selbst entscheiden.

it is desirable for many kinds of religion (properly speaking, forms of ecclesiastical faith) to exist in a state. And this is, in fact, desirable to the extent that it is a good sign—a sign, namely, that the people are allowed freedom of belief. But it is only the government that is to be commended here. In itself, such a public state of affairs in religion is not a good thing unless the principle underlying it is of such a nature as to bring with it universal agreement on the essential maxims of belief, as the concept of religion requires, and to distinguish this agreement from conflicts arising from its non-essentials. Differences of opinion about the relative efficacy of the vehicle of religion in promoting its final aim, religion itself (that is, the moral improvement of men), may therefore produce, at most, different church sects, but not different religious sects; for this is directly opposed to the unity and universality of religion (and so of the invisible church). Enlightened Catholics and Protestants, while still holding to their own dogmas, could thus look upon each other as brothers in faith, while expecting and striving toward this end: that, with the government's favor, time will gradually bring the formalities of faith closer to the dignity of their end, religion itself (and for this reason the faith in question cannot be faith that we can obtain God's favor or pardon by anything other than a pure moral attitude of will). Without dreaming of a conversion of all Jews* (to Christianity in the sense of a *messianic* faith), we can consider it possible even in their case if, as is now happening, purified religious concepts awaken among them and throw off the garb of the ancient cult, which now serves no purpose and even suppresses any true religious attitude. Since they have long had

---

*Moses Mendelssohn rejects this demand in a way that does credit to his *cleverness* (by an *argumentatio ad hominem*).[16] Until (he says) God, from Mount Sinai, revokes our law as solemnly as He gave it (in thunder and lightning)—that is, until the end of time—we are bound by it. By this he apparently meant to say: Christians, first get rid of the Judaism in *your own* faith, and then we will give up ours. But it is for his co-religionists to decide whether this does credit to his good will; for by this stern challenge he cut off their hope for any relief whatsoever from the burden that oppresses them, though he apparently considered only the smallest part of it essential to his faith.

wahre Religionsgesinnung verdrängenden alten Cultus abwerfen. Da sie nun so lange das Kleid ohne Mann (Kirche ohne Religion) gehabt haben, gleichwohl aber der Mann ohne Kleid (Religion ohne Kirche) auch nicht gut verwahrt ist, sie also gewisse Förmlichkeiten einer Kirche, die dem Endzweck in ihrer jetzigen Lage am angemessensten wäre, bedürfen: so kann man den Gedanken eines sehr guten Kopfs dieser Nation, Ben=david's, die Religion Jesu (vermuthlich mit ihrem Vehikel, dem Evan=gelium) öffentlich anzunehmen, nicht allein für sehr glücklich, sondern auch für den einzigen Vorschlag halten, dessen Ausführung dieses Volk, auch ohne sich mit andern in Glaubenssachen zu vermischen, bald als ein gelehrtes, wohlgesittetes und aller Rechte des bürgerlichen Zustandes fähiges Volk, dessen Glaube auch von der Regierung sanctionirt werden könnte, bemerklich machen würde; wobei freilich ihr die Schriftauslegung (der Thora und des Evangeliums) frei gelassen werden müßte, um die Art, wie Jesus als Jude zu Juden, von der Art, wie er als moralischer Lehrer zu Menschen überhaupt redete, zu unterscheiden. — Die Euthanasie des Judenthums ist die reine moralische Religion mit Verlassung aller alten Satzungslehren, deren einige doch im Christenthum (als messiani=schen Glauben) noch zurück behalten bleiben müssen: welcher Sectenunter=schied endlich doch auch verschwinden muß und so das, was man als den Beschluß des großen Drama des Religionswechsels auf Erden nennt, (die Wiederbringung aller Dinge) wenigstens im Geiste herbeiführt, da nur ein Hirt und eine Heerde Statt findet.

*   *
*

Wenn aber gefragt wird: nicht blos was Christenthum sei, sondern wie es der Lehrer desselben anzufangen habe, damit ein solches in den Herzen der Menschen wirklich angetroffen werde (welches mit der Aufgabe einerlei ist: was ist zu thun, damit der Religionsglaube zugleich bessere Menschen mache?), so ist der Zweck zwar einerlei und kann keinen Secten=unterschied veranlassen, aber die Wahl des Mittels zu demselben kann diesen doch herbei führen, weil zu einer und derselben Wirkung sich mehr wie eine Ursache denken läßt und sofern also Verschiedenheit und Streit der Meinungen, ob das eine oder das andere demselben angemessen und göttlich sei, mithin eine Trennung in Principien bewirken kann, die selbst

garments without a man in them (a church without religion) and since, moreover, a *man without garments* (religion without a church) is not well protected, they need certain formalities of a church—the church best able to lead them, in their present state, to the final end. So we can consider the proposal of Ben David, [17] a highly intelligent Jew, to adopt publicly the religion of *Jesus* (presumably with its vehicle, the *Gospel*), a most fortunate one. Moreover it is the only plan which, if carried out, would leave the Jews a distinctive faith and yet quickly call attention to them as an educated and civilized people who are ready for all the rights of citizenship and whose faith could also be sanctioned by the government. If this were to happen, the Jews would have to be left free, in their interpretation of the Scriptures (the Torah and the Gospels), to distinguish the way in which Jesus spoke as a Jew to Jews from the way he spoke as a moral teacher to men in general. The euthanasia of Judaism is pure moral religion, freed from all the ancient statutory teachings, some of which were bound to be retained in Christianity (as a messianic faith). But this division of sects, too, must disappear in time, leading, at least in spirit, to what we call the conclusion of the great drama of religious change on earth (the restoration of all things), when there will be only one shepherd and one flock.

*   *
*

But if we ask not only what Christianity is but also how to set about teaching it so that it will really be present in the hearts of men (and this is one with the question of what to do so that religious faith will also make men better), there can be no division into sects regarding the end, since this is always the same. But our choice of means to the end can bring about a division of sects; since we can conceive of more than one cause for the same effect, we can hold different and conflicting views as to which means is fitting and divine and so disagree in our

das Wesentliche (in subjectiver Bedeutung) der Religion überhaupt an=
gehen.

Da die Mittel zu diesem Zwecke nicht empirisch sein können — weil
diese allenfalls wohl auf die That, aber nicht auf die Gesinnung hinwirken
—, so muß für den, der alles Übersinnliche zugleich für übernatür=
lich hält, die obige Aufgabe sich in die Frage verwandeln: wie ist die
Wiedergeburt (als die Folge der Bekehrung, wodurch jemand ein anderer,
neuer Mensch wird) durch göttlichen unmittelbaren Einfluß möglich, und
was hat der Mensch zu thun, um diesen herbei zu ziehen? Ich behaupte,
daß, ohne die Geschichte zu Rathe zu ziehen (als welche zwar Meinungen,
aber nicht die Nothwendigkeit derselben vorstellig machen kann), man a pri=
ori einen unausbleiblichen Sectenunterschied, den blos diese Aufgabe bei
denen bewirkt, welchen es eine Kleinigkeit ist, zu einer natürlichen Wirkung
übernatürliche Ursachen herbei zu rufen, vorher sagen kann, ja daß diese
Spaltung auch die einzige sei, welche zur Benennung zweier verschiedener
Religionssecten berechtigt; denn die anderen, welche man fälschlich so be=
nennt, sind nur Kirchensecten und gehen das Innere der Religion nicht
an. — Ein jedes Problem aber besteht erstlich aus der Quästion der
Aufgabe, zweitens der Auflösung und drittens dem Beweis, daß das
Verlangte durch die letztere geleistet werde. Also:

1) Die Aufgabe (die der wackere Spener mit Eifer allen Lehrern
der Kirche zurief) ist: der Religionsvortrag muß zum Zweck haben, aus
uns andere, nicht blos bessere Menschen (gleich als ob wir so schon gute,
aber nur dem Grade nach vernachlässigte wären) zu machen. Dieser Satz
ward den Orthodoxisten (ein nicht übel ausgedachter Name) in den
Weg geworfen, welche in dem Glauben an die reine Offenbarungslehre
und den von der Kirche vorgeschriebenen Observanzen (dem Beten, dem
Kirchengehen und den Sacramenten) neben dem ehrbaren (zwar mit Über=
tretungen untermengten, durch jene aber immer wieder gut zu machenden)
Lebenswandel die Art setzten, Gott wohlgefällig zu werden. — Die Auf=
gabe ist also ganz in der Vernunft gegründet.

2) Die Auflösung aber ist völlig mystisch ausgefallen: so wie man
es vom Supernaturalism in Principien der Religion erwarten konnte, der,
weil der Mensch von Natur in Sünden todt sei, keine Besserung aus eige=
nen Kräften hoffen lasse, selbst nicht aus der ursprünglichen unverfälsch=
baren moralischen Anlage in seiner Natur, die, ob sie gleich übersinnlich
ist, dennoch Fleisch genannt wird, darum weil ihre Wirkung nicht zugleich

principles, even in those having to do with what is essential (in a subjective sense) in religion as such.

Now the means to this end cannot be empirical, since empirical means could undoubtedly affect our actions but not our attitude. And so, for one who thinks that the *supersensible* must also be *supernatural*, the above problem turns into the question: how is rebirth (resulting from a conversion by which one becomes an other, new man) possible by God's direct influence, and what must man do to bring it about? I maintain that, without consulting history (which can say only that certain opinions have been held but not that they arose necessarily), we can predict a priori that people who consider it a trifling matter to call in a supernatural cause for a natural effect must inevitably divide into sects over this problem. Indeed, I maintain that this division is the only one that entitles us to speak of two different religious sects, since other so-called religious sects are merely church sects, and their divisions do not concern the core of religion. In handling any problem, however, one must first *state* the problem, then *solve* it, and finally *prove* that the solution does what was required of it. Accordingly:

1) The problem (which the valiant Spener [18] called out fervently to all ecclesiastical teachers) is this: the aim of religious instruction must be to make us *other* men and not merely better men (as if we were already good but only negligent about the degree of our goodness). This thesis was thrown in the path of the *orthodox* (a not inappropriate name), who hold that the way to become pleasing to God consists in believing pure revealed doctrine and observing the practices prescribed by the church (prayer, churchgoing, and the sacraments)—to which they add the requirement of honorable conduct (mixed, admittedly, with transgressions, but these can always be made good by faith and the rites prescribed). The problem, therefore, has a solid basis in reason.

2) But the solution turns out to be completely *mystical*, as one might expect from supernaturalism in principles of religion; for, according to it, the original, incorruptible moral predisposition in man's nature, though supersensible, is still to be called flesh because its effect is not supernatural as well; only

übernatürlich ist, als in welchem Falle die unmittelbare Ursache der=
selben allein der Geist (Gottes) sein würde. — Die mystische Auflösung
jener Aufgabe theilt nun die Gläubigen in zwei Secten des Gefühls
übernatürlicher Einflüsse: die eine, wo das Gefühl als von herzzermal=
mender (zerknirschender), die andere, wo es von herzzerschmelzender
(in die selige Gemeinschaft mit Gott sich auflösender) Art sein müsse, so
daß die Auflösung des Problems (aus bösen Menschen gute zu machen)
von zwei entgegengesetzten Standpunkten ausgeht („wo das Wollen zwar
gut ist, aber das Vollbringen mangelt"). In der einen Secte kommt es
nämlich nur darauf an, von der Herrschaft des Bösen in sich los zu kom=
men, worauf dann das gute Princip sich von selbst einfinden würde: in
der andern, das gute Princip in seine Gesinnung aufzunehmen, worauf
vermittelst eines übernatürlichen Einflusses das Böse für sich keinen Platz
mehr finden und das Gute allein herrschend sein würde.

Die Idee von einer moralischen, aber nur durch übernatürlichen Ein=
fluß möglichen Metamorphose des Menschen mag wohl schon längst in
den Köpfen der Gläubigen rumort haben: sie ist aber in neueren Zeiten
allererst recht zur Sprache gekommen und hat den Spener= Francki=
schen und den Mährisch = Zinzendorfschen Sectenunterschied (den
Pietism und Moravianism) in der Bekehrungslehre hervorgebracht.

Nach der ersteren Hypothese geschieht die Scheidung des Guten vom
Bösen (womit die menschliche Natur amalgamirt ist) durch eine übernatür=
liche Operation, die Zerknirschung und Zermalmung des Herzens in der
Buße, als einem nahe an Verzweiflung grenzenden, aber doch auch nur
durch den Einfluß eines himmlischen Geistes in seinem nöthigen Grade
erreichbaren Gram (maeror animi), um welchen der Mensch selbst bitten
müsse, indem er sich selbst darüber grämt, daß er sich nicht genug gräme
(mithin das Leidsein ihm doch nicht so ganz von Herzen gehen kann).
Diese „Höllenfahrt des Selbsterkenntnisses bahnt nun, wie der sel. Ha=
mann sagt, den Weg zur Vergötterung". Nämlich nachdem diese Glut
der Buße ihre größte Höhe erreicht hat, geschehe der Durchbruch, und
der Regulus des Wiedergebornen glänze unter den Schlacken, die ihn
zwar umgeben, aber nicht verunreinigen, tüchtig zu dem Gott wohlgefäl=
ligen Gebrauch in einem guten Lebenswandel. — Diese radicale Verände=
rung fängt also mit einem Wunder an und endigt mit dem, was man
sonst als natürlich anzusehen pflegt, weil es die Vernunft vorschreibt,
nämlich mit dem moralisch=guten Lebenswandel. Weil man aber selbst

if spirit (God) were the direct cause of man's improvement would this effect be a supernatural one. So man, being by nature dead in sin, cannot hope to improve by his own powers, not even by his moral predisposition. Now those who believe in a mystical solution to the difficulty divide into two sects with regard to the *feeling* of this supernatural influence: according to one sect, it has to be the kind that *dashes the heart to pieces* (crushes it with remorse): according to the other, the kind that *melts the heart* (so that man dissolves in blessed communion with God). Thus the solution to the problem (of making good men out of bad) begins from two opposed standpoints ("where the volition is indeed good, but its fulfillment is wanting"). In one sect it is only a question of *freeing* ourselves from the power of evil within us, and then the good principle will appear of itself; in the other, of admitting the good principle in our attitude of will, and then, by a supernatural influence, there is no longer room for the evil, and the good rules alone.

The idea of a moral metamorphosis of man that could yet take place only by supernatural influence may well have been *rumbling around* in believers' heads for a long time; but only in more recent times has it been clearly enunciated and given rise to a division of sects between the followers of *Spener* and *Franck* [19] (Pietists) and the *Moravian Brethren* of *Zinzendorf* [20] (*Moravians*) on the doctrine of conversion.

According to the Pietist hypothesis, the operation that separates good from evil (of which human nature is compounded) is a supernatural one—a breaking and crushing of the heart in *repentance*, a grief (*maeror animi*) bordering on despair which can, however, reach the necessary intensity only by the influence of a heavenly spirit. Man must himself beg for this grief, while grieving over the fact that his grief is not great enough (to drive the pain completely from his heart). Now as the late Hamann [21] says: "This descent into the hell of self-knowledge paves the way to deification." In other words, when the fire of repentance has reached its height, the amalgam of good and evil *breaks up* and the purer metal of the *reborn* gleams through the dross, which surrounds but does not contaminate it, ready for service pleasing to God in good conduct. This radical change, therefore, begins with a *miracle*

beim höchsten Fluge einer mystisch=gestimmten Einbildungskraft den Men=
schen doch nicht von allem Selbstthun lossprechen kann, ohne ihn gänzlich
zur Maschine zu machen, so ist das anhaltende inbrünstige Gebet das,
was ihm noch zu thun obliegt, (wofern man es überhaupt für ein Thun
will gelten lassen) und wovon er sich jene übernatürliche Wirkung allein
versprechen kann; wobei doch auch der Scrupel eintritt: daß, da das Gebet,
wie es heißt, nur sofern erhörlich ist, als es im Glauben geschieht, dieser
selbst aber eine Gnadenwirkung ist, d. i. etwas, wozu der Mensch aus
eigenen Kräften nicht gelangen kann, er mit seinen Gnadenmitteln im
Cirkel geführt wird und am Ende eigentlich nicht weiß, wie er das Ding
angreifen solle.

Nach der zweiten Secte Meinung geschieht der erste Schritt, den der
sich seiner sündigen Beschaffenheit bewußt werdende Mensch zum Besseren
thut, ganz natürlich, durch die Vernunft, die, indem sie ihm im morali=
schen Gesetz den Spiegel vorhält, worin er seine Verwerflichkeit erblickt,
die moralische Anlage zum Guten benutzt, um ihn zur Entschließung zu
bringen, es fortmehr zu seiner Maxime zu machen: aber die Ausführung
dieses Vorsatzes ist ein Wunder. Er wendet sich nämlich von der Fahne
des bösen Geistes ab und begiebt sich unter die des guten, welches eine
leichte Sache ist. Aber nun bei dieser zu beharren, nicht wieder ins Böse
zurück zu fallen, vielmehr im Guten immer mehr fortzuschreiten, das ist
die Sache, wozu er natürlicher Weise unvermögend sei, vielmehr nichts
Geringeres als Gefühl einer übernatürlichen Gemeinschaft und sogar das
Bewußtsein eines continuirlichen Umganges mit einem himmlischen Geiste
erfordert werde; wobei es zwischen ihm und dem letzteren zwar auf einer
Seite nicht an Verweisen, auf der andern nicht an Abbitten fehlen kann:
doch ohne daß eine Entzweiung oder Rückfall (aus der Gnade) zu besorgen
ist; wenn er nur darauf Bedacht nimmt, diesen Umgang, der selbst ein
continuirliches Gebet ist, ununterbrochen zu cultiviren.

Hier ist nun eine zwiefache mystische Gefühlstheorie zum Schlüssel
der Aufgabe: ein neuer Mensch zu werden, vorgelegt, wo es nicht um das
Object und den Zweck aller Religion (den Gott gefälligen Lebenswandel,
denn darüber stimmen beide Theile überein), sondern um die subjective
Bedingungen zu thun ist, unter denen wir allein Kraft dazu bekommen,
jene Theorie in uns zur Ausführung zu bringen; wobei dann von Tu=
gend (die ein leerer Name sei) nicht die Rede sein kann, sondern nur
von der Gnade, weil beide Parteien darüber einig sind, daß es hiemit

and ends with what we would ordinarily consider natural, since *reason* prescribes it: namely, morally good conduct. But even in the highest flight of a mystically inclined imagination, one cannot exempt man from doing anything himself, without making him a mere machine; and so what man has to do is *pray* fervidly and incessantly (in so far as we are willing to count prayer as a *deed*), and only from this can he expect that supernatural effect. But since prayer, as they say, can be heard only if it is made in faith, and faith itself is an effect of grace—that is, something man cannot achieve by his own powers—the scruple arises that this view gets involved in a vicious circle with its means of grace and, in the final analysis, really does not know how to handle the thing.

According to the *Moravian* view, as man becomes aware of his sinful state he takes the first step toward his improvement quite naturally, by his *reason*; for as reason holds before him, in the moral law, the mirror in which he sees his guilt, it leads him, using his moral disposition to the good, to decide that from now on he will make the law his maxim. But his carrying out of this resolution is a *miracle*. In other words, it is an easy thing for man to turn his back on the banner of the evil spirit and set out under that of the good; but what he is naturally incapable of doing is to persevere in this, not to relapse into evil but, on the contrary, to advance constantly in goodness. For this, he needs nothing less than the feeling of supernatural communion with a heavenly spirit and even continuous awareness of intercourse with it. It is true that in this relationship between God and man one side cannot fail to reprove and the other to beg forgiveness; but man need not worry about an estrangement or a relapse (from grace), if only he takes care to cultivate, without interruption, this intercourse which is itself a continuous prayer.

Here we have two mystical theories of feeling offered as keys to the problem of becoming a new man. What is at issue between them is not the *object* and end of all religion (which, both agree, is conduct pleasing to God), but the *subjective* conditions which are necessary for us to acquire the power to work out that theory in ourselves. The subjective condition in question cannot be virtue (which is an empty name to them), but only *grace*; for both

nicht natürlich zugehen könne, sich aber wieder darin von einander trennen, daß der eine Theil den fürchterlichen Kampf mit dem bösen Geiste, um von dessen Gewalt los zu kommen, bestehen muß, der andere aber dieses gar nicht nöthig, ja als Werkheiligkeit verwerflich findet, sondern geradezu mit dem guten Geiste Allianz schließt, weil die vorige mit dem bösen (als pactum turpe) gar keinen Einspruch dagegen verursachen kann; da dann die Wiedergeburt als einmal für allemal vorgehende übernatürliche und radicale Revolution im Seelenzustande auch wohl äußerlich einen Secten= unterschied aus so sehr gegen einander abstechenden Gefühlen beider Par= teien, kennbar machen dürfte.*)

3) Der Beweis: daß, wenn, was Nr. 2 verlangt worden, geschehen, die Aufgabe Nr. 1 dadurch aufgelöset sein werde. — Dieser Beweis ist unmöglich. Denn der Mensch müßte beweisen, daß in ihm eine übernatür= liche Erfahrung, die an sich selbst ein Widerspruch ist, vorgegangen sei. Es könnte allenfalls eingeräumt werden, daß der Mensch in sich eine Er= fahrung (z. B. von neuen und besseren Willensbestimmungen) gemacht hätte, von einer Veränderung, die er sich nicht anders als durch ein Wunder zu erklären weiß, also von etwas übernatürlichem. Aber eine Erfahrung, von der er sich sogar nicht einmal, daß sie in der That Erfahrung sei, überführen kann, weil sie (als übernatürlich) auf keine Regel der Natur unseres Verstandes zurückgeführt und dadurch bewährt werden kann, ist eine Ausdeutung gewisser Empfindungen, von denen man nicht weiß, was man aus ihnen machen soll, ob sie als zum Erkenntniß gehörig einen wirklichen Gegenstand haben, oder bloße Träumereien sein mögen. Den

---

*) Welche Nationalphysiognomie möchte wohl ein ganzes Volk, welches (wenn dergleichen möglich wäre) in einer dieser Secten erzogen wäre, haben? Denn daß ein solcher sich zeigen würde, ist wohl nicht zu zweifeln: weil oft wiederholte, vor= nehmlich widernatürliche Eindrücke aufs Gemüth sich in Geberdung und Ton der Sprache äußeren, und Mienen endlich stehende Gesichtszüge werden. Beate, oder wie sie Hr. Nicolai nennt, gebenedeiete Gesichter würden es von anderen ge= sitteten und aufgeweckten Völkern (eben nicht zu seinem Vortheil) unterscheiden; denn es ist Zeichnung der Frömmigkeit in Caricatur. Aber nicht die Verachtung der Frömmigkeit ist es, was den Namen der Pietisten zum Sectennamen gemacht hat (mit dem immer eine gewisse Verachtung verbunden ist), sondern die phantastische und bei allem Schein der Demuth stolze Annaßung sich als übernatürlich=begünstigte Kinder des Himmels auszuzeichnen, wenn gleich ihr Wandel, so viel man sehen kann, vor dem der von ihnen so benannten Weltkinder in der Moralität nicht den mindesten Vorzug zeigt.

sides agree that we cannot acquire this power naturally. But their theories then diverge, since one side thinks we can escape from the dominion of the evil spirit only by a *fearful* struggle with it, whereas the other finds this quite unnecessary and even censures it as hypocritical; instead, it straightaway concludes an alliance with the good spirit, since the earlier pact with the evil spirit (as *pactum turpe*) can give rise to no objection to this. When the kinds of feeling involved in man's rebirth are as sharply contrasted as in the theories of these two parties, their different theories of rebirth, as a supernatural and radical spiritual revolution that takes place once and for all, may well appear outwardly as a division of sects.*

3) The *proof:* that number 2 happens, so that the problem posed in number 1 is solved. This proof is impossible. For we would have to prove that we have had a supernatural experience, and this is a contradiction in terms. The most we could grant is that we have experienced a change in ourselves (new and better volitions, for example) which we do not know how to explain except by a miracle and so by something supernatural. But an experience which we cannot even convince ourselves is actually an experience, since (as supernatural) it cannot be traced back to any rule in the nature of our understanding and established by it, is an interpretation of certain sensations that we do not know what to make of, not knowing whether they are elements in knowledge and so have real objects or whether they are mere

---

*If it were possible for a whole people to be brought up in one of these sects, what sort of national physiognomy would this people be likely to have? For there is no doubt that such a physiognomy would emerge, since frequently repeated mental impressions, especially if they are contrary to nature, express themselves in one's appearance and tone of voice, and facial expressions eventually become permanent features. *Sanctified* or, as Herr Nicolai [22] calls them, *divinely blessed* faces would distinguish such a people from other civilized and enlightened peoples (not exactly to its advantage); for this is a caricature of piety. But it was not contempt for piety that made "Pietist" a sect name (and a certain contempt is always connected with such a name); it was rather the Pietists' fantastic and—despite all their show of humility—proud claim to be marked out as supernaturally favored children of heaven, even though their conduct, as far as we can see, is not the least bit better in moral terms than that of the people they call children of the world.

unmittelbaren Einfluß der Gottheit als einer solchen fühlen wollen, ist, weil die Idee von dieser blos in der Vernunft liegt, eine sich selbst wider= sprechende Anmaßung. — Also ist hier eine Aufgabe sammt ihrer Auf= lösung ohne irgend einen möglichen Beweis; woraus denn auch nie etwas Vernünftiges gemacht werden wird.

Es kommt nun noch darauf an, nachzusuchen, ob die Bibel nicht noch ein anderes Princip der Auflösung jenes Spenerischen Problems, als die zwei angeführte sectenmäßige enthalte, welches die Unfruchtbarkeit des kirchlichen Grundsatzes der bloßen Orthodoxie ersetzen könne. In der That ist nicht allein in die Augen fallend, daß ein solches in der Bibel anzu= treffen sei, sondern auch überzeugend gewiß, daß nur durch dasselbe und das in diesem Princip enthaltene Christenthum dieses Buch seinen so weit ausgebreiteten Wirkungskreis und dauernden Einfluß auf die Welt hat erwerben können, eine Wirkung, die keine Offenbarungslehre (als solche), kein Glaube an Wunder, keine vereinigte Stimme vieler Bekenner je her= vorgebracht hätte, weil sie nicht aus der Seele des Menschen selbst geschöpft gewesen wäre und ihm also immer hätte fremd bleiben müssen.

Es ist nämlich etwas in uns, was zu bewundern wir niemals auf= hören können, wenn wir es einmal ins Auge gefaßt haben, und dieses ist zugleich dasjenige, was die Menschheit in der Idee zu einer Würde er= hebt, die man am Menschen als Gegenstande der Erfahrung nicht ver= muthen sollte. Daß wir den moralischen Gesetzen unterworfene und zu deren Beobachtung selbst mit Aufopferung aller ihnen widerstreitenden Lebensannehmlichkeiten durch unsere Vernunft bestimmte Wesen sind, dar= über wundert man sich nicht, weil es objectiv in der natürlichen Ordnung der Dinge als Objecte der reinen Vernunft liegt, jenen Gesetzen zu ge= horchen: ohne daß es dem gemeinen und gesunden Verstande nur einmal einfällt, zu fragen, woher uns jene Gesetze kommen mögen, um vielleicht, bis wir ihren Ursprung wissen, die Befolgung derselben aufzuschieben, oder wohl gar ihre Wahrheit zu bezweifeln. — Aber daß wir auch das Ver= mögen dazu haben, der Moral mit unserer sinnlichen Natur so große Opfer zu bringen, daß wir das auch können, wovon wir ganz leicht und klar begreifen, daß wir es sollen, diese Überlegenheit des übersinn= lichen Menschen in uns über den sinnlichen, desjenigen, gegen den der letztere (wenn es zum Widerstreit kommt) nichts ist, ob dieser zwar in seinen eigenen Augen Alles ist, diese moralische, von der Menschheit unzer= trennliche Anlage in uns ist ein Gegenstand der höchsten Bewunderung,

fancies. To claim that we *feel* as such the immediate influence of God is self-contradictory, because the Idea of God lies only in reason. Here, then, we have a problem along with a solution to it, for which no proof of any kind is possible; and so we can never make anything rational out of it.

Now we still have to inquire whether the Bible may not contain another principle for solving Spener's problem—a principle, different from the sectarian principles we have just discussed, which could replace the unfruitful ecclesiastical principle of sheer orthodoxy. As a matter of fact, it not only leaps to the eye that there is such a principle in the Bible; it is also conclusively certain that only by this principle and the Christianity it contains could the Bible have acquired so extensive a sphere of efficacy and achieved such lasting influence on the world, an effect that no revealed doctrine (as such), no belief in miracles, and no number of the faithful crying out in unison could ever have produced, because in that case it would not have been drawn from man's own soul and must, accordingly, always have remained foreign to him.

For there is something in us that we cannot cease to wonder at when we have once seen it, the same thing that raises *humanity* in its Idea to a dignity we should never have suspected in *man* as an object of experience. We do not wonder at the fact that we are beings subject to moral laws and destined by our reason to obey them, even if this means sacrificing whatever pleasures may conflict with them; for obedience to moral laws lies objectively in the natural order of things as the object of pure reason, and it never occurs to ordinary, sound understanding to ask where these laws come from, in order, perhaps, to put off obeying them until we know their source, or even to doubt their validity. But we do wonder at our *ability* so to sacrifice our sensuous nature to morality that we *can* do what we quite readily and clearly conceive we *ought* to do. This ascendancy of the *supersensible* man in us over the *sensible*, such that (when it comes to a conflict between them) the sensible is *nothing*, though in its own eyes it is *everything*, is an object of the greatest *wonder*; and our wonder

die, je länger man dieses wahre (nicht erdachte) Ideal ansieht, nur immer desto höher steigt: so daß diejenigen wohl zu entschuldigen sind, welche, durch die Unbegreiflichkeit desselben verleitet, dieses Übersinnliche in uns, weil es doch praktisch ist, für übernatürlich, d. i. für etwas, was gar nicht in unserer Macht steht und uns als eigen zugehört, sondern vielmehr für den Einfluß von einem andern und höheren Geiste halten; worin sie aber sehr fehlen: weil die Wirkung dieses Vermögens alsdann nicht unsere That sein, mithin uns auch nicht zugerechnet werden könnte, das Vermögen dazu also nicht das unsrige sein würde. — Die Benutzung der Idee dieses uns unbegreiflicher Weise beiwohnenden Vermögens und die Ansherzlegung derselben von der frühesten Jugend an und fernerhin im öffentlichen Vortrage enthält nun die ächte Auflösung jenes Problems (vom neuen Menschen), und selbst die Bibel scheint nichts anders vor Augen gehabt zu haben, nämlich nicht auf übernatürliche Erfahrungen und schwärmerische Gefühle hin zu weisen, die statt der Vernunft diese Revolution bewirken sollten: sondern auf den Geist Christi, um ihn, so wie er ihn in Lehre und Beispiel bewies, zu dem unsrigen zu machen, oder vielmehr, da er mit der ursprünglichen moralischen Anlage schon in uns liegt, ihm nur Raum zu verschaffen. Und so ist zwischen dem seelenlosen Orthodoxism und dem vernunfttödtenden Mysticism die biblische Glaubenslehre, so wie sie vermittelst der Vernunft aus uns selbst entwickelt werden kann, die mit göttlicher Kraft auf aller Menschen Herzen zur gründlichen Besserung hinwirkende und sie in einer allgemeinen (obzwar unsichtbaren) Kirche vereinigende, auf dem Kriticism der praktischen Vernunft gegründete wahre Religionslehre.

*　　　*　　　*

Das aber, worauf es in dieser Anmerkung eigentlich ankommt, ist die Beantwortung der Frage: ob die Regierung wohl einer Secte des Gefühlglaubens die Sanction einer Kirche könne angedeihen lassen; oder ob sie eine solche zwar dulden und schützen, mit jenem Prärogativ aber nicht beehren könne, ohne ihrer eigenen Absicht zuwider zu handeln.

Wenn man annehmen darf (wie man es denn mit Grunde thun kann), daß es der Regierung Sache gar nicht sei, für die künftige Seligkeit der Unterthanen Sorge zu tragen und ihnen den Weg dazu anzuweisen (denn das muß sie wohl diesen selbst überlassen, wie denn auch der Regent selbst

at this moral predisposition in us, inseparable from our humanity, only increases the longer we contemplate this true (not fabricated) ideal. Since the *supersensible* in us is inconceivable and yet practical, we can well excuse those who are led to consider it supernatural—that is, to regard it as the influence of another and higher spirit, something not within our power and not belonging to us as our own. Yet they are greatly mistaken in this, since on their view the effect of this power would not be our deed and could not be imputed to us, and so the power to produce it would not be our own. Now the real solution to the problem (of the new man) consists in putting to use the Idea of this power, which dwells in us in a way we cannot understand, and impressing it on men, beginning in their earliest youth and continuing on by public instruction. Even the Bible seems to have nothing else in view: it seems to refer, not to supernatural experiences and fantastic feelings which should take reason's place in bringing about this revolution, but to the spirit of Christ, which he manifested in teachings and examples so that we might make it our own—or rather, since it is already present in us by our moral predisposition, so that we might simply make room for it. And so, between *orthodoxy* which has no soul and *mysticism* which kills reason, there is the teaching of the Bible, a faith which our reason can develop out of itself. This teaching is the true religious doctrine, based on the *criticism* of practical reason, that works with divine power on all men's hearts toward their fundamental improvement and unites them in one universal (though invisible) church.

*   *

*

But the main purpose of this note is really to answer the question: could the government confer on a mystical sect the sanction of a church or could it, consistently with its own aim, tolerate and protect such a sect, without giving it the honor of that prerogative?

If we admit (as we have reason to do) that it is not the government's business to concern itself with the future happiness of the subjects and show them the way to it (for it must leave that to the subjects, since the ruler usually gets his own religion from

seine eigene Religion gewöhnlicher Weise vom Volk und dessen Lehrern her hat): so kann ihre Absicht nur sein, auch durch dieses Mittel (den Kirchenglauben) lenksame und moralisch=gute Unterthanen zu haben.

Zu dem Ende wird sie erstlich keinen Naturalism (Kirchenglau= ben ohne Bibel) sanctioniren, weil es bei dem gar keine dem Einfluß der Regierung unterworfene kirchliche Form geben würde, welches der Vor= aussetzung widerspricht. — Die biblische Orthodoxie würde also das sein, woran sie die öffentliche Volkslehrer bände, in Ansehung deren diese wiederum unter der Beurtheilung der Facultäten stehen würden, die es angeht, weil sonst ein Pfaffenthum, d. i. eine Herrschaft der Werkleute des Kirchenglaubens, entstehen würde, das Volk nach ihren Absichten zu beherrschen. Aber den Orthodoxism, d. i. die Meinung von der Hin= länglichkeit des Kirchenglaubens zur Religion, würde sie durch ihre Auto= rität nicht bestätigen: weil diese die natürliche Grundsätze der Sittlichkeit zur Nebensache macht, da sie vielmehr die Hauptstütze ist, worauf die Re= gierung muß rechnen können, wenn sie in ihr Volk Vertrauen setzen soll.*) Endlich kann sie am wenigsten den Mysticism als Meinung des Volks, übernatürlicher Inspiration selbst theilhaftig werden zu können, zum Rang eines öffentlichen Kirchenglaubens erheben, weil er gar nichts Öffentliches ist und sich also dem Einfluß der Regierung gänzlich entzieht.

---

*) Was den Staat in Religionsdingen allein interessiren darf, ist: wozu die Lehrer derselben anzuhalten sind, damit er nützliche Bürger, gute Soldaten und überhaupt getreue Unterthanen habe. Wenn er nun dazu die Einschärfung der Rechtgläubigkeit in statutarischen Glaubenslehren und eben solcher Gnadenmittel wählt, so kann er hiebei sehr übel fahren. Denn da das Annehmen dieser Sta= tute eine leichte und dem schlechtdenkendsten Menschen weit leichtere Sache ist als dem Guten, dagegen die moralische Besserung der Gesinnung viel und lange Mühe macht, er aber von der ersteren hauptsächlich seine Seligkeit zu hoffen gelehrt wor= den ist, so darf er sich eben kein groß Bedenken machen, seine Pflicht (doch behut= sam) zu übertreten, weil er ein unfehlbares Mittel bei der Hand hat, der gött= lichen Strafgerechtigkeit (nur daß er sich nicht verspäten muß) durch seinen rechten Glauben an alle Geheimnisse und inständige Benutzung der Gnadenmittel zu ent= gehen; dagegen, wenn jene Lehre der Kirche geradezu auf die Moralität gerichtet sein würde, das Urtheil seines Gewissens ganz anders lauten würde: nämlich daß, so viel er von dem Bösen, was er that, nicht ersetzen kann, dafür müsse er einem künftigen Richter antworten, und dieses Schicksal abzuwenden, vermöge kein kirch= liches Mittel, kein durch Angst herausgedrängter Glaube, noch ein solches Gebet (desine fata deum flecti sperare precando). — Bei welchem Glauben ist nun der Staat sicherer?

the people and their teachers), then the government's purpose with regard to ecclesiastical faith can be only to have, through this means too, subjects who are tractable and morally good.

With this end in view the government will, first, refuse to sanction any kind of *naturalism* (ecclesiastical faith without the Bible); for naturalism would not provide the form of a church subject to the government's influence, and this contradicts our supposition. It will, therefore, bind the public teachers of the people to biblical orthodoxy; and these teachers, again, will be subject to the judgment of the relevant faculties with regard to orthodoxy, since otherwise clericalism would spring up—that is, the working men of ecclesiastical faith would assume control and rule the people according to their own purposes. But the government would not endorse *orthodoxy* by its authority; for orthodoxy—the view that belief in dogma is sufficient for religion—regards the natural principles of morality as of secondary importance, whereas morality is rather the mainstay on which the government must be able to count if it wants to trust the people.* Least of all can the government raise mysticism, as the people's view that they themselves can share in supernatural inspiration, to the rank of a public ecclesiastical faith, because mysticism has nothing public about it and so escapes entirely the government's influence.

---

*In religious matters the only thing that can interest the state is: to what doctrines it must bind teachers of religion in order to have useful citizens, good soldiers, and, in general, faithful subjects. Now if, to that end, it chooses to enjoin orthodox statutory doctrines and means of grace, it can fare very badly. For it is an easy thing for a man to accept these statutes, and far easier for the evil-minded man than for the good, whereas the moral improvement of his attitude of will is a long and difficult struggle. And so, if a man is taught to hope for salvation primarily from these statutes, he need not hesitate greatly about transgressing his duty (though cautiously), because he has an infallible means at hand to evade God's punitive justice (if only he does not wait too long) by his orthodox belief in every mystery and his urgent use of the means of grace. On the other hand, if the teaching of the church were directed straight to morality, the judgment of his conscience would be quite different: namely, that he must answer to a future judge for any evil he has done that he cannot repair, and that no ecclesiastical means, no faith or prayer extorted by dread, can avert this fate (*desine fata deum flecti sperare pecando* [cease hoping that you will alter the divine will by prayer]). With which belief, now, is the state more secure?

Friedens-Abschluß und Beilegung des Streits der Facultäten.

In Streitigkeiten, welche blos die reine, aber praktische Vernunft angehen, hat die philosophische Facultät ohne Widerrede das Vorrecht, den Vortrag zu thun und, was das Formale betrifft, den Proceß zu instruiren; was aber das Materiale anlangt, so ist die theologische im Besitz den Lehnstuhl, der den Vorrang bezeichnet, einzunehmen, nicht weil sie etwa in Sachen der Vernunft auf mehr Einsicht Anspruch machen kann als die übrigen, sondern weil es die wichtigste menschliche Angelegenheit betrifft, und führt daher den Titel der obersten Facultät (doch nur als prima inter pares). — Sie spricht aber nicht nach Gesetzen der reinen und a priori erkennbaren Vernunftreligion (denn da würde sie sich erniedrigen und auf die philosophische Bank herabsetzen), sondern nach statutarischen, in einem Buche, vorzugsweise Bibel genannt, enthaltenen Glaubensvorschriften, d. i. in einem Codex der Offenbarung eines vor viel hundert Jahren geschlossenen alten und neuen Bundes der Menschen mit Gott, dessen Authenticität als eines Geschichtsglaubens (nicht eben des moralischen; denn der würde auch aus der Philosophie gezogen werden können) doch mehr von der Wirkung, welche die Lesung der Bibel auf das Herz der Menschen thun mag, als von mit kritischer Prüfung der darin enthaltenen Lehren und Erzählungen aufgestellten Beweisen erwartet werden darf, dessen Auslegung auch nicht der natürlichen Vernunft der Laien, sondern nur der Scharfsinnigkeit der Schriftgelehrten überlassen wird.*)

---

*) Im römisch-katholischen System des Kirchenglaubens ist diesen Punkt (das Bibellesen) betreffend mehr Consequenz als im protestantischen. — Der reformirte Prediger La Coste sagt zu seinen Glaubensgenossen: „Schöpft das göttliche Wort aus der Quelle (der Bibel) selbst, wo ihr es dann lauter und unverfälscht einnehmen könnt; aber ihr müßt ja nichts anders in der Bibel finden, als was wir darin finden. — Nun, liebe Freunde, sagt uns lieber, was ihr in der Bibel findet, damit wir nicht unnöthiger Weise darin selbst suchen und am Ende, was wir darin gefunden zu haben vermeinten, von euch für unrichtige Auslegung derselben erklärt werde." — Auch spricht die katholische Kirche in dem Satze: „Außer der Kirche (der katholischen) ist kein Heil", consequenter als die protestantische, wenn diese sagt: daß man auch als Katholik selig werden könne. Denn wenn das ist (sagt Bossuet), so wählt man ja am sichersten, sich zur ersteren zu schlagen. Denn noch seliger als selig kann doch kein Mensch zu werden verlangen.

Conclusion of Peace and Settlement of the Conflict of the Faculties

In any conflict having to do only with pure but practical reason, no one can dispute the prerogative of the philosophy faculty to make the report and, as far as the formal rules of procedure are concerned, *draw up* the case. But with regard to its content, the theology faculty occupies the armchair, the sign of precedence—not because it can claim more insight than the others in matters of reason, but because it deals with man's most important concern and is therefore entitled the *highest* faculty (yet only as *prima inter pares*). But it does not speak according to laws of pure rational religion which can be known a priori (for then it would degrade itself and descend to the philosophers' bench): it speaks, rather, according to *statutory* precepts of faith contained in a book, particularly the book called the *Bible*—that is, in a code that reveals an old and a new covenant which man concluded with God many centuries ago. Its authenticity, as an object of historical belief (not moral belief, since that could also be drawn from philosophy), can be better established by the effect its reading can produce in the hearts of men than by proofs based on critical examination of the teachings and tales it contains. Its interpretation, moreover, is not left to laymen's reason, but reserved for the acumen of experts.*

---

*On this point (the reading of the Bible), the Roman Catholic system of dogma is more consistent than the Protestant. The reformed preacher La Coste [23] says to his co-religionists: "Draw the divine word from the spring itself (the Bible), where you can take it purer and unadulterated; but you must find in the Bible nothing other than what we find there. Now, dear friends, please tell us what you find in the Bible so that we won't waste our time searching for it ourselves, only to have you explain, in the end, that what we supposed we had found in it is a false interpretation." Again, when the Catholic Church says: Outside the (Catholic) Church there is no salvation, it speaks more consistently than the Protestant Church when it says: Catholics too can be saved. For if that is so (says Bossuet), then the safer choice is to join the Catholic Church; for no one can ask for *more* salvation.

Der biblische Glaube ist ein messianischer Geschichtsglaube, dem ein Buch des Bundes Gottes mit Abraham zum Grunde liegt, und besteht aus einem mosaisch-messianischen und einem evangelisch-messianischen Kirchenglauben, der den Ursprung und die Schicksale des Volks Gottes so vollständig erzählt, daß er, von dem, was in der Weltgeschichte überhaupt das oberste ist, und wobei kein Mensch zugegen war, nämlich dem Weltanfang (in der Genesis), anhebend, sie bis zum Ende aller Dinge (in der Apokalypsis) verfolgt, — welches freilich von keinem Andern, als einem göttlich-inspirirten Verfasser erwartet werden darf; — wobei sich doch eine bedenkliche Zahlen-Kabbala in Ansehung der wichtigsten Epochen der heiligen Chronologie darbietet, welche den Glauben an die Authenticität dieser biblischen Geschichtserzählung etwas schwächen dürfte.*)

---

*) 70 apokalyptische Monate (deren es in diesem Cyklus 4 giebt), jeden zu $29\frac{1}{2}$ Jahren, geben 2065 Jahr. Davon jedes 49ste Jahr, als das große Ruhejahr, (deren in diesem Zeitlaufe 42 sind) abgezogen: bleiben gerade 2023, als das Jahr, da Abraham aus dem Lande Kanaan, das ihm Gott geschenkt hatte, nach Ägypten ging. — Von da an bis zur Einnahme jenes Landes durch die Kinder Israel 70 apokalyptische Wochen (= 490 Jahr) — und so 4mal solcher Jahrwochen zusammengezählt (= 1960) und mit 2023 addirt, geben nach P. Petau's Rechnung das Jahr der Geburt Christi (= 3983) so genau, daß auch nicht ein Jahr daran fehlt. — Siebzig Jahr hernach die Zerstörung Jerusalems (auch eine mystische Epoche). — — Aber Bengel, in ordine temporum pag. 9. it. p. 218 seqq., bringt 3939 als die Zahl der Geburt Christi heraus? Aber das ändert nichts an der Heiligkeit des Numerus septenarius. Denn die Zahl der Jahre vom Rufe Gottes an Abraham bis zur Geburt Christi ist 1960, welches 4 apokalyptische Perioden austrägt, jeden zu 490, oder auch 40 apok. Perioden, jeden zu 7mal 7 = 49 Jahr. Zieht man nun von jedem neunundvierzigsten das große Ruhejahr und von jedem größten Ruhejahr, welches das 490ste ist, eines ab (zusammen 44), so bleibt gerade 3939. — Also sind die Jahrzahlen 3983 und 3939, als das verschieden angegebene Jahr der Geburt Christi, nur darin unterschieden: daß die letztere entspringt, wenn in der Zeit der ersteren das, was zur Zeit der 4 großen Epochen gehört, um die Zahl der Ruhejahre vermindert wird. Nach Bengeln würde die Tafel der heil. Geschichte so aussehen:

2023: Verheißung an Abraham, das Land Kanaan zu besitzen;
2502: Besitzerlangung desselben;
2981: Einweihung des ersten Tempels;
3460: Gegebener Befehl zur Erbauung des zweiten Tempels;
3939: Geburt Christi.

Auch das Jahr der Sündfluth läßt sich so a priori ausrechnen. Nämlich 4 Epochen zu 490 (= 70×7) Jahr machen 1960. Davon jedes 7te (= 280) abgezogen,

Biblical faith is historical belief in a *messiah*, which has as its basis a book of God's covenant with Abraham. It consists in a *Mosaic-messianic* and an *evangelical-messianic* dogma, and gives such a complete account of the origin and destiny of God's people that, starting (in Genesis) with the beginning of the world, the first moment in the world's history at which no man was present, it follows it to the end of all things (in the Apocalypse)—a narrative that one could, indeed, expect only from a divinely inspired author. Still, the existence of a questionable cabala of numbers regarding the most important epochs of sacred chronology might somewhat weaken one's faith in the authenticity of the *historical narrative* the Bible contains.*

---

*70 Apocalyptic months (of which there are 4 in this cycle), each 29½ years long, equal 2065 years. Subtract every 49th year of this, as the great year of rest (there are 42 of them in this period) and we get exactly 2023 as the year Abraham left the land of Canaan, which God had given him, for Egypt. From then to the occupation of that land by the children of Israel 70 Apocalyptic weeks (= 490 years)—multiply these week-years by 4 (= 1960) and add 2023, and this gives, according to P. Petaus's [24] reckoning, the year of Christ's birth (3983) so exactly that it is not even a year off. 70 years after this, the destruction of Jerusalem (also a mystical epoch). But Bengel (*in ordine temporum,* page 9 and pages 218 ff.) [25] gets 3939 as the date of Christ's birth? That changes nothing in the sacred character of the *numerus septenarius;* for the number of years between God's call to Abraham and the birth of Christ is 1960, which comprises 4 Apocalyptic periods each of 490 years, or also 40 Apocalyptic periods each of 7 x 7 or 49 years. Now if we subtract 1 from every 49th year for the great year of rest, and 1 for every greatest year of rest, which is the 490th (44 altogether), there remains exactly 3939. Hence the dates 3983 and 3939, as different years assigned to the birth of Christ, differ only in this: that 3939 is obtained from 3983 by subtracting the number of years of rest from what is included in the time of the 4 great epochs. According to Bengel, the table of sacred history is as follows:

2023 Promise to Abraham that he would possess the land of Canaan
2502 He takes possession of it
2981 Consecration of the first temple
3460 Command given to build the second temple
3939 Birth of Christ

The year of the Flood, too, can be calculated a priori in the same way: 4 epochs of 490 (70 x 7) years makes 1960. Subtract from this every 7th (280) and this leaves 1680. From this 1680 subtract every 70th year contained in it

Ein Gesetzbuch des nicht aus der menschlichen Vernunft gezogenen, aber doch mit ihr, als moralisch=praktischer Vernunft, dem Endzwecke nach vollkommen einstimmigen statutarischen (mithin aus einer Offenba= rung hervorgehenden) göttlichen Willens, die Bibel, würde nun das kräf= tigste Organ der Leitung des Menschen und des Bürgers zum zeitlichen und ewigen Wohl sein, wenn sie nur als Gottes Wort beglaubigt und ihre Authenticität documentirt werden könnte. — Diesem Umstande aber stehen viele Schwierigkeiten entgegen.

Denn wenn Gott zum Menschen wirklich spräche, so kann dieser doch niemals wissen, daß es Gott sei, der zu ihm spricht. Es ist schlechter= dings unmöglich, daß der Mensch durch seine Sinne den Unendlichen fassen, ihn von Sinnenwesen unterscheiden und ihn woran kennen solle. — Daß es aber nicht Gott sein könne, dessen Stimme er zu hören glaubt, davon kann er sich wohl in einigen Fällen überzeugen; denn wenn das, was ihm durch sie geboten wird, dem moralischen Gesetz zuwider ist, so mag die Erscheinung ihm noch so majestätisch und die ganze Natur über= schreitend dünken: er muß sie doch für Täuschung halten.*)

Die Beglaubigung der Bibel nun, als eines in Lehre und Beispiel zur Norm dienenden evangelisch=messianischen Glaubens, kann nicht aus der Gottesgelahrtheit ihrer Verfasser (denn der war immer ein dem mög= lichen Irrthum ausgesetzter Mensch), sondern muß aus der Wirkung ihres Inhalts auf die Moralität des Volks von Lehrern aus diesem Volk selbst, als Idioten (im Wissenschaftlichen), an sich, mithin als aus dem reinen Quell der allgemeinen, jedem gemeinen Menschen beiwohnenden Vernunft= religion geschöpft betrachtet werden, die eben durch diese Einfalt auf die

---

bleiben 1680. Von diesen 1680 jedes darin enthaltene 70 ste Jahr abgezogen (= 24), bleiben 1656, als das Jahr der Sündfluth. — Auch von dieser bis zum R. G. an Abraham sind 366 volle Jahre, davon eines ein Schaltjahr ist.

Was soll man nun hiezu sagen? Haben die heilige Zahlen etwa den Welt= lauf bestimmt? — Frank's Cyclus iobilaeus dreht sich ebenfalls um diesen Mittel= punkt der mystischen Chronologie herum.

*) Zum Beispiel kann die Mythe von dem Opfer dienen, das Abraham auf göttlichen Befehl durch Abschlachtung und Verbrennung seines einzigen Sohnes — (das arme Kind trug unwissend noch das Holz hinzu) — bringen wollte. Abra= ham hätte auf diese vermeinte göttliche Stimme antworten müssen: „Daß ich meinen guten Sohn nicht tödten solle, ist ganz gewiß; daß aber du, der du mir erscheinst, Gott sei, davon bin ich nicht gewiß und kann es auch nicht werden", wenn sie auch vom (sichtbaren) Himmel herabschallte.

Now a code of God's *statutory* (and so revealed) will, not derived from human reason but harmonizing perfectly with morally practical reason toward the final end—in other words, the Bible—would be the most effective organ for guiding men and citizens to their temporal and eternal well-being, if only it could be accredited as the word of God and its authenticity could be proved by documents. But there are many difficulties in the way of validating it.

For if God should really speak to man, man could still never *know* that it was God speaking. It is quite impossible for man to apprehend the infinite by his senses, distinguish it from sensible beings, and *recognize* it as such. But in some cases man can be sure that the voice he hears is *not* God's; for if the voice commands him to do something contrary to the moral law, then no matter how majestic the apparition may be, and no matter how it may seem to surpass the whole of nature, he must consider it an illusion.*

Now the source from which we draw the credentials of the Bible, as an evangelical-messianic faith whose teachings and examples serve as a norm, cannot be the divine learning of its author (for he remained a man, exposed to possible error). It must rather be the effect which its content has on the morality of the people, when it is preached to them by teachers from these same people. And since these teachers, themselves, are incompetent (in scientific matters), we must regard the credentials of the Bible as drawn from the pure spring of universal rational religion dwelling in every ordinary man; and it is this very

---

(= 24), and this leaves 1656 as the year of the Flood. Also, from this to God's call to Abraham are 366 full years, of which 1 is a leap year.

What are we to say to this? Have the sacred numbers perhaps determined the course of events in the world? Frank's *Cyclus iobilaeus* also revolves around the center of this mystical chronology. [26]

*We can use, as an example, the myth of the sacrifice that Abraham was going to make by butchering and burning his only son at God's command (the poor child, without knowing it, even brought the wood for the fire). Abraham should have replied to this supposedly divine voice: "That I ought not to kill my good son is quite certain. But that you, this apparition, are God—of that I am not certain, and never can be, not even is this voice rings down to me from (visible) heaven."

115

Herzen desselben den ausgebreitetsten und kräftigsten Einfluß haben mußte. — Die Bibel war das Vehikel derselben vermittelst gewisser statutarischer Vorschriften, welche der Ausübung der Religion in der bürgerlichen Gesellschaft eine Form als einer Regierung gab, und die Authenticität dieses Gesetzbuchs als eines göttlichen (des Inbegriffs aller unserer Pflichten als göttlicher Gebote) beglaubigt also und documentirt sich selbst, was den Geist desselben (das Moralische) betrifft; was aber den Buchstaben (das Statutarische) desselben anlangt, so bedürfen die Satzungen in diesem Buche keiner Beglaubigung, weil sie nicht zum Wesentlichen (principale), sondern nur zum Beigesellten (accessorium) desselben gehören. — — Den Ursprung aber dieses Buchs auf Inspiration seiner Verfasser (deus ex machina) zu gründen, um auch die unwesentliche Statute desselben zu heiligen, muß eher das Zutrauen zu seinem moralischen Werth schwächen, als es stärken.

Die Beurkundung einer solchen Schrift, als einer göttlichen, kann von keiner Geschichtserzählung, sondern nur von der erprobten Kraft derselben, Religion in menschlichen Herzen zu gründen und, wenn sie durch mancherlei (alte oder neue) Satzungen verunartet wäre, sie durch ihre Einfalt selbst wieder in ihre Reinigkeit herzustellen, abgeleitet werden, welches Werk darum nicht aufhört, Wirkung der Natur und Erfolg der fortschreitenden moralischen Cultur in dem allgemeinen Gange der Vorsehung zu sein, und als eine solche erklärt zu werden bedarf, damit die Existenz dieses Buchs nicht ungläubisch dem bloßen Zufall, oder abergläubisch einem Wunder zugeschrieben werde, und die Vernunft in beiden Fällen auf den Strand gerathe.

Der Schluß hieraus ist nun dieser:

Die Bibel enthält in sich selbst einen in praktischer Absicht hinreichenden Beglaubigungsgrund ihrer (moralischen) Göttlichkeit durch den Einfluß, den sie als Text einer systematischen Glaubenslehre von jeher sowohl in katechetischem als homiletischem Vortrage auf das Herz der Menschen ausgeübt hat, um sie als Organ nicht allein der allgemeinen und inneren Vernunftreligion, sondern auch als Vermächtniß (neues Testament) einer statutarischen, auf unabsehliche Zeiten zum Leitfaden dienenden Glaubenslehre aufzubehalten: es mag ihr auch in theoretischer Rücksicht für Gelehrte, die ihren Ursprung theoretisch und historisch nachsuchen, und für die kritische Behandlung ihrer Geschichte an Beweisthümern viel oder wenig abgehen. — Die Göttlichkeit ihres moralischen Inhalts ent-

simplicity that accounts for the Bible's extremely widespread and powerful influence on the hearts of the people. Through certain statutory precepts by which it gave a *form*, as of a government, to the practice of religion in civil society, the Bible was the vehicle of religion. As far as its spirit (its moral content) is concerned, then, this code of laws accredits itself and is itself the document that establishes its authenticity as a divine code (the sum of all our duties as divine commands). As for the letter of the code (the statutory element), the decrees of this book do not need to be accredited because they do not belong to what is essential in it (*principale*) but only to what is associated with this (*accessorium*). But to base the origin of this book on the inspiration of its author (*deus ex machina*), in order to sanctify its non-essential statutes as well, must weaken, rather than strengthen, our confidence in its moral worth.

No historical account can verify the divine origin of such a writing. The proof can be derived only from its tested power to establish religion in the human heart and, by its very simplicity, to reestablish it in its purity should it be corrupted by various (ancient or modern) dogmas. The working of the Bible does not thereby cease to be an act of *nature* and a result of advancing moral cultivation in the general course of *Providence*; and we must explain it as such, so that we do not attribute the Bible's existence *sceptically* to mere accident or *superstitiously* to a *miracle*, both of which would cause reason to run aground.

Now the conclusion from this is as follows:

The Bible contains within itself a credential of its (moral) divinity that is sufficient for practical purposes—the influence that, as the text of a systematic doctrine of faith, it has always exercised on the hearts of men, both in catechetical instruction and in preaching. This is sufficient reason for preserving it, not only as the organ of universal inner rational religion, but also as the legacy (new testament) of a statutory doctrine of faith which will serve us indefinitely as a guiding line. It matters little that scholars who investigate its origin theoretically and historically and study its historical content critically may find it more or less wanting in proofs from a theoretical point of view. The *divinity* of its moral content adequately compensates reason for the

schädigt die Vernunft hinreichend wegen der Menschlichkeit der Geschichts=
erzählung, die, gleich einem alten Pergamente hin und wieder unleserlich,
durch Accommodationen und Conjecturen im Zusammenhange mit dem
Ganzen muß verständlich gemacht werden, und berechtigt dabei doch zu
dem Satz: daß die Bibel, gleich als ob sie eine göttliche Offen=
barung wäre, aufbewahrt, moralisch benutzt und der Religion als ihr
Leitmittel untergelegt zu werden verdiene.

Die Keckheit der Kraftgenies, welche diesem Leitbande des Kirchen=
glaubens sich jetzt schon entwachsen zu sein wähnen, sie mögen nun als
Theophilanthropen in öffentlichen dazu errichteten Kirchen, oder als
Mystiker bei der Lampe innerer Offenbarungen schwärmen, würde die
Regierung bald ihre Nachsicht bedauren machen, jenes große Stiftungs=
und Leitungsmittel der bürgerlichen Ordnung und Ruhe vernachlässigt
und leichtsinnigen Händen überlassen zu haben. — Auch ist nicht zu er=
warten, daß, wenn die Bibel, die wir haben, außer Credit kommen sollte,
eine andere an ihrer Stelle emporkommen würde; denn öffentliche Wun=
der machen sich nicht zum zweitenmale in derselben Sache: weil das Fehl=
schlagen des vorigen in Absicht auf die Dauer dem folgenden allen Glau=
ben benimmt; — wiewohl doch auch andererseits auf das Geschrei der
Alarmisten (das Reich ist in Gefahr) nicht zu achten ist, wenn in ge=
wissen Statuten der Bibel, welche mehr die Förmlichkeiten als den inne=
ren Glaubensgehalt der Schrift betreffen, selbst an den Verfassern der=
selben einiges gerügt werden sollte: weil das Verbot der Prüfung einer
Lehre der Glaubensfreiheit zuwider ist. — Daß aber ein Geschichtsglaube
Pflicht sei und zur Seligkeit gehöre, ist Aberglaube.*)

---

*) Aberglaube ist der Hang in das, was als nicht natürlicher Weise zu=
gehend vermeint wird, ein größeres Vertrauen zu setzen, als was sich nach Natur=
gesetzen erklären läßt — es sei im Physischen oder Moralischen. — Man kann also
die Frage aufwerfen: ob der Bibelglaube (als empirischer), oder ob umgekehrt die
Moral (als reiner Vernunft= und Religionsglaube) dem Lehrer zum Leitfaden
dienen solle; mit anderen Worten: ist die Lehre von Gott, weil sie in der Bibel
steht, oder steht sie in der Bibel, weil sie von Gott ist? — Der erstere Satz ist
augenscheinlich inconsequent: weil das göttliche Ansehen des Buchs hier voraus=
gesetzt werden muß, um die Göttlichkeit der Lehre desselben zu beweisen. Also
kann nur der zweite Satz Statt finden, der aber schlechterdings keines Beweises
fähig ist (Supernaturalium non datur scientia). — — Hievon ein Beispiel. —
Die Jünger des mosaisch=messianischen Glaubens sahen ihre Hoffnung aus dem
Bunde Gottes mit Abraham nach Jesu Tode ganz sinken (wir hofften, er würde

Kant's Schriften. Werke. VII.   5

humanity of its historical narrative which, like an old parchment that is illegible in places, has to be made intelligible by adjustments and conjectures consistent with the whole. And the divinity of its moral content justifies this statement: that the Bible deserves to be kept, put to moral use, and assigned to religion as its guide *just as if it is a divine revelation.*

If the government were to neglect that great means for establishing and administering civil order and peace and abandon it to frivolous hands, the audacity of those prodigies of strength who imagine they have already outgrown this leading-string of dogma and express their raptures either in public churches devoted to theophilanthropy or in mysticism, with its lamp of private revelations, would soon make it regret its indulgence. Moreover, we cannot expect that, if the Bible we have were once discredited, another would arise in its place; for public miracles do not happen twice in the same affair, since the failure of the first one to endure would prevent anyone from believing in the second. On the other hand, we should pay no attention to the outcry raised by *alarmists* (that the state is in danger) when some fault is found with the authors of the Bible in certain of its statues having to do more with formalities presented in the text than with its inner content of faith; for a prohibition against examining a doctrine is contrary to freedom of belief. But it is superstition to hold that historical belief is a duty and essential to salvation.*

Superstition is the tendency to put greater trust in what is supposed to be non-natural than in what can be explained by laws of nature, whether in physical or in moral matters. The question can therefore be raised: whether biblical faith (as empirical belief) or morality (as pure rational and religious belief) should serve as the teacher's guide? In other words, is the teaching from God because it is in the Bible, or is it in the Bible because it is from God? The first proposition is obviously inconsistent, because it requires us to presuppose the divine authority of the book in order to prove the divinity of its doctrine. Hence only the second proposition is acceptable, though it admits of no proof whatsoever *(Supernaturalium non datur scientia* [there is no scientific knowledge of supernatural matters]). Here is an example of this. The disciples of the Mosaic-messianic faith saw their hopes, based on God's covenant with Abraham, fail completely after Jesus' death (we had hoped that

Von der biblischen Auslegungskunst (hermeneutica sacra), da sie nicht den Laien überlassen werden kann (denn sie betrifft ein wissen= schaftliches System), darf nun lediglich in Ansehung dessen, was in der Religion statutarisch ist, verlangt werden: daß der Ausleger sich erkläre, ob sein Ausspruch als authentisch, oder als doctrinal verstanden werden solle. — Im ersteren Falle muß die Auslegung dem Sinne des Verfassers buchstäblich (philologisch) angemessen sein; im zweiten aber hat der Schriftsteller die Freiheit, der Schriftstelle (philosophisch) denjeni= gen Sinn unterzulegen, den sie in moralisch=praktischer Absicht (zur Er= bauung des Lehrlings) in der Exegese annimmt; denn der Glaube an einen bloßen Geschichtssatz ist todt an ihm selber. — Nun mag wohl die erstere für den Schriftgelehrten und indirect auch für das Volk in ge= wisser pragmatischen Absicht wichtig genug sein, aber der eigentliche Zweck der Religionslehre, moralisch bessere Menschen zu bilden, kann auch da= bei nicht allein verfehlt, sondern wohl gar verhindert werden. — Denn die heilige Schriftsteller können als Menschen auch geirrt haben (wenn man nicht ein durch die Bibel beständig fortlaufendes Wunder annimmt), wie z. B. der h. Paul mit seiner Gnadenwahl, welche er aus der mo= saisch=messianischen Schriftlehre in die evangelische treuherzig überträgt, ob er zwar über die Unbegreiflichkeit der Verwerfung gewisser Menschen, ehe sie noch geboren waren, sich in großer Verlegenheit befindet und so, wenn man die Hermeneutik der Schriftgelehrten als continuirlich dem

---

Israel erlösen); denn nur den Kindern Abrahams war in ihrer Bibel das Heil verheißen. Nun trug es sich zu, daß, da am Pfingstfeste die Jünger versammelt waren, einer derselben auf den glücklichen, der subtilen jüdischen Auslegungskunst angemessenen Einfall gerieth, daß auch die Heiden (Griechen und Römer) als in diesen Bund aufgenommen betrachtet werden könnten: wenn sie an das Opfer, welches Abraham Gotte mit seinem einzigen Sohne bringen wollte (als dem Sinnbilde des einigen Opfers des Weltheilandes) glaubten; denn da wären sie Kinder Abrahams im Glauben (zuerst unter, dann aber auch ohne die Beschnei= dung). — Es ist kein Wunder, daß diese Entdeckung, die in einer großen Volks= versammlung eine so unermeßliche Aussicht eröffnete, mit dem größten Jubel, und als ob sie unmittelbare Wirkung des heil. Geistes gewesen wäre, aufgenommen und für ein Wunder gehalten wurde und als ein solches in die biblische (Apostel=) Ge= schichte kam, bei der es aber gar nicht zur Religion gehört, sie als Factum zu glauben und diesen Glauben der natürlichen Menschenvernunft aufzudringen. Der durch Furcht abgenöthigte Gehorsam in Ansehung eines solchen Kirchenglaubens, als zur Seligkeit erforderlich, ist also Aberglaube.

With regard to what is statutory in religion, we may require biblical hermeneutics (*hermeneutica sacra*)—which, since it has to do with a scientific system, cannot be left to the laity—to tell us whether the exegete's findings are to be taken as *authentic* or *doctrinal*. In the first case, exegesis must conform literally (philologically) with the author's meaning. But in the second case the writer is free, in his exegesis, to ascribe to the text (philosophically) the meaning it admits of for morally practical purposes (the pupil's edification); for faith in a merely historical proposition is, in itself, dead. Now the literal interpretation may well be important enough for biblical scholars and, indirectly, for the people as well, for certain pragmatic purposes. But this kind of interpretation can not only fail to promote but even hinder the real end of religious teaching—the development of morally better men. For even the authors of sacred Scripture, being human, could have made mistakes (unless we admit a miracle running continuously throughout the Bible), as, for example, St. Paul in good faith carried over the doctrine of predestination from the doctrines of the Mosaic-messianic Scriptures to those of the Gospels, although he was greatly embarrassed over the inconceivability of certain individuals being damned before they were even born. And so, if the hermeneutics of scriptural scholars is supposed to be a continuous revelation the interpreter receives, the divine

---

he would deliver Israel); for their Bible promised salvation only to the children of Abraham. Now it happened that when the disciples were gathered at Pentecost, one of them hit upon the happy idea, in keeping with the subtle Jewish art of exegesis, that pagans (Greeks and Romans) could also be regarded as admitted into this covenant, if they believed in the sacrifice of his only son that Abraham was willing to offer God (as the symbol of the world-savior's own sacrifice); for then they would be children of Abraham in faith (at first subject to circumcision, but later even without it). It is no wonder that this discovery which, in a great gathering of people, opened so immense a prospect, was received with the greatest rejoicing as if it had been the direct working of the Holy Spirit, and was considered a miracle and recorded as such in biblical (apostolic) history. But religion does not require us to believe this as a fact, or obtrude this belief on natural human reason. Consequently, if a church commands us to believe such a dogma, as necessary for salvation, and we obey out of fear, our belief is superstition.

Ausleger zu Theil gewordene Offenbarung annimmt, der Göttlichkeit der Religion beständig Abbruch thun muß. — Also ist nur die doctrinale Auslegung, welche nicht (empirisch) zu wissen verlangt, was der heilige Verfasser mit seinen Worten für einen Sinn verbunden haben mag, sondern was die Vernunft (a priori) in moralischer Rücksicht bei Veranlassung einer Spruchstelle als Text der Bibel für eine Lehre unterlegen kann, die einzige evangelisch-biblische Methode der Belehrung des Volks in der wahren, inneren und allgemeinen Religion, die von dem particulären Kirchenglauben als Geschichtsglauben — unterschieden ist; wobei dann alles mit Ehrlichkeit und Offenheit, ohne Täuschung zugeht, da hingegen das Volk, mit einem Geschichtsglauben, den keiner desselben sich zu beweisen vermag, statt des moralischen (allein seligmachenden), den ein jeder faßt, in seiner Absicht (die es haben muß) getäuscht, seinen Lehrer anklagen kann.

In Absicht auf die Religion eines Volks, das eine heilige Schrift zu verehren gelehrt worden ist, ist nun die doctrinale Auslegung derselben, welche sich auf sein (des Volks) moralisches Interesse — der Erbauung, sittlichen Besserung und so der Seligwerdung — bezieht, zugleich die authentische: d. i. so will Gott seinen in der Bibel geoffenbarten Willen verstanden wissen. Denn es ist hier nicht von einer bürgerlichen, das Volk unter Disciplin haltenden (politischen), sondern einer auf das Innere der moralischen Gesinnung abzweckenden (mithin göttlichen) Regierung die Rede. Der Gott, der durch unsere eigene (moralisch-praktische) Vernunft spricht, ist ein untrüglicher, allgemein verständlicher Ausleger dieses seines Worts, und es kann auch schlechterdings keinen anderen (etwa auf historische Art) beglaubigten Ausleger seines Worts geben: weil Religion eine reine Vernunftsache ist.

*   *   *

*

Und so haben die Theologen der Facultät die Pflicht auf sich, mithin auch die Befugniß, den Bibelglauben aufrecht zu erhalten: doch unbeschadet der Freiheit der Philosophen, ihn jederzeit der Kritik der Vernunft zu unterwerfen, welche im Falle einer Dictatur (des Religionsedicts), die jener oberen etwa auf kurze Zeit eingeräumt werden dürfte, sich durch die solenne Formel bestens verwahren: Provideant consules, ne quid respublica detrimenti capiat.

5*

character of religion must be constantly prejudiced. Hence *doctrinal* interpretation—which does not seek to know (empirically) what meaning the sacred author may have connected to his words but rather what teaching reason can ascribe (a priori), for the sake of morality, to a biblical text it is presented with—is the only way of handling the Gospels to instruct the people in true, inner and universal religion, which must be distinguished from particular church dogma, as a matter of historical belief. In this way everything takes place honestly and openly, without deception. On the other hand, the people can reproach their teachers for *deceiving* them in their purpose (which they must have) if they are given historical belief, which none of them can prove, instead of moral faith (the only kind that brings salvation), which everyone grasps.

If a people has been taught to revere a sacred Scripture, the doctrinal interpretation of that Scripture, which looks to the people's moral interest—its edification, moral improvement, and hence salvation—is also the authentic one with regard to its religion: in other words, this is how God wants this people to understand His will as revealed in the Bible. For it is not a question here of a civil (political) government keeping the people under discipline, but of a government which has as its end the essence of this people's moral attitude of will (hence, a divine government). The God Who speaks through our own (morally practical) reason is an infallible interpreter of His words in the Scriptures, Whom everyone can understand. And it is quite impossible for there to be any other accredited interpreter of His words (one, for example, who would interpret them in a historical way); for religion is a purely rational affair.

*   *
*

And so the theologians of the faculty have the duty incumbent on them, and consequently the title, to uphold biblical faith; but this does not impair the freedom of the philosophers to subject it always to the critique of reason. And should a dictatorship be granted to the higher faculty for a short time (by religious edict), this freedom can best be secured by the solemn formula: *Provideant consules, ne quid respublica detrimenti capiat* ["Let the consuls see to it that no harm befalls the republic"].

123

Anhang biblisch=historischer Fragen
über die praktische Benutzung und muthmaßliche Zeit der
Fortdauer dieses heiligen Buchs.

Daß es bei allem Wechsel der Meinungen noch lange Zeit im An=
sehen bleiben werde, dafür bürgt die Weisheit der Regierung, als deren
Interesse in Ansehung der Eintracht und Ruhe des Volks in einem Staat
hiemit in enger Verbindung steht. Aber ihm die Ewigkeit zu verbürgen,
oder auch es chiliastisch in ein neues Reich Gottes auf Erden übergehen
zu lassen, das übersteigt unser ganzes Vermögen der Wahrsagung. —
Was würde also geschehen, wenn der Kirchenglaube dieses große Mittel
der Volksleitung einmal entbehren müßte?

Wer ist der Redacteur der biblischen Bücher (alten und neuen Testa=
ments), und zu welcher Zeit ist der Kanon zu Stande gekommen?

Werden philologisch=antiquarische Kenntnisse immer zur Erhaltung
der einmal angenommenen Glaubensnorm nöthig sein, oder wird die Ver=
nunft den Gebrauch derselben zur Religion dereinst von selbst und mit
allgemeiner Einstimmung anzuordnen im Stande sein?

Hat man hinreichende Documente der Authenticität der Bibel nach
den sogenannten 70 Dolmetschern, und von welcher Zeit kann man sie mit
Sicherheit datiren? u. s. w.

Die praktische, vornehmlich öffentliche Benutzung dieses Buchs in
Predigten ist ohne Zweifel diejenige, welche zur Besserung der Menschen
und Belebung ihrer moralischen Triebfedern (zur Erbauung) beiträgt.
Alle andere Absicht muß ihr nachstehen, wenn sie hiemit in Collision kommt.
— Man muß sich daher wundern: daß diese Maxime noch hat bezweifelt
werden können, und eine paraphrastische Behandlung eines Texts der
paränetischen, wenn gleich nicht vorgezogen, doch durch die erstere
wenigstens hat in Schatten gestellt werden sollen. — Nicht die Schrift=
gelahrtheit, und was man vermittelst ihrer aus der Bibel durch philolo=
gische Kenntnisse, die oft nur verunglückte Conjecturen sind, herauszieht,
sondern was man mit moralischer Denkungsart (also nach dem Geiste
Gottes) in sie hineinträgt, und Lehren, die nie trügen, auch nie ohne
heilsame Wirkung sein können, das muß diesem Vortrage ans Volk die

Appendix: Historical Questions about the Bible
Concerning the Practical Use and Probable Duration of This
Sacred Book

The government's wisdom guarantees that, whatever changes our opinions may undergo, the Bible will continue to hold a place of honor among us for a long time, since the government's interest in the harmony and peace of people in civil society is closely bound up with it. But to guarantee that the Bible will last forever, or even have it pass over into the millenium of a new kingdom of God on earth, goes far beyond our powers of prediction. What would happen, then, should ecclesiastical faith eventually have to do without this great instrument for guiding the people?

Who edited the books of the Bible (Old and New Testaments), and from what period does the canon date?

Once the norm of faith has been accepted, will philological and antiquarian knowledge always be needed to preserve it, or will reason, by itself and with universal agreement, some day be able to direct it to the service of religion?

Have we documents adequate to establish the authenticity of the so-called Septuagint version of the Bible? From what time can we date it with certainty? And so forth.

The practical use of this book—especially its public use in sermons—is undoubtedly the one that is conducive to man's improvement and to quickening his moral motive (his edification). All other aims must give way to this, if they conflict with it. It is surprising, then, that this maxim could have been doubted and that a *periphrastic* treatment of the text should have overshadowed, if not eclipsed, a *hortatory* treatment. In explaining the Bible to the people the preacher must be guided, not by what scholarship *draws out* of Scripture by philological studies, which are often no more than misleading guesses, but by what a moral cast of mind (according to the spirit of God) *puts into* it, and by teachings that can never mislead and can never fail to produce beneficial results. In other words, he must treat the

Leitung geben: nämlich den Text nur (wenigstens hauptsächlich) als
Veranlassung zu allem Sittenbessernden, was sich dabei denken läßt, zu
behandeln, ohne was die heil. Schriftsteller dabei selbst im Sinne gehabt
haben möchten, nachforschen zu dürfen. — Eine auf Erbauung als End=
zweck gerichtete Predigt (wie denn das eine jede sein soll) muß die Beleh=
rung aus den Herzen der Zuhörer, nämlich der natürlichen moralischen
Anlage, selbst des unbelehrtesten Menschen, entwickeln, wenn die dadurch
zu bewirkende Gesinnung lauter sein soll. Die damit verbundene Zeug=
nisse der Schrift sollen auch nicht die Wahrheit dieser Lehren bestäti=
genden historische Beweisgründe sein (denn deren bedarf die sittlich=thätige
Vernunft hiebei nicht: und das empirische Erkenntniß vermag es auch
nicht), sondern blos Beispiele der Anwendung der praktischen Vernunft=
principien auf Facta der h. Geschichte, um ihre Wahrheit anschaulicher zu
machen; welches aber auch ein sehr schätzbarer Vortheil für Volk und Staat
auf der ganzen Erde ist.

Anhang
Von einer reinen Mystik in der Religion.*)

Ich habe aus der Kritik der reinen Vernunft gelernt, daß Philosophie
nicht etwa eine Wissenschaft der Vorstellungen, Begriffe und Ideen, oder
eine Wissenschaft aller Wissenschaften, oder sonst etwas Ähnliches sei; son=
dern eine Wissenschaft des Menschen, seines Vorstellens, Denkens und
Handelns; — sie soll den Menschen nach allen seinen Bestandtheilen dar=
stellen, wie er ist und sein soll, d. h. sowohl nach seinen Naturbestimmun=
gen, als auch nach seinem Moralitäts= und Freiheitsverhältniß. Hier
wies nun die alte Philosophie dem Menschen einen ganz unrichtigen Stand=
punkt in der Welt an, indem sie ihn in dieser zu einer Maschine machte,
die als solche gänzlich von der Welt oder von den Außendingen und Um=
ständen abhängig sein mußte; sie machte also den Menschen zu einem bei=

*) In einem seiner Dissertation: De similitudine inter Mysticismum purum
et Kantianam religionis doctrinam. Auctore Carol. Arnold. Wilmans, Bielefelda-Guestphalo, Halis Saxonum 1797. beigefügten Briefe, welchen ich mit seiner
Erlaubniß und mit Weglassung der Einleitungs= und Schlußhöflichkeitsstellen hiemit liefere, und welcher diesen jetzt der Arzneiwissenschaft sich widmenden jungen
Mann als einen solchen bezeichnet, von dem sich auch in anderen Fächern der
Wissenschaft viel erwarten läßt. Wobei ich gleichwohl jene Ähnlichkeit meiner Vorstellungsart mit der seinigen unbedingt einzugestehen nicht gemeint bin.

text *only* (or at least *primarily*) as an occasion for anything morally improving that can be made of it, without venturing to search for what the sacred authors themselves might have meant by it. A sermon directed to edification as its final end (as any sermon should be) must develop its lesson from the *hearts* of the listeners, namely, from the natural moral predisposition that is present in even the most ignorant man; for only then will the attitude of will it brings forth be pure. The *testimony of* Scripture connected with these teachings should also not be treated as historical arguments confirming their truth (for morally active reason needs no such argument, and besides, empirical knowledge could not yield anything of the sort), but merely as examples in which the truth of reason's practical principles is made more perceptible through their application to facts of sacred history. But this, too, is a very valuable gain for peoples and states throughout the world.

Appendix

On a Pure Mysticism in Religion*

I have learned from the Critique of Pure Reason that philosophy is not a science of representations, concepts and Ideas, or a science of all the sciences, or anything else of this sort. It is rather a science of man, of his representations, thoughts and actions: it should present all the components of man both as he is and as he should be—that is, in terms both of his natural functions and of his relations of morality and freedom. Ancient philosophers were quite mistaken in the role they assigned man in the world, since they considered him a machine within it, entirely dependent on the world or on external things and circumstances, and so made him an all but passive part of the world. Now the

---

*This is a letter by Carol. Arnold. Wilmans, who enclosed it with his dissertation *De similitudine inter Mysticismum purum et Kantianam religionis doctrinam* (Bielefelda-Guestphalo, Halis Saxonum 1797). With his permission I publish it here, except for the salutation and the complimentary close. It singles out this young man—now devoted to the science of medicine—as one from whom much can be expected in other fields of science as well. In doing this, however, I do not mean to guarantee that my views coincide entirely with his. [27]

nahe bloß paſſiven Theile der Welt. — Jetzt erſchien die Kritik der Ver=
nunft und beſtimmte dem Menſchen in der Welt eine durchaus active
Exiſtenz. Der Menſch ſelbſt iſt urſprünglich Schöpfer aller ſeiner Vor=
ſtellungen und Begriffe und ſoll einziger Urheber aller ſeiner Handlungen
ſein. Jenes „iſt“ und dieſes „ſoll“ führt auf zwei ganz verſchiedene Be=
ſtimmungen am Menſchen. Wir bemerken daher auch im Menſchen zweier=
lei ganz verſchiedenartige Theile, nämlich auf der einen Seite Sinnlichkeit
und Verſtand und auf der andern Vernunft und freien Willen, die ſich
ſehr weſentlich von einander unterſcheiden. In der Natur iſt alles; es iſt
von keinem Soll in ihr die Rede; Sinnlichkeit und Verſtand gehen aber
nur immer darauf aus, zu beſtimmen, was und wie es iſt; ſie müſſen alſo
für die Natur, für dieſe Erdenwelt, beſtimmt ſein und mithin zu ihr ge=
hören. Die Vernunft will beſtändig ins Überſinnliche, wie es wohl über
die ſinnliche Natur hinaus beſchaffen ſein möchte: ſie ſcheint alſo, obzwar
ein theoretiſches Vermögen, dennoch gar nicht für dieſe Sinnlichkeit be=
ſtimmt zu ſein; der freie Wille aber beſteht ja in einer Unabhängigkeit von
den Außendingen; dieſe ſollen nicht Triebfedern des Handlens für den
Menſchen ſein; er kann alſo noch weniger zur Natur gehören. Aber wohin
denn? Der Menſch muß für zwei ganz verſchiedene Welten beſtimmt ſein,
einmal für das Reich der Sinne und des Verſtandes, alſo für dieſe Erden=
welt: dann aber auch noch für eine andere Welt, die wir nicht kennen, für
ein Reich der Sitten.

Was den Verſtand betrifft, ſo iſt dieſer ſchon für ſich durch ſeine Form
auf dieſe Erdenwelt eingeſchränkt; denn er beſteht bloß aus Kategorien,
d. h. Äußerungsarten, die bloß auf ſinnliche Dinge ſich beziehen können.
Seine Gränzen ſind ihm alſo ſcharf geſteckt. Wo die Kategorien aufhören,
da hört auch der Verſtand auf: weil ſie ihn erſt bilden und zuſammenſetzen.
[Ein Beweis für die bloß irdiſche oder Naturbeſtimmung des Verſtandes
ſcheint mir auch dieſes zu ſein, daß wir in Rückſicht der Verſtandeskräfte
eine Stufenleiter in der Natur finden, vom klügſten Menſchen bis zum
dümmſten Thiere (indem wir doch den Inſtinct auch als eine Art von
Verſtand anſehen können, in ſofern zum bloßen Verſtande der freie Wille
nicht gehört).] Aber nicht ſo in Rückſicht der Moralität, die da aufhört,
wo die Menſchheit aufhört, und die in allen Menſchen urſprünglich daſſelbe
Ding iſt. Der Verſtand muß alſo bloß zur Natur gehören, und wenn der
Menſch bloß Verſtand hätte ohne Vernunft und freien Willen, oder ohne
Moralität, ſo würde er ſich in nichts von den Thieren unterſcheiden und

critique of reason has appeared and assigned man a thoroughly *active* existence in the world. Man himself is the original maker of all his representations and concepts, and ought to be the sole author of all his actions. That *"is"* and this *"ought"* lead to two quite different functions in man. Accordingly, we also find in man two quite different elements, namely sensibility and understanding on the one hand, and on the other hand reason and free will; and these two are essentially distinct. In nature, everything *is*: the question of *ought* does not arise there. And since sensibility and understanding aim only at determining what *is* and how it comes to be, they must have their function in nature, in the physical world, and so belong to it. Reason tries constantly to enter the supersensible, to see what there *might be* beyond sensible nature. Although it is a theoretical power, it thus appears not to have its function in what is sensible. Free will, however, consists in independence from external things, since these ought not to be motives in man's actions; still less, then, can it belong to nature. But where does this lead us? To the fact that man must be destined for two entirely different worlds: for the realm of sense and understanding and so for this terrestrial world, but also for another world, which we do not know—a moral kingdom.

As for understanding, it is, by its form, intrinsically limited to this terrestrial world; for it consists merely in categories, that is, modes of expression which can refer only to sensible things. Its limits are therefore sharply defined: where the categories stop, so too does understanding: for the categories form and compose it. (It seems to me that we can also find evidence for the merely terrestrial and natural vocation of understanding in the fact that we find in nature a ladder of powers of understanding, from the most intelligent man to the dumbest beast [since we can consider instinct, too, a kind of understanding in so far as free will does not belong to mere understanding]). But this is not the case with morality, which comes into being along with humanity and which is originally the same thing in all men. Understanding must, therefore, belong merely to nature; and if man had only understanding, without reason and free will, or without morality, there would be nothing to distinguish him from the beasts—he might merely stand at the top of their ladder.

vielleicht bloß an der Spitze ihrer Stufenleiter stehen, da er hingegen jetzt,
im Besitz der Moralität, als freies Wesen, durchaus und wesentlich von den
Thieren verschieden ist, auch von dem klügsten (dessen Instinct oft deutlicher
und bestimmter wirkt, als der Verstand der Menschen). — Dieser Verstand
aber ist ein gänzlich actives Vermögen des Menschen; alle seine Vorstellungen und Begriffe sind bloß seine Geschöpfe, der Mensch denkt mit
seinem Verstande ursprünglich, und er schafft sich also seine Welt. Die
Außendinge sind nur Gelegenheitsursachen der Wirkung des Verstandes,
sie reizen ihn zur Action, und das Product dieser Action sind Vorstellungen
und Begriffe. Die Dinge also, worauf sich diese Vorstellungen und Begriffe beziehen, können nicht das sein, was unser Verstand vorstellt; denn
der Verstand kann nur Vorstellungen und seine Gegenstände, nicht aber
wirkliche Dinge schaffen, d. h. die Dinge können unmöglich durch diese
Vorstellungen und Begriffe vom Verstande als solche, wie sie an sich sein
mögen, erkannt werden; die Dinge, die unsere Sinne und unser Verstand
darstellen, sind vielmehr an sich nur Erscheinungen, d. i. Gegenstände
unserer Sinne und unseres Verstandes, die das Product aus dem Zusammentreffen der Gelegenheitsursachen und der Wirkung des Verstandes
sind, die aber deswegen doch nicht Schein sind, sondern die wir im praktischen Leben für uns als wirkliche Dinge und Gegenstände unserer Vorstellungen ansehen können; eben weil wir die wirklichen Dinge als jene
Gelegenheitsursachen supponiren müssen. Ein Beispiel giebt die Natur-
wissenschaft. Außendinge wirken auf einen actionsfähigen Körper und
reizen diesen dadurch zur Action; das Product hievon ist Leben. — Was
ist aber Leben? Physisches Anerkennen seiner Existenz in der Welt und
seines Verhältnisses zu den Außendingen; der Körper lebt dadurch, daß er
auf die Außendinge reagirt, sie als seine Welt ansieht und sie zu seinem
Zweck gebraucht, ohne sich weiter um ihr Wesen zu bekümmern. Ohne
Außendinge wäre dieser Körper kein lebender Körper, und ohne Actions-
fähigkeit des Körpers wären die Außendinge nicht seine Welt. Eben so
mit dem Verstande. Erst durch sein Zusammentreffen mit den Außendingen entsteht diese seine Welt; ohne Außendinge wäre er todt, — ohne
Verstand aber wären keine Vorstellungen, ohne Vorstellungen keine Gegenstände und ohne diese nicht diese seine Welt; so wie mit einem anderen
Verstande auch eine andere Welt da sein würde, welches durch das Beispiel von Wahnsinnigen klar wird. Also der Verstand ist Schöpfer seiner
Gegenstände und der Welt, die aus ihnen besteht; aber so, daß wirkliche

But because man does have morality he is completely and essentially different, as a free being, from the beasts, even from the most intelligent of them (whose instinct often works more clearly and precisely than man's understanding). Understanding, however, is a thoroughly active power of man; all his representations and concepts are purely *his* works: he thinks spontaneously with his understanding, and he therefore makes *his* world. External things are only occasional causes for understanding's activity: they stimulate it to act and the products of this action are representations and concepts. Thus the things to which these representations and concepts refer cannot be that which our understanding represents; for understanding can make only representations and *its* own objects, not real things. In other words, we cannot possibly know, by these representations and concepts of understanding as such, things as they might be in themselves. Things that our senses and understanding express are in themselves only appearances, that is, objects of our senses and understanding produced by the cooperation of occasional causes and the activity of understanding. But this does not mean that they are illusions: in practical life we can regard them as real things for us and objects of our representations, just because we must suppose real things as occasional causes. Natural science provides an example. External things work on a body capable of action and, by so doing, stimulate it to act. The result of this is life. But what is life? Physical recognition of one's existence in the world and one's relation to external things. The body lives in so far as it reacts to external things, takes them for its world, and uses them to its advantage, without concerning itself further about their essence. Without external things, this body would not be a living body; and without the body's capacity for action, external things would not be its world. It is the same with understanding. Its world arises from its encounter with external things, and without them it would be dead. But without understanding there would be no representations, without representations there would be no objects, and without objects its world would not exist. So too, given another understanding, another world would also exist, as the example of insanity makes clear. Understanding, therefore, makes its objects and the world

Dinge die Gelegenheitsursachen seiner Action und also der Vorstellungen sind.

Dadurch unterscheiden sich nun diese Naturkräfte des Menschen wesentlich von der Vernunft und dem freien Willen. Beide machen zwar auch active Vermögen aus, aber die Gelegenheitsursachen ihrer Action sollen nicht aus dieser Sinnenwelt genommen sein. Die Vernunft als theoretisches Vermögen kann also hier gar keine Gegenstände haben, ihre Wirkungen können nur Ideen sein, d. h. Vorstellungen der Vernunft, denen keine Gegenstände entsprechen, weil nicht wirkliche Dinge, sondern etwa nur Spiele des Verstandes die Gelegenheitsursachen ihrer Action sind. Also kann die Vernunft als theoretisches, speculatives Vermögen hier in dieser Sinnenwelt gar nicht gebraucht werden (und muß folglich, weil sie doch einmal als solches da ist, für eine andere Welt bestimmt sein), sondern nur als praktisches Vermögen zum Behuf des freien Willens. Dieser nun ist bloß und allein praktisch; das Wesentliche desselben besteht darin, daß seine Action nicht Reaction, sondern eine reine objective Handlung sein soll, oder daß die Triebfedern seiner Action nicht mit den Gegenständen derselben zusammenfallen sollen; daß er also unabhängig von den Vorstellungen des Verstandes, weil dieses eine verkehrte und verderbte Wirkungsart derselben veranlassen würde, als auch unabhängig von den Ideen der speculativen Vernunft handeln soll, weil diese, da ihnen nichts Wirkliches entspricht, leicht eine falsche und grundlose Willensbestimmung verursachen könnten. Also muß die Triebfeder der Action des freien Willens etwas sein, was im innern Wesen des Menschen selbst gegründet und von der Freiheit des Willens selbst unzertrennlich ist. Dieses ist nun das moralische Gesetz, welches uns durchaus so aus der Natur herausreißt und über sie erhebt, daß wir als moralische Wesen die Naturdinge weder zu Ursachen und Triebfedern der Action des Willens bedürfen, noch sie als Gegenstände unseres Wollens ansehen können, in deren Stelle vielmehr nur die moralische Person der Menschheit tritt. Jenes Gesetz sichert uns also eine bloß dem Menschen eigenthümliche und ihn von allen übrigen Naturtheilen unterscheidende Eigenschaft, die Moralität, vermöge welcher wir unabhängige und freie Wesen sind, und die selbst wieder durch diese Freiheit begründet ist. — Diese Moralität und nicht der Verstand ist es also, was den Menschen erst zum Menschen macht. So sehr auch der Verstand ein völlig actives und in sofern selbstständiges Vermögen ist, so bedarf er doch zu seiner Action der Außendinge und ist auch zugleich auf sie

that is composed of them, but in such a way that real things are occasional causes of its activity and so of its representations.

This essentially distinguishes these natural powers of man from his reason and free will. For while both reason and free will are also active powers, they should not take the occasional causes of their action from the sensible world. So reason as a theoretical power can have no objects in the sensible world; because the occasional causes of its action are not real things but only, perhaps, the play of understanding, it can produce only Ideas—that is, representations of reason to which no objects correspond. This is why reason cannot be used as a theoretical, speculative power here in this world of sense (and must, because it nevertheless exists as a power in it, be destined for another world), but only as a practical power on behalf of free will. Now free will is purely and simply practical. Its essence consists in this: that its action should not be reaction but rather a pure objective act, or that the motive and the object of its volition should not coincide; and that it should, accordingly, act independently of understanding's representations, since dependence on them would produce a perverted and corrupt kind of act, just as it should act independently of the Ideas of speculative reason, since nothing real corresponds to them and they could easily give rise to a false and unfounded determination of the will. The motive of free will's action must therefore have its ground in the inner being of man himself and be inseparable from this very freedom of the will. Now this motive is the moral law, which so thoroughly frees us from nature and raises us above it that, as moral beings, we have no need of natural things as causes and motives in our acts of will and cannot consider them objects of our volition. The moral person of humanity, alone, takes their place. This law, then, guarantees us a specific characteristic that belongs only to man and distinguishes him from all the rest of nature: morality, which makes us independent and free beings and which is itself, in turn, based on this freedom. Thus morality, not understanding, is what first makes us men. Although understanding is a fully active power and, to this extent, an independent power, it still needs external things for its action and is limited to them. Free will, on the contrary, is completely

eingeschränkt; da hingegen der freie Wille völlig unabhängig ist und einzig durch das innere Gesetz bestimmt werden soll: d. h. der Mensch bloß durch sich selbst, sofern er sich nur zu seiner ursprünglichen Würde und Unab= hängigkeit von allem, was nicht das Gesetz ist, erhoben hat. Wenn also dieser unser Verstand ohne diese seine Außendinge nichts, wenigstens nicht dieser Verstand sein würde, so bleiben Vernunft und freier Wille diesel= ben, ihr Wirkungskreis sei, welcher er wolle. (Sollte hier der freilich hyper= physische Schluß wohl mit einiger Wahrscheinlichkeit gemacht werden kön= nen: „daß mit dem Tode des Menschenkörpers auch dieser sein Verstand stirbt und verloren geht mit allen seinen irdischen Vorstellungen, Begriffen und Kenntnissen: weil doch dieser Verstand immer nur für irdische, sinn= liche Dinge brauchbar ist, und, sobald der Mensch ins Übersinnliche sich versteigen will, hier sogleich aller Verstandesgebrauch aufhört, und der Vernunftgebrauch dagegen eintritt"? Es ist dieses eine Idee, die ich nach= her auch bei den Mystikern, aber nur dunkel gedacht, nicht behauptet ge= funden habe, und die gewiß zur Beruhigung und vielleicht auch morali= schen Verbesserung vieler Menschen beitragen würde. Der Verstand hängt so wenig wie der Körper vom Menschen selbst ab. Bei einem fehlerhaften Körperbau beruhigt man sich, weil man weiß, er ist nichts Wesentliches — ein gutgebaueter Körper hat nur hier auf der Erde seine Vorzüge. Gesetzt, die Idee würde allgemein, daß es mit dem Verstande eben so wäre, sollte das nicht für die Moralität der Menschen ersprießlich sein? Die neuere Naturlehre des Menschen harmonirt sehr mit dieser Idee, indem sie den Verstand bloß als etwas vom Körper Abhängiges und als ein Product der Gehirnwirkung ansieht. S. Reils physiologische Schriften. Auch die ältern Meinungen von der Materialität der Seele ließen sich hierdurch auf etwas Reales zurückbringen.) —

Der fernere Verlauf der kritischen Untersuchung der menschlichen Seelenvermögen stellte die natürliche Frage auf: hat die unvermeidliche und nicht zu unterdrückende Idee der Vernunft von einem Urheber des Weltalls und also unserer selbst und des moralischen Gesetzes auch wohl einen gültigen Grund, da jeder theoretische Grund seiner Natur nach un= tauglich zur Befestigung und Sicherstellung jener Idee ist? Hieraus ent= stand der so schöne moralische Beweis für das Dasein Gottes, der jedem, auch wenn er nicht wollte, doch insgeheim auch deutlich und hinlänglich beweisend sein muß. Aus der durch ihn nun begründeten Idee von einem Weltschöpfer aber ging endlich die praktische Idee hervor von einem all=

independent and should be determined solely by the inner law: in other words, man should be determined solely by himself in so far as he has raised himself to his original dignity and independence from everything but the law. Without its external things our understanding would be nothing—at least it would not be *this* understanding; but reason and free will remain the same in whatever realm they might carry on their activity. (Could we, with some plausibility, draw from this the admittedly hyperphysical conclusion: "With the death of the human body, man's understanding with all its earthly representations, concepts and knowledge also dies and vanishes, since the use of this understanding is limited to earthly, sensible things and ceases as soon as man tries to rise into the supersensible, where it is replaced by the use of reason"? This is an idea that I later found among the mystics too, though they have only an obscure conception of it and do not assert it. Certainly, it would be conducive to the comfort of many men, and perhaps also to their moral improvement. Man is no more responsible for his understanding than for his body. A man with a defective body consoles himself with the knowledge that a good physical constitution is not essential: it is advantageous only here on earth. Were the same view generally accepted with regard to understanding, should not men's morality profit from it? Modern physiology harmonizes thoroughly with this idea, since it considers understanding dependent on the body and produced by the working of the brain. See Reil's [27a] writings on physiology. Even ancient views on the material nature of the soul could, in this way, be reduced to something real.)

As we continue the critical investigation of man's powers of soul, the question naturally arises: is there valid ground for reason's inevitable and irrepressible Idea of a moral author of the universe and so of ourselves and of the moral law, even though no theoretical ground, by its very nature, can adequately establish and guarantee that Idea? From this arises the beautiful moral argument for God's existence, which is bound to be a clear and adequate proof for everyone in private—even for those who are reluctant to have it proved. And from the Idea of a world-creator, which it has now established, there finally issues

gemeinen moralischen Gesetzgeber für alle unsere Pflichten, als Urheber
des uns inwohnenden moralischen Gesetzes.   Diese Idee bietet dem
Menschen eine ganz neue Welt dar. Er fühlt sich für ein anderes Reich
geschaffen, als für das Reich der Sinne und des Verstandes, — nämlich
für ein moralisches Reich, für ein Reich Gottes. Er erkennt nun seine
Pflichten zugleich als göttliche Gebote, und es entsteht in ihm ein neues
Erkenntniß, ein neues Gefühl, nämlich Religion. — So weit, ehrwürdi-
ger Vater, war ich in dem Studio Ihrer Schriften gekommen, als ich eine
Classe von Menschen kennen lernte, die man Separatisten nennt, die aber
sich selbst Mystiker nennen, bei welchen ich fast buchstäblich Ihre Lehre in
Ausübung gebracht fand. Es hielt freilich anfangs schwer, diese in der
mystischen Sprache dieser Leute wieder zu finden; aber es gelang mir nach
anhaltendem Suchen. Es fiel mir auf, daß diese Menschen ganz ohne
Gottesdienst lebten; alles verwarfen, was Gottesdienst heißt und nicht
in Erfüllung seiner Pflichten besteht; daß sie sich für religiöse Menschen,
ja für Christen hielten und doch die Bibel nicht als ihr Gesetzbuch an-
sahen, sondern nur von einem inneren, von Ewigkeit her in uns einwoh-
nenden Christenthum sprachen. — Ich forschte nach dem Lebenswandel
dieser Leute und fand (räudige Schafe ausgenommen, die man in jeder
Heerde ihres Eigennutzes wegen findet) bei ihnen reine moralische Gesinnungen und eine beinahe stoische Consequenz in ihren Handlungen.
Ich untersuchte ihre Lehre und ihre Grundsätze und fand im Wesentlichen
ganz Ihre Moral und Religionslehre wieder, jedoch immer mit dem Unterschiede, daß sie das innere Gesetz, wie sie es nennen, für eine innere
Offenbarung und also bestimmt Gott für den Urheber desselben halten.
Es ist wahr, sie halten die Bibel für ein Buch, welches auf irgend eine
Art, worauf sie sich nicht weiter einlassen, göttlichen Ursprungs ist; aber
wenn man genauer forscht, so findet man, daß sie diesen Ursprung der
Bibel erst aus der Übereinstimmung der Bibel, der in ihr enthaltenen
Lehren, mit ihrem inneren Gesetze schließen: denn wenn man sie z. B.
fragt: warum? so ist ihre Antwort: sie legitimirt sich in meinem Inneren,
und ihr werdet es eben so finden, wenn ihr der Weisung eures inneren
Gesetzes oder den Lehren der Bibel Folge leistet. Eben deswegen halten
sie sie auch nicht für ihr Gesetzbuch, sondern nur für eine historische Bestätigung, worin sie das, was in ihnen selbst ursprünglich gegründet ist,
wiederfinden. Mit einem Worte, diese Leute würden (verzeihen Sie mir
den Ausdruck!) wahre Kantianer sein, wenn sie Philosophen wären. Aber

the practical Idea of a universal moral law-giver who, as the author of the moral law dwelling in us, prescribes all our duties. This Idea presents an entirely new world to man. He feels that he was created for another realm than that of sense and understanding—namely, for a moral realm, a kingdom of God. Now he recognizes his duties as divine commands also, and there arises in him a new awareness, a new feeling—namely, religion. I had reached this point in my study of your writings, venerable father, when I became acquainted with a group of people, called separatists but calling themselves *mystics*, among whom I found your teachings put into practice almost verbatim. It was indeed difficult to recognize your teachings, at first, in their mystical terms, but after persistent probing I succeeded. It struck me as strange that these people live entirely without public worship: that they repudiate all "divine service" that does not consist in fulfilling one's duties: that they consider themselves religious people and indeed Christians, though they take as their code not the Bible, but only the precepts of an inward Christianity dwelling in us from eternity. I inquired into their conduct and found in them (except for the mangy sheep that, from self-interest, get into every flock) a pure moral attitude of will and an almost Stoic consistency in their actions. I examined their teachings and principles and recognized the essentials of your entire moral and religious doctrine, though with this difference: that they consider the inner law, as they call it, an inward revelation and so regard God as definitely its author. It is true that they regard the Bible as a book which in some way or other—they do not discuss it further—is of divine origin; but, inquiring more closely, one finds that they infer the divine origin of the Bible from the consistency of the doctrine it contains with their inner law. For if one asks their reason, they reply: The Bible is validated in my heart, as you will find it in yours if you obey the precepts of your inner law or the teachings of the Bible. For the same reason they do not regard the Bible as their code of laws but only as a historical confirmation in which they recognize what is originally grounded in themselves. In a word, if these people were philosophers they would be (pardon the term!) true

137

sie sind größtentheils aus der Classe der Kaufleute, Handwerker und Land=
bauern; doch habe ich hin und wieder auch in höheren Ständen und un=
ter den Gelehrten einige gefunden; aber nie einen Theologen, denen diese
Leute ein wahrer Dorn im Auge sind, weil sie ihren Gottesdienst nicht
von ihnen unterstützt sehen und ihnen doch wegen ihres exemplarischen
Lebenswandels und Unterwerfung in jede bürgerliche Ordnung durchaus
nichts anhaben können. Von den Quäkern unterscheiden sich diese Sepa=
ratisten nicht in ihren Religionsgrundsätzen, aber wohl in der Anwen=
dung derselben aufs gemeine Leben. Denn sie kleiden sich z. B., wie es
gerade Sitte ist, und bezahlen alle sowohl Staats= als kirchliche Abgaben.
Bei dem gebildeten Theile derselben habe ich nie Schwärmerei gefunden,
sondern freies, vorurtheilloses Räsonnement und Urtheil über religiöse
Gegenstände.

Kantians. But most of them are merchants, artisans, and peasants, although I have now and then found them in higher stations, and a few of them among the educated. But I have never found a theologian among them—for to theologians, they are a real thorn in the eye because, while they do not support public worship, their exemplary conduct and complete submission to the civil order put them quite beyond reproach. What distinguishes these separatists from Quakers is not their religious *principles*, but the way they apply them to their everyday life; for example, they adopt no distinctive dress and pay both their state and church taxes. Among the educated members I have never encountered fanaticism, but rather free, unprejudiced reasoning and judgment in religious matters.

Zweiter Abschnitt.

Der Streit der philosophischen Facultät mit der juristischen.

SECOND PART

The Conflict of the Philosophy Faculty with the Faculty of Law

Erneuerte Frage:
Ob das menschliche Geschlecht im beständigen Fortschreiten zum Besseren sei.

1.
Was will man hier wissen?

Man verlangt ein Stück von der Menschengeschichte und zwar nicht das von der vergangenen, sondern der künftigen Zeit, mithin eine vor= hersagende, welche, wenn sie nicht nach bekannten Naturgesetzen (wie Sonnen= und Mondfinsternisse) geführt wird, wahrsagend und doch natürlich, kann sie aber nicht anders, als durch übernatürliche Mittheilung und Erweiterung der Aussicht in die künftige Zeit erworben werden, weissagend (prophetisch) genannt wird.*) — Übrigens ist es hier auch nicht um die Naturgeschichte des Menschen (ob etwa künftig neue Racen derselben entstehen möchten), sondern um die Sittengeschichte und zwar nicht nach dem Gattungsbegriff (singulorum), sondern dem Ganzen der gesellschaftlich auf Erden vereinigten, in Völkerschaften ver= theilten Menschen (universorum) zu thun, wenn gefragt wird: ob das menschliche Geschlecht (im Großen) zum Besseren beständig fortschreite.

2.
Wie kann man es wissen?

Als wahrsagende Geschichtserzählung des Bevorstehenden in der künftigen Zeit: mithin als eine a priori mögliche Darstellung der Bege= benheiten, die da kommen sollen. — Wie ist aber eine Geschichte a priori

---

*) Wer ins Wahrsagen pfuschert (es ohne Kenntniß oder Ehrlichkeit thut), von dem heißt es: er wahrsagert, von der Pythia an bis zur Zigeunerin.

AN OLD QUESTION RAISED AGAIN: IS THE HUMAN RACE CONSTANTLY PROGRESSING?

1.

What Do We *Want* To Know in this Matter?

We desire a fragment of human history and one, indeed, that is drawn not from past but future time, therefore a predictive history; if it is not based on known laws (like eclipses of the sun and moon), this history is designated as divinatory, and yet natural; but if it can be acquired in no other way than through a supernatural communication and widening of one's view of future time, this history is called premonitory (prophetic).* If it is asked whether the human race at large is progressing perpetually toward the better, the important thing is not the natural history of man (whether new races may arise in the future), but rather his moral history and, more precisely, his history not as a species according to the generic notion (*singulorum*), but as the totality of men united socially on earth and apportioned into peoples (*universorum*).

2.

How *Can* We Know It?

As a divinatory historical narrative of things imminent in future time, consequently as a possible representation a priori of events which are supposed to happen then. But how is a history a

---

*From Pythia to the gipsy girl, whoever dabbles in divination (doing it without knowledge or honesty) is said to be a *soothsayer*.

141

möglich? — Antwort: wenn der Wahrsager die Begebenheiten selber macht und veranstaltet, die er zum Voraus verkündigt.

Jüdische Propheten hatten gut weissagen, daß über kurz oder lang nicht bloß Verfall, sondern gänzliche Auflösung ihrem Staat bevorstehe; denn sie waren selbst die Urheber dieses ihres Schicksals. — Sie hatten als Volksleiter ihre Verfassung mit so viel kirchlichen und daraus abflie=ßenden bürgerlichen Lasten beschwert, daß ihr Staat völlig untauglich wurde, für sich selbst, vornehmlich mit benachbarten Völkern zusammen zu bestehen, und die Jeremiaden ihrer Priester mußten daher natürlicher Weise vergeblich in der Luft verhallen: weil diese hartnäckicht auf ihrem Vorsatz einer unhaltbaren, von ihnen selbst gemachten Verfassung beharr=ten, und so von ihnen selbst der Ausgang mit Unfehlbarkeit vorausgesehen werden konnte.

Unsere Politiker machen, so weit ihr Einfluß reicht, es eben so und sind auch im Wahrsagen eben so glücklich. — Man muß, sagen sie, die Menschen nehmen, wie sie sind, nicht wie der Welt unkundige Pedanten oder gutmüthige Phantasten träumen, daß sie sein sollten. Das wie sie sind aber sollte heißen: wozu wir sie durch ungerechten Zwang, durch verrätherische, der Regierung an die Hand gegebene Anschläge gemacht haben, nämlich halsstarrig und zur Empörung geneigt; wo dann frei=lich, wenn sie ihre Zügel ein wenig sinken läßt, sich traurige Folgen er=äugnen, welche die Prophezeiung jener vermeintlich=klugen Staatsmänner wahrmachen.

Auch Geistliche weissagen gelegentlich den gänzlichen Verfall der Re=ligion und die nahe Erscheinung des Antichrists, während dessen sie ge=rade das thun, was erforderlich ist, ihn einzuführen: indem sie nämlich ihrer Gemeine nicht sittliche Grundsätze ans Herz zu legen bedacht sind, die geradezu aufs Bessern führen, sondern Observanzen und historischen Glauben zur wesentlichen Pflicht machen, die es indirect bewirken sollen, woraus zwar mechanische Einhelligkeit als in einer bürgerlichen Verfas=sung, aber keine in der moralischen Gesinnung erwachsen kann; alsdann aber über Irreligiosität klagen, welche sie selber gemacht haben, die sie also auch ohne besondere Wahrsagergabe vorherverkündigen konnten.

priori possible? Answer: if the diviner himself creates and contrives the events which he announces in advance.

It was all very well for the Jewish prophets to prophesy that sooner or later not simply decadence but complete dissolution awaited their state, for they themselves were the authors of this fate. As national leaders they had loaded their constitution with so much ecclesiastical freight, and civil freight tied to it, that their state became utterly unfit to subsist of itself, and especially unfit to subsist together with neighboring nations. Hence the jeremiads of their priests were naturally bound to be lost upon the winds, because the priests obstinately persisted in their design for an untenable constitution created by themselves; and thus they could infallibly foresee the issue.

So far as their influence extends, our politicians do precisely the same thing and are just as lucky in their prophecies. We must, they say, take men as they are, not as pedants ignorant of the world or good-natured visionaries fancy they ought to be. But in place of that "as they are" it would be better to say what they "have made" them—stubborn and inclined to revolt—through unjust constraint, through perfidious plots placed in the hands of the government; obviously then, if the government allows the reins to relax a little, sad consequences ensue which verify the prophecy of those supposedly sagacious statesmen.

Ecclesiastics, too, occasionally prophesy the complete destruction of religion and the imminent appearance of Antichrist; and in doing so they are performing precisely what is requisite to call him up. This happens because they have not seen to impressing on their parishes moral principles which lead directly to the better, but rather fabricate into essential duty observances and historical beliefs which are supposed to effect it indirectly; from this, of course, can grow the mechanical unanimity as in a civil constitution, but none in moral disposition. But then they complain about irreligion, which they themselves have caused and thus could predict even without any special prophetic talent.

3.

Eintheilung des Begriffs von dem, was man für die Zu= kunft vorherwissen will.

Der Fälle, die eine Vorhersagung enthalten können, sind drei. Das menschliche Geschlecht ist entweder im continuirlichen Rückgange zum Ärgeren, oder im beständigen Fortgange zum Besseren in seiner mo= ralischen Bestimmung, oder im ewigen Stillstande auf der jetzigen Stufe seines sittlichen Werths unter den Gliedern der Schöpfung (mit welchem die ewige Umdrehung im Kreise um denselben Punkt einerlei ist).

Die erste Behauptung kann man den moralischen Terrorismus, die zweite den Eudämonismus (der, das Ziel des Fortschreitens im weiten Prospect gesehen, auch Chiliasmus genannt werden würde), die dritte aber den Abderitismus nennen: weil, da ein wahrer Stillstand im Moralischen nicht möglich ist, ein beständig wechselndes Steigen und eben so öfteres und tiefes Zurückfallen (gleichsam ein ewiges Schwanken) nichts mehr austrägt, als ob das Subject auf derselben Stelle und im Stillstande geblieben wäre.

a.

Von der terroristischen Vorstellungsart der Menschen= geschichte.

Der Verfall ins Ärgere kann im menschlichen Geschlechte nicht be= ständig fortwährend sein; denn bei einem gewissen Grade desselben würde es sich selbst aufreiben. Daher beim Anwachs großer, wie Berge sich auf= thürmenden Greuelthaten und ihnen angemessenen Übel gesagt wird: nun kann es nicht mehr ärger werden; der jüngste Tag ist vor der Thür, und der fromme Schwärmer träumt nun schon von der Wiederbringung aller Dinge und einer erneuerten Welt, nachdem diese im Feuer untergegan= gen ist.

b.

Von der eudämonistischen Vorstellungsart der Menschen= geschichte.

Daß die Masse des unserer Natur angearteten Guten und Bösen in der Anlage immer dieselbe bleibe und in demselben Individuum weder

3.
Classification of the Concept of That Which We Wish to Foreknow As Regards the Future

In three cases one could make predictions. The human race exists either in continual retrogression toward wickedness, or in perpetual progression toward improvement in its moral destination, or in eternal stagnation in its present stage of moral worth among creatures (a stagnation with which eternal rotation in orbit around the same point is one and the same).

The first assertion we can call moral terrorism, and the second eudaemonism (which could also be called chiliasm if we view the goal of progress within a broad prospectus); but the third we can term abderitism [28] because, since a true stagnation in matters of morality is not possible, a perpetually changing upward tendency and an equally frequent and profound relapse (an eternal oscillation, as it were) amounts to nothing more than if the subject had remained in the same place, standing still.

a.
Concerning the Terroristic Manner of Representing Human History

Decline into wickedness cannot be incessant in the human race, for at a certain stage of disintegration it would destroy itself. Hence in connection with the increase of great atrocities looming up like mountains, and evils commensurate with them, it is said: now things cannot grow worse; Doomsday is at our doorstep; and the pious enthusiast by this time is already dreaming of the restoration of all things and a renovated world after the time that this one will have perished in flames.

b.
Concerning the Eudaemonistic Manner of Representing Human History

It may always be conceded that the proportion of good and evil elements inherent in our predisposition remains constant and can be neither augmented nor diminished in the same individual;

vermehrt noch vermindert werden könne, mag immer eingeräumt werden;
— und wie sollte sich auch dieses Quantum des Guten in der Anlage ver=
mehren lassen, da es durch die Freiheit des Subjects geschehen müßte,
wozu dieses aber wiederum eines größeren Fonds des Guten bedürfen
würde, als es einmal hat? — Die Wirkungen können das Vermögen der
wirkenden Ursache nicht übersteigen; und so kann das Quantum des mit
dem Bösen im Menschen vermischten Guten ein gewisses Maß des letz=
teren nicht überschreiten, über welches er sich emporarbeiten und so auch
immer zum noch Besseren fortschreiten könnte. Der Eudämonism mit
seinen sanguinischen Hoffnungen scheint also unhaltbar zu sein und zu
Gunsten einer weissagenden Menschengeschichte in Ansehung des immer=
während weitern Fortschreitens auf der Bahn des Guten wenig zu ver=
sprechen.

c.

Von der Hypothese des Abderitisms des Menschengeschlechts zur Vorherbestimmung seiner Geschichte.

Diese Meinung möchte wohl die Mehrheit der Stimmen auf ihrer
Seite haben. Geschäftige Thorheit ist der Charakter unserer Gattung:
in die Bahn des Guten schnell einzutreten, aber darauf nicht zu beharren,
sondern, um ja nicht an einen einzigen Zweck gebunden zu sein, wenn es
auch nur der Abwechselung wegen geschähe, den Plan des Fortschritts
umzukehren, zu bauen, um niederreißen zu können, und sich selbst die hoff=
nungslose Bemühung aufzulegen, den Stein des Sisyphus bergan zu
wälzen, um ihn wieder zurückrollen zu lassen. — Das Princip des Bösen
in der Naturanlage des menschlichen Geschlechts scheint also hier mit dem
des Guten nicht sowohl amalgamirt (verschmolzen), als vielmehr Eines
durchs Andere neutralisirt zu sein, welches Thatlosigkeit zu Folge haben
würde (die hier der Stillstand heißt): eine leere Geschäftigkeit, das Gute
mit dem Bösen durch Vorwärts und Rückwärts gehen so abwechseln zu
lassen, daß das ganze Spiel des Verkehrs unserer Gattung mit sich selbst
auf diesem Glob als ein bloßes Possenspiel angesehen werden müßte, was
ihr keinen größeren Werth in den Augen der Vernunft verschaffen kann,
als den die andere Thiergeschlechter haben, die dieses Spiel mit weniger
Kosten und ohne Verstandesaufwand treiben.

how then should the quantity of good in our predisposition increase? For that would happen only through the freedom of the subject, for which purpose the subject would in turn require a greater reservoir of good than it now possesses. The effects cannot surpass the power of the efficient cause; thus the quantity of good mixed in man with the evil cannot exceed a certain measure beyond which it would be able to work its way up and thus ever proceed toward the better. Eudaemonism, with its sanguine hopes, therefore, appears to be untenable and to promise little in a prophetic history of humanity in favor of progress endlessly broadening its course toward the good.

c.

Concerning the Abderitic Hypothesis of the Human Race for the Predetermination of Its History

This opinion may well have the majority of voices on its side. Bustling folly is the character of our species: people hastily set off on the path of the good, but do not persevere steadfastly upon it; indeed, in order to avoid being bound to a single goal, even if only for the sake of variety they reverse the plan of progress, build in order to demolish, and impose upon themselves the hopeless effort of rolling the stone of Sisyphus uphill in order to let it roll back down again. The principle of evil in the natural predisposition of the human race, therefore, does not seem to be amalgamated (blended) here with that of the good, but each principle appears rather to be neutralized by the other. Inertia (which is called here stagnation) would be the result of this. It is a vain affair to have good so alternate with evil that the whole traffic of our species with itself on this globe would have to be considered as a mere farcical comedy, for this can endow our species with no greater value in the eyes of reason than that which other animal species possess, species which carry on this game with fewer costs and without expenditure of thought.

4.

Durch Erfahrung unmittelbar ist die Aufgabe des Fort= schreitens nicht aufzulösen.

Wenn das menschliche Geschlecht, im Ganzen betrachtet, eine noch so lange Zeit vorwärts gehend und im Fortschreiten begriffen gewesen zu sein befunden würde, so kann doch niemand dafür stehen, daß nun nicht gerade jetzt vermöge der physischen Anlage unserer Gattung die Epoche seines Rückganges eintrete; und umgekehrt, wenn es rücklings und mit beschleunigtem Falle zum Ärgeren geht, so darf man nicht verzagen, daß nicht eben da der Umwendungspunkt (punctum flexus contrarii) anzutref= fen wäre, wo vermöge der moralischen Anlage in unserem Geschlecht der Gang desselben sich wiederum zum Besseren wendete. Denn wir haben es mit freihandelnden Wesen zu thun, denen sich zwar vorher dictiren läßt, was sie thun sollen, aber nicht vorhersagen läßt, was sie thun wer= den, und die aus dem Gefühl der Übel, die sie sich selbst zufügten, wenn es recht böse wird, eine verstärkte Triebfeder zu nehmen wissen, es nun doch besser zu machen, als es vor jenem Zustande war. — Aber „arme Sterbliche (sagt der Abt Coyer), unter euch ist nichts beständig, als die Unbeständigkeit!"

Vielleicht liegt es auch an unserer unrecht genommenen Wahl des Standpunkts, aus dem wir den Lauf menschlicher Dinge ansehen, daß dieser uns so widersinnisch scheint. Die Planeten, von der Erde aus ge= sehen, sind bald rückgängig, bald stillstehend, bald fortgängig. Den Stand= punkt aber von der Sonne aus genommen, welches nur die Vernunft thun kann, gehen sie nach der Kopernikanischen Hypothese beständig ihren regel= mäßigen Gang fort. Es gefällt aber einigen sonst nicht Unweisen, steif auf ihrer Erklärungsart der Erscheinungen und dem Standpunkte zu be= harren, den sie einmal genommen haben: sollten sie sich darüber auch in Tychonische Cyklen und Epicyklen bis zur Ungereimtheit verwickeln. — Aber das ist eben das Unglück, daß wir uns in diesen Standpunkt, wenn es die Vorhersagung freier Handlungen angeht, zu versetzen nicht ver= mögend sind. Denn das wäre der Standpunkt der Vorsehung, der über alle menschliche Weisheit hinausliegt, welche sich auch auf freie Hand= lungen des Menschen erstreckt, die von diesem zwar gesehen, aber mit Gewißheit nicht vorhergesehen werden können (für das göttliche Auge

6*

4.

The Problem of Progress Is Not to Be
Resolved Directly through Experience

Even if we felt that the human race, considered as a whole, was to be conceived as progressing and proceeding forward for however long a time, still no one can guarantee that now, this very moment, with regard to the physical disposition of our species, the epoch of its decline would not be liable to occur; and inversely, if it is moving backwards, and in an accelerated fall into baseness, a person may not despair even then of encountering a juncture (*punctum flexus contrarii*) where the moral predisposition in our race would be able to turn anew toward the better. For we are dealing with beings that act freely, to whom, it is true, what they ought to do may be dictated in advance, but of whom it may not be predicted what they will do: we are dealing with beings who, from the feeling of self-inflicted evil, when things disintegrate altogether, know how to adopt a strengthened motive for making them even better than they were before that state. But "miserable mortals," says the Abbot Coyer, "nothing is constant in your lives except inconstancy!"

If the course of human affairs seems so senseless to us, perhaps it lies in a poor choice of position from which we regard it. Viewed from the earth, the planets sometimes move backwards, sometimes forward, and sometimes not at all. But if the standpoint selected is the sun, an act which only reason can perform, according to the Copernican hypothesis they move constantly in their regular course. Some people, however, who in other respects are not stupid, like to persist obstinately in their way of explaining the phenomena and in the point of view which they have once adopted, even if they should thereby entangle themselves to the point of absurdity in Tychonic cycles and epicycles.[29] But, and this is precisely the misfortune, we are not capable of placing ourselves in this position when it is a question of the prediction of free actions. For that would be the standpoint of Providence which is situated beyond all human wisdom, and which likewise extends to the free actions of man; these actions, of course, man can *see*, but not *foresee* with

ist hier kein Unterschied), weil er zu dem letzteren den Zusammenhang nach
Naturgesetzen bedarf, in Ansehung der künftigen freien Handlungen aber
dieser Leitung oder Hinweisung entbehren muß.

Wenn man den Menschen einen angebornen und unveränderlich=guten,
obzwar eingeschränkten Willen beilegen dürfte, so würde er dieses Fort=
schreiten seiner Gattung zum Besseren mit Sicherheit vorhersagen können:
weil es eine Begebenheit träfe, die er selbst machen kann. Bei der Mi=
schung des Bösen aber mit dem Guten in der Anlage, deren Maß er nicht
kennt, weiß er selbst nicht, welcher Wirkung er sich davon gewärtigen könne.

5.

**An irgend eine Erfahrung muß doch die wahrsagende Geschichte
des Menschengeschlechts angeknüpft werden.**

Es muß irgend eine Erfahrung im Menschengeschlechte vorkommen,
die als Begebenheit auf eine Beschaffenheit und ein Vermögen desselben
hinweiset, Ursache von dem Fortrücken desselben zum Besseren und (da
dieses die That eines mit Freiheit begabten Wesens sein soll) Urheber des=
selben zu sein; aus einer gegebenen Ursache aber läßt sich eine Begebenheit
als Wirkung vorhersagen, wenn sich die Umstände eräugnen, welche dazu
mitwirkend sind. Daß diese letztere sich aber irgend einmal eräugnen
müssen, kann wie beim Calcul der Wahrscheinlichkeit im Spiel wohl im
Allgemeinen vorhergesagt, aber nicht bestimmt werden, ob es sich in meinem
Leben zutragen und ich die Erfahrung davon haben werde, die jene Vor=
hersagung bestätigte. — Also muß eine Begebenheit nachgesucht werden,
welche auf das Dasein einer solchen Ursache und auch auf den Act ihrer
Causalität im Menschengeschlechte unbestimmt in Ansehung der Zeit hin=
weise, und die auf das Fortschreiten zum Besseren als unausbleibliche
Folge schließen ließe, welcher Schluß dann auch auf die Geschichte der ver=
gangenen Zeit (daß es immer im Fortschritt gewesen sei) ausgedehnt wer=
den könnte, doch so, daß jene Begebenheit nicht selbst als Ursache des letz=
teren, sondern nur als hindeutend, als Geschichtszeichen (signum rememorativum, demonstrativum, prognostikon), angesehen werden müsse
und so die Tendenz des menschlichen Geschlechts im Ganzen, d. i. nicht
nach den Individuen betrachtet (denn das würde eine nicht zu beendigende
Aufzählung und Berechnung abgeben), sondern wie es in Völkerschaften
und Staaten getheilt auf Erden angetroffen wird, beweisen könnte.

certitude (for the divine eye there is no distinction in this matter); because, in the final analysis, man requires coherency according to natural laws, but with respect to his future free actions he must dispense with this guidance or direction.

If we were able to attribute to man an inherent and unalterably good, albeit limited, will, he would be able to predict with certainty the progress of his species toward the better, because it would concern an event that he himself could produce. But in connection with the mixture of good and evil in his predisposition, the proportion of which he is incognizant, he himself does not know what effect he might expect from it.

5.

Yet the Prophetic History of the Human Race Must Be Connected to Some Experience

There must be some experience in the human race which, as an event, points to the disposition and capacity of the human race to be the cause of its own advance toward the better, and (since this should be the act of a being endowed with freedom), toward the human race as being the author of this advance. But from a given cause an event as an effect can be predicted [only] if the circumstances prevail which contribute to it. That these conditions must come to pass some time or other can, of course, be predicted in general, as in the calculation of probability in games of chance; but that prediction cannot enable us to know whether what is predicted is to happen in my life and I am to have the experience of it. Therefore, an event must be sought which points to the existence of such a cause and to its effectiveness in the human race, undetermined with regard to time, and which would allow progress toward the better to be concluded as an inevitable consequence. This conclusion then could also be extended to the history of the past (that it has always been in progress) in such a way that that event would have to be considered not itself as the cause of history, but only as an intimation, a historical sign (*signum rememorativum, demonstrativum, prognostikon*) demonstrating the tendency of the human race viewed in its entirety, that is, seen not as [a sum of] individuals (for that would yield an interminable enumeration and computation), but rather as divided into nations and states (as it is encountered on earth).

6.

Von einer Begebenheit unserer Zeit, welche diese moralische Tendenz des Menschengeschlechts beweiset.

Diese Begebenheit besteht nicht etwa in wichtigen, von Menschen ver=
richteten Thaten oder Unthaten, wodurch, was groß war, unter Menschen
klein oder, was klein war, groß gemacht wird, und wie gleich als durch
Zauberei alte, glänzende Staatsgebäude verschwinden, und andere an deren
Statt wie aus den Tiefen der Erde hervorkommen. Nein: nichts von allem
dem. Es ist bloß die Denkungsart der Zuschauer, welche sich bei diesem
Spiele großer Umwandlungen öffentlich verräth und eine so allgemeine
und doch uneigennützige Theilnehmung der Spielenden auf einer Seite ge=
gen die auf der andern, selbst mit Gefahr, diese Parteilichkeit könne ihnen
sehr nachtheilig werden, dennoch laut werden läßt, so aber (der Allgemein=
heit wegen) einen Charakter des Menschengeschlechts im Ganzen und zu=
gleich (der Uneigennützigkeit wegen) einen moralischen Charakter desselben
wenigstens in der Anlage beweiset, der das Fortschreiten zum Besseren
nicht allein hoffen läßt, sondern selbst schon ein solches ist, so weit das Ver=
mögen desselben für jetzt zureicht.

Die Revolution eines geistreichen Volks, die wir in unseren Tagen
haben vor sich gehen sehen, mag gelingen oder scheitern; sie mag mit Elend
und Greuelthaten dermaßen angefüllt sein, daß ein wohldenkender Mensch
sie, wenn er sie zum zweitenmale unternehmend glücklich auszuführen
hoffen könnte, doch das Experiment auf solche Kosten zu machen nie be=
schließen würde, — diese Revolution, sage ich, findet doch in den Ge=
müthern aller Zuschauer (die nicht selbst in diesem Spiele mit verwickelt
sind) eine Theilnehmung dem Wunsche nach, die nahe an Enthusiasm
grenzt, und deren Äußerung selbst mit Gefahr verbunden war, die also
keine andere als eine moralische Anlage im Menschengeschlecht zur Ursache
haben kann.

Diese moralische einfließende Ursache ist zwiefach: erstens die des
Rechts, daß ein Volk von anderen Mächten nicht gehindert werden müsse,
sich eine bürgerliche Verfassung zu geben, wie sie ihm selbst gut zu sein
dünkt; zweitens die des Zwecks (der zugleich Pflicht ist), daß diejenige
Verfassung eines Volks allein an sich rechtlich und moralisch=gut sei,
welche ihrer Natur nach so beschaffen ist, den Angriffskrieg nach Grund=
sätzen zu meiden, welche keine andere als die republicanische Verfassung,

6.

Concerning an Event of Our Time Which Demonstrates this Moral Tendency of the Human Race

This event consists neither in momentous deeds nor crimes committed by men whereby what was great among men is made small or what was small is made great, nor in ancient splendid political structures which vanish as if by magic while others come forth in their place as if from the depths of the earth. No, nothing of the sort. It is simply the mode of thinking of the spectators which reveals itself publicly in this game of great revolutions, and manifests such a universal yet disinterested sympathy for the players on one side against those on the other, even at the risk that this partiality could become very disadvantageous for them if discovered. Owing to its universality, this mode of thinking demonstrates a character of the human race at large and all at once; owing to its disinterestedness, a moral character of humanity, at least in its predisposition, a character which not only permits people to hope for progress toward the better, but is already itself progress in so far as its capacity is sufficient for the present.

The revolution[30] of a gifted people which we have seen unfolding in our day may succeed or miscarry; it may be filled with misery and atrocities to the point that a sensible man, were he boldly to hope to execute it successfully the second time, would never resolve to make the experiment at such cost—this revolution, I say, nonetheless finds in the hearts of all spectators (who are not engaged in this game themselves) a wishful participation that borders closely on enthusiasm, the very expression of which is fraught with danger; this sympathy, therefore, can have no other cause than a moral predisposition in the human race.

This moral cause inserting itself [in the course of events] is twofold: first, that of the *right*, that a nation must not be hindered in providing itself with a civil constitution, which appears good to the people themselves; and second, that of the *end* (which is, at the same time, a duty), that that same national constitution alone be just and morally good in itself, created in such a way as to avoid, by its very nature, principles permitting offensive war. It can be no other than a republican constitution,

wenigstens der Idee nach, sein kann,*) mithin in die Bedingung einzutreten, wodurch der Krieg (der Quell aller Übel und Verderbniß der Sitten)
abgehalten und so dem Menschengeschlechte bei aller seiner Gebrechlichkeit
der Fortschritt zum Besseren negativ gesichert wird, im Fortschreiten
wenigstens nicht gestört zu werden.

Dies also und die Theilnehmung am Guten mit Affect, der Enthusiasm, ob er zwar, weil aller Affect als ein solcher Tadel verdient,
nicht ganz zu billigen ist, giebt doch vermittelst dieser Geschichte zu der
für die Anthropologie wichtigen Bemerkung Anlaß: daß wahrer Enthusiasm nur immer aufs Idealische und zwar rein Moralische geht,
dergleichen der Rechtsbegriff ist, und nicht auf den Eigennutz gepfropft
werden kann. Durch Geldbelohnungen konnten die Gegner der Revolutio-
nirenden zu dem Eifer und der Seelengröße nicht gespannt werden, den
der bloße Rechtsbegriff in ihnen hervorbrachte, und selbst der Ehrbegriff
des alten kriegerischen Adels (ein Analogon des Enthusiasm) verschwand
vor den Waffen derer, welche das Recht des Volks, wozu sie gehörten, ins
Auge gefaßt hatten**) und sich als Beschützer desselben dachten; mit welcher

---

*) Es ist aber hiemit nicht gemeint, daß ein Volk, welches eine monarchische
Constitution hat, sich damit das Recht anmaße, ja auch nur in sich geheim den
Wunsch hege, sie abgeändert zu wissen; denn seine vielleicht sehr verbreitete Lage in
Europa kann ihm jene Verfassung als die einzige anempfehlen, bei der es sich
zwischen mächtigen Nachbaren erhalten kann. Auch ist das Murren der Unterthanen nicht des Innern der Regierung halber, sondern wegen des Benehmens derselben gegen Auswärtige, wenn sie diese etwa am Republicanisiren hinderte, gar
kein Beweis der Unzufriedenheit des Volks mit seiner eigenen Verfassung, sondern
vielmehr der Liebe für dieselbe, weil es wider eigene Gefahr desto mehr gesichert
ist, je mehr sich andere Völker republicanisiren. — Dennoch haben verläumderische
Sykophanten, um sich wichtig zu machen, diese unschuldige Kannegießerei für Neue-
rungssucht, Jacobinerei und Rottirung, die dem Staat Gefahr drohe, auszugeben
gesucht: indessen daß auch nicht der mindeste Grund zu diesem Vorgeben da war,
vornehmlich nicht in einem Lande, was vom Schauplatz der Revolution mehr als
hundert Meilen entfernt war.

**) Von einem solchen Enthusiasm der Rechtsbehauptung für das menschliche
Geschlecht kann man sagen: postquam ad arma Vulcania ventum est, — mortalis
mucro glacies ceu futilis ictu dissiluit. — Warum hat es noch nie ein Herrscher
gewagt, frei herauszusagen, daß er gar kein Recht des Volks gegen ihn anerkenne;
daß dieses seine Glückseligkeit bloß der Wohlthätigkeit einer Regierung, die
diese ihm angedeihen läßt, verdanke, und alle Anmaßung des Unterthans zu einem
Recht gegen dieselbe (weil dieses den Begriff eines erlaubten Widerstands in sich

republican at least in essence;* it thus establishes the condition whereby war (the source of all evil and corruption of morals) is deterred; and, at least negatively, progress toward the better is assured humanity in spite of all its infirmity, for it is at least left undisturbed in its advance.

This, then, plus the passionate participation in the good, i.e., enthusiasm (although not to be wholly esteemed, since passion as such deserves censure), provide through this history the occasion for the following remark which is important for anthropology: genuine enthusiasm always moves only toward what is ideal and, indeed, to what is purely moral, such as the concept of right, and it cannot be grafted onto self-interest. Monetary rewards will not elevate the adversaries of the revolution to the zeal and grandeur of soul which the pure concept of right produced in them; and even the concept of honor among the old martial nobility (an analogue to enthusiasm) vanished before the weapons of those who kept in view** the right of the nation to which they belonged and of which they considered themselves the guardians; with what

----

*But this is not to say that a nation which has a monarchical constitution should therewith usurp the law, nor even only cherish the secret wish of seeing it changed; for its position in Europe, perhaps very extended, can recommend that constitution as the only one by which that nation can maintain itself among powerful neighbors. Likewise the grumbling of the subjects, provoked not by the internal policy of the government but by the conduct of the latter toward foreigners, if perchance that conduct should hinder the subjects in their republican tendencies, is no proof at all of the nation's dissatisfaction with its own constitution, but rather of love for it; because the nation is the more assured against any danger the more other nations pursue a republican policy. Nevertheless, some slanderous sycophants, to make themselves important, have sought to pass off this innocuous political twaddle as fondness for innovation, Jacobinism and mob action which would threaten the state; yet, under the circumstances, there was not even the least reason for these allegations, particularly in a country more than a hundred miles removed from the scene of the revolution.

**Of such an enthusiasm for upholding justice for the human race we can say: "postquam ad arma Vulcania ventum est, mortalis mucro glacies ceu futilis ictu dissiluit." [30a] Why has a ruler never dared openly to declare that he recognizes absolutely no right of the people opposed to him, that his people owe their happiness solely to the beneficence of a government which confers

Exaltation das äußere, zuschauende Publicum dann ohne die mindeste Absicht der Mitwirkung sympathisirte.

7.
Wahrsagende Geschichte der Menschheit.

Es muß etwas Moralisches im Grundsatze sein, welches die Vernunft als rein, zugleich aber auch wegen des großen und Epoche machenden Einflusses als etwas, das die dazu anerkannte Pflicht der Seele des Menschen vor Augen stellt, und das menschliche Geschlecht im Ganzen seiner Vereinigung (non singulorum, sed universorum) angeht, dessen verhofftem Gelingen und den Versuchen zu demselben es mit so allgemeiner und uneigennütziger Theilnehmung zujauchzt. — Diese Begebenheit ist das Phänomen nicht einer Revolution, sondern (wie es Hr. Erhard ausdrückt) der Evolution einer naturrechtlichen Verfassung, die zwar nur unter wilden Kämpfen noch nicht selbst errungen wird — indem der

enthält) ungereimt, ja gar strafbar sei? — Die Ursache ist: weil eine solche öffentliche Erklärung alle Unterthanen gegen ihn empören würde, ob sie gleich, wie folgsame Schafe von einem gütigen und verständigen Herren geleitet, wohlgefüttert und kräftig beschützt, über nichts, was ihrer Wohlfahrt abginge, zu klagen hätten. — Denn mit Freiheit begabten Wesen gnügt nicht der Genuß der Lebensannehmlichkeit, die ihm auch von Anderen (und hier von der Regierung) zu Theil werden kann; sondern auf das Princip kommt es an, nach welchem es sich solche verschafft. Wohlfahrt aber hat kein Princip, weder für den, der sie empfängt, noch der sie austheilt (der eine setzt sie hierin, der andere darin): weil es dabei auf das Materiale des Willens ankommt, welches empirisch und so der Allgemeinheit einer Regel unfähig ist. Ein mit Freiheit begabtes Wesen kann und soll also im Bewußtsein dieses seines Vorzuges vor dem vernunftlosen Thier nach dem formalen Princip seiner Willkür keine andere Regierung für das Volk, wozu es gehört, verlangen, als eine solche, in welcher dieses mit gesetzgebend ist: d. i. das Recht der Menschen, welche gehorchen sollen, muß nothwendig vor aller Rücksicht auf Wohlbefinden vorhergehen, und dieses ist ein Heiligthum, das über allen Preis (der Nützlichkeit) erhaben ist, und welches keine Regierung, so wohlthätig sie auch immer sein mag, antasten darf. — Aber dieses Recht ist doch immer nur eine Idee, deren Ausführung auf die Bedingung der Zusammenstimmung ihrer Mittel mit der Moralität eingeschränkt ist, welche das Volk nicht überschreiten darf; welches nicht durch Revolution, die jederzeit ungerecht ist, geschehen darf. — Autokratisch herrschen und dabei doch republicanisch, d. h. im Geiste des Republicanism und nach einer Analogie mit demselben, regieren, ist das, was ein Volk mit seiner Verfassung zufrieden macht.

exaltation the uninvolved public looking on sympathized then without the least intention of assisting.

7.
Prophetic History of Humanity

In the principle there must be something moral, which reason presents as pure; but because of its great and epoch-making influence, reason must present it as the acknowledged duty of the human soul, concerning mankind as a whole (*non singularum, sed universorum*), which hails, with such universal and impartial sympathy, the hopes for its success and the efforts toward realizing it. This even is the phenomenon, not of revolution, but (as Erhard expresses it)   a phenomenon of the evolution of a constitution in accordance with natural law which, to be sure, is still not won solely by desperate battles—for war, both civil and foreign, destroys all previously existing

this happiness upon them, and that all presumption of the subject to a right opposed to the government (since this right comprehends the concept of permissible resistance) is absurd and even culpable? The reason is that such a public declaration would rouse all of his subjects against him; although, as docile sheep, led by a benevolent and sensible master, well-fed and powerfully protected, they would have nothing wanting in their welfare for which to lament. For a being endowed with freedom is not satisfied with the pleasure of life's comforts which fall to his lot by the act of another (in this case the government); what matters rather is the principle according to which the individual provides such things for himself. But welfare possesses no principle either for him who receives it or for him who dispenses it (one places it here, the other there), inasmuch as what matters in welfare is the material of the will, which is empirical, and which is thus unfit for the universality of a rule. A being endowed with freedom in the consciousness of his superiority over the irrational animal, can and should therefore, according to the formal principle of his will, demand no other government for the people to which he belongs than one in which the people are co-legislative; that is, the right of men who are supposed to obey must necessarily precede all regard for well-being, and this right is a blessing that is exalted above all price (of utility), and one upon which no government, however beneficent it may persistently be, is permitted to infringe. But this right is still always only an Idea of which the realization is restricted to the condition of accord of its means with the morality which the nation may not transgress; and this may not come to pass through revolution which is always unjust. To rule autocratically and yet to govern in a republican way, that is, in the spirit of republicanism and on an analogy with it—that is what makes a nation satisfied with its constitution.

Krieg von innen und außen alle bisher bestandene statutarische zer=
stört —, die aber doch dahin führt, zu einer Verfassung hinzustreben,
welche nicht kriegssüchtig sein kann, nämlich der republicanischen; die es
entweder selbst der Staatsform nach sein mag, oder auch nur nach der
Regierungsart, bei der Einheit des Oberhaupts (des Monarchen) den
Gesetzen analogisch, die sich ein Volk selbst nach allgemeinen Rechtsprin=
cipien geben würde, den Staat verwalten zu lassen.

Nun behaupte ich dem Menschengeschlechte nach den Aspecten und
Vorzeichen unserer Tage die Erreichung dieses Zwecks und hiemit zugleich
das von da an nicht mehr gänzlich rückgängig werdende Fortschreiten des=
selben zum Besseren auch ohne Sehergeist vorhersagen zu können. Denn
ein solches Phänomen in der Menschengeschichte vergißt sich nicht mehr,
weil es eine Anlage und ein Vermögen in der menschlichen Natur zum
Besseren aufgedeckt hat, dergleichen kein Politiker aus dem bisherigen
Laufe der Dinge herausgeklügelt hätte, und welches allein Natur und
Freiheit, nach inneren Rechtsprincipien im Menschengeschlechte vereinigt,
aber, was die Zeit betrifft, nur als unbestimmt und Begebenheit aus Zu=
fall verheißen konnte.

Aber wenn der bei dieser Begebenheit beabsichtigte Zweck auch jetzt
nicht erreicht würde, wenn die Revolution oder Reform der Verfassung
eines Volks gegen das Ende doch fehlschlüge, oder, nachdem diese einige
Zeit gewährt hätte, doch wiederum alles ins vorige Gleis zurückgebracht
würde (wie Politiker jetzt wahrsagern), so verliert jene philosophische Vor=
hersagung doch nichts von ihrer Kraft. — Denn jene Begebenheit ist zu
groß, zu sehr mit dem Interesse der Menschheit verwebt und ihrem Ein=
flusse nach auf die Welt in allen ihren Theilen zu ausgebreitet, als daß
sie nicht den Völkern bei irgend einer Veranlassung günstiger Umstände in
Erinnerung gebracht und zu Wiederholung neuer Versuche dieser Art er=
weckt werden sollte; da dann bei einer für das Menschengeschlecht so wich=
tigen Angelegenheit endlich doch zu irgend einer Zeit die beabsichtigte Ver=
fassung diejenige Festigkeit erreichen muß, welche die Belehrung durch
öftere Erfahrung in den Gemüthern Aller zu bewirken nicht ermangeln
würde.

Es ist also ein nicht bloß gutgemeinter und in praktischer Absicht
empfehlungswürdiger, sondern allen Ungläubigen zum Trotz auch für die
strengste Theorie haltbarer Satz: daß das menschliche Geschlecht im Fort=
schreiten zum Besseren immer gewesen sei und so fernerhin fortgehen werde,

statutory constitutions. This evolution leads to striving after a constitution that cannot be bellicose, that is to say, a republican constitution. The constitution may be republican either in its *political form* or only in its *manner of governing*, in having the state ruled through the unity of the sovereign (the monarch) by analogy with the laws that a nation would provide itself in accordance with the universal principles of legality.

Now I claim to be able to predict to the human race—even without prophetic insight—according to the aspects and omens of our day, the attainment of this goal. That is, I predict its progress toward the better which, from now on, turns out to be no longer completely retrogressive. For such a phenomenon in human history *is not to be forgotten*, because it has revealed a tendency and faculty in human nature for improvement such that no politician, affecting wisdom, might have conjured out of the course of things hitherto existing, and one which nature and freedom alone, united in the human race in conformity with inner principles of right, could have promised. But so far as time is concerned, it can promise this only indefinitely and as a contingent event.

But even if the end viewed in connection with this event should not now be attained, even if the revolution or reform of a national constitution should finally miscarry, or, after some time had elapsed, everything should relapse into its former rut (as politicians now predict), that philosophical prophecy still would lose nothing of its force. For that event is too important, too much interwoven with the interest of humanity, and its influence too widely propagated in all areas of the world to not be recalled on any favorable occasion by the nations which would then be roused to a repetition of new efforts of this kind; because then, in an affair so important for humanity, the intended constitution, at a certain time, must finally attain that constancy which instruction by repeated experience suffices to establish in the minds of all men.

Here, therefore, is a proposition valid for the most rigorous theory, in spite of all skeptics, and not just a well-meaning and practically commendable proposition: the human race has always been in progress toward the better and will continue to be so henceforth. To him who does not consider what happens in

welches, wenn man nicht bloß auf das sieht, was in irgend einem Volk geschehen kann, sondern auch auf die Verbreitung über alle Völker der Erde, die nach und nach daran Theil nehmen dürften, die Aussicht in eine unabsehliche Zeit eröffnet; wofern nicht etwa auf die erste Epoche einer Naturrevolution, die (nach Camper und Blumenbach) bloß das Thier- und Pflanzenreich, ehe noch Menschen waren, vergrub, noch eine zweite folgt, welche auch dem Menschengeschlechte eben so mitspielt, um andere Geschöpfe auf diese Bühne treten zu lassen, u. s. w. Denn für die Allgewalt der Natur, oder vielmehr ihrer uns unerreichbaren obersten Ursache ist der Mensch wiederum nur eine Kleinigkeit. Daß ihn aber auch die Herrscher von seiner eigenen Gattung dafür nehmen und als eine solche behandeln, indem sie ihn theils thierisch, als bloßes Werkzeug ihrer Absichten, belasten, theils in ihren Streitigkeiten gegen einander aufstellen, um sie schlachten zu lassen, — das ist keine Kleinigkeit, sondern Umkehrung des Endzwecks der Schöpfung selbst.

8.

Von der Schwierigkeit der auf das Fortschreiten zum Weltbesten angelegten Maximen in Ansehung ihrer Publicität.

Volksaufklärung ist die öffentliche Belehrung des Volks von seinen Pflichten und Rechten in Ansehung des Staats, dem es angehört. Weil es hier nur natürliche und aus dem gemeinen Menschenverstande hervorgehende Rechte betrifft, so sind die natürlichen Verkündiger und Ausleger derselben im Volk nicht die vom Staat bestellte amtsmäßige, sondern freie Rechtslehrer, d. i. die Philosophen, welche eben um dieser Freiheit willen, die sie sich erlauben, dem Staate, der immer nur herrschen will, anstößig sind, und werden unter dem Namen Aufklärer als für den Staat gefährliche Leute verschrieen; obzwar ihre Stimme nicht vertraulich ans Volk (als welches davon und von ihren Schriften wenig oder gar keine Notiz nimmt), sondern ehrerbietig an den Staat gerichtet und dieser jenes sein rechtliches Bedürfniß zu beherzigen angefleht wird; welches durch keinen andern Weg als den der Publicität geschehen kann, wenn ein ganzes Volk seine Beschwerde (gravamen) vortragen will. So verhindert das Verbot der Publicität den Fortschritt eines Volks zum Besseren, selbst in dem, was das Mindeste seiner Forderung, nämlich bloß sein natürliches Recht, angeht.

just some one nation but also has regard to the whole scope of all the peoples on earth who will gradually come to participate in progress, this reveals the prospect of an immeasurable time—provided at least that there does not, by some chance, occur a second epoch of natural revolution which will push aside the human race to clear the stage for other creatures, like that which (according to Camper and Blumenbach) [32] submerged the plant and animal kingdoms before men ever existed. For in the face of the omnipotence of nature, or rather its supreme first cause which is inaccessible to us, the human being is, in his turn, but a trifle. But for the sovereigns of his own species also to consider and treat him as such, whether by burdening him as an animal, regarding him as a mere tool of their designs, or exposing him in their conflicts with one another in order to have him massacred—that is no trifle, but a subversion of the ultimate purpose of creation itself.

8.

Concerning the Difficulty of the Maxims Applying to World Progress with Regard to Their Publicity

Enlightenment of the masses is the public instruction of the people in its duties and rights vis-a-vis the state to which they belong. Since only natural rights and rights arising out of the common human understanding are concerned here, then the natural heralds and expositors of these among the people are not officially appointed by the state but are free professors of law, that is philosophers who, precisely because this freedom is allowed to them, are objectionable to the state, which always desires to rule alone; and they are decried, under the name of enlighteners, as persons dangerous to the state, although their voice is not addressed confidentially to the people (as the people take scarcely any or no notice at all of it and of their writings) but is addressed respectfully to the state; and they implore the state to take to heart that need which is felt to be legitimate. This can happen by no other means than that of publicity in the event that an entire people cares to bring forward its grievances (gravamen). Thus the prohibition of publicity impedes the progress of a people toward improvement, even in that which applies to the least of its claims, namely its simple, natural right.

Eine andere, obzwar leicht durchzuschauende, aber doch gesetzmäßig einem Volk befohlene Verheimlichung ist die von der wahren Beschaffenheit seiner Constitution. Es wäre Verletzung der Majestät des großbritannischen Volks, von ihm zu sagen, es sei eine unbeschränkte Monarchie: sondern man will, es soll eine durch die zwei Häuser des Parlaments, als Volksrepräsentanten, den Willen des Monarchen einschränkende Verfassung sein, und doch weiß ein jeder sehr gut, daß der Einfluß desselben auf diese Repräsentanten so groß und so unfehlbar ist, daß von gedachten Häusern nichts anderes beschlossen wird, als was Er will und durch seinen Minister anträgt; der dann auch wohl einmal auf Beschlüsse anträgt, bei denen er weiß und es auch macht, daß ihm werde widersprochen werden (z. B. wegen des Negerhandels), um von der Freiheit des Parlaments einen scheinbaren Beweis zu geben. — Diese Vorstellung der Beschaffenheit der Sache hat das Trügliche an sich, daß die wahre, zu Recht beständige Verfassung gar nicht mehr gesucht wird: weil man sie in einem schon vorhandenen Beispiel gefunden zu haben vermeint, und eine lügenhafte Publicität das Volk mit Vorspiegelung einer durch das von ihm ausgehende Gesetz eingeschränkten Monarchie*) täuscht, indessen daß seine Stellvertreter, durch Bestechung gewonnen, es ingeheim einem absoluten Monarchen unterwarfen.

*   *   *

Die Idee einer mit dem natürlichen Rechte der Menschen zusammenstimmenden Constitution: daß nämlich die dem Gesetz Gehorchenden auch

---

*) Eine Ursache, deren Beschaffenheit man nicht unmittelbar einsieht, entdeckt sich durch die Wirkung, die ihr unausbleiblich anhängt. — Was ist ein absoluter Monarch? Es ist derjenige, auf dessen Befehl, wenn er sagt: es soll Krieg sein, sofort Krieg ist. — Was ist dagegen ein eingeschränkter Monarch? Der, welcher vorher das Volk befragen muß, ob Krieg sein solle oder nicht, und sagt das Volk: es soll nicht Krieg sein, so ist kein Krieg. — Denn Krieg ist ein Zustand, in welchem dem Staatsoberhaupte alle Staatskräfte zu Gebot stehen müssen. Nun hat der großbritannische Monarch recht viel Kriege geführt, ohne dazu jene Einwilligung zu suchen. Also ist dieser König ein absoluter Monarch, der er zwar der Constitution nach nicht sein sollte; die er aber immer vorbei gehen kann, weil er eben durch jene Staatskräfte, nämlich daß er alle Ämter und Würden zu vergeben in seiner Macht hat, sich der Beistimmung der Volksrepräsentanten versichert halten kann. Dieses Bestechungssystem muß aber freilich nicht Publicität haben, um zu gelingen. Es bleibt daher unter dem sehr durchsichtigen Schleier des Geheimnisses.

Another disguise, which is easily penetrated indeed, but is one to which a nation, nevertheless, is legally committed, is that pertaining to the true nature of its constitution. It would be an insult to its majesty to say of the British nation that it is an absolute monarchy: some rather maintain that a constitution limiting the will of the monarch through the two Houses of Parliament, acting as representatives of the people, is supposed to exist; and yet everyone knows perfectly well that the monarch's influence on these representatives is so great and so certain that nothing is resolved by the Houses except what he wills and purposes through his minister. The latter then probably even proposes resolutions in connection with which he knows that he will be contradicted, and even arranges it that way (for example, with regard to slave-trade) in order to provide a fictitious proof of the freedom of Parliament. This representation of the nature of the case has something delusive about it so that the true constitution, faithful to law, is no longer sought at all; for a person imagines he has found it in an example already at hand, and a false publicity deceives the people with the illusion of a limited monarchy* in power by a law which issues from them, while their representatives, won over by bribery, have secretly subjected them to an absolute monarchy.

*   *
*

The Idea of a constitution in harmony with the natural right of man, one namely in which the citizens obedient to the law,

---

*A cause, the nature of which one does directly understand, makes itself known through the effect which unfailingly attaches to it. What is an *absolute* monarch? He is one at whose command, if he says, "war is necessary," a state of war immediately exists. What is a *limited* monarch, on the other hand? He who must first consult the people as to whether war is or is not to be; and the people say, "there is to be no war," so there is no war. For war is a situation in which *all* political power must be at the disposal of the sovereign. Now the British monarch has conducted wars aplenty without seeking the consent for them. Therefore, this king is an absolute monarch who ought not to be one, of course, according to the constitution; but he is always able to bypass it because precisely through those political powers, namely, that he has it in his power to dispense all appointments and posts, he can consider assured the assent of the representatives of the people. In order to succeed, however, this system of bribery must certainly not be publicized. Hence it remains under the highly transparent veil of secrecy.

163

zugleich, vereinigt, gesetzgebend sein sollen, liegt bei allen Staatsformen zum Grunde, und das gemeine Wesen, welches, ihr gemäß durch reine Vernunftbegriffe gedacht, ein platonisches Ideal heißt (respublica noume-non), ist nicht ein leeres Hirngespinnst, sondern die ewige Norm für alle bürgerliche Verfassung überhaupt und entfernt allen Krieg. Eine dieser gemäß organisirte bürgerliche Gesellschaft ist die Darstellung derselben nach Freiheitsgesetzen durch ein Beispiel in der Erfahrung (respublica phaenomenon) und kann nur nach mannigfaltigen Befehdungen und Kriegen mühsam erworben werden; ihre Verfassung aber, wenn sie im Großen einmal errungen worden, qualificirt sich zur besten unter allen, um den Krieg, den Zerstörer alles Guten, entfernt zu halten; mithin ist es Pflicht in eine solche einzutreten, vorläufig aber (weil jenes nicht so bald zu Stande kommt) Pflicht der Monarchen, ob sie gleich autokratisch herrschen, dennoch republicanisch (nicht demokratisch) zu regieren, d. i. das Volk nach Principien zu behandeln, die dem Geist der Freiheits= gesetze (wie ein Volk mit reifer Vernunft sie sich selbst vorschreiben würde) gemäß sind, wenn gleich dem Buchstaben nach es um seine Einwilligung nicht befragt würde.

9.

Welchen Ertrag wird der Fortschritt zum Besseren dem Menschengeschlecht abwerfen?

Nicht ein immer wachsendes Quantum der Moralität in der Ge= sinnung, sondern Vermehrung der Producte ihrer Legalität in pflicht= mäßigen Handlungen, durch welche Triebfeder sie auch veranlaßt sein mögen; d. i. in den guten Thaten der Menschen, die immer zahlreicher und besser ausfallen werden, also in den Phänomenen der sittlichen Be= schaffenheit des Menschengeschlechts, wird der Ertrag (das Resultat) der Bearbeitung desselben zum Besseren allein gesetzt werden können. — Denn wir haben nur empirische Data (Erfahrungen), worauf wir diese Vor= hersagung gründen: nämlich auf die physische Ursache unserer Handlungen, in sofern sie geschehen, die also selbst Erscheinungen sind, nicht die mora= lische, welche den Pflichtbegriff von dem enthält, was geschehen sollte, und der allein rein, a priori, aufgestellt werden kann.

Allmählich wird der Gewaltthätigkeit von Seiten der Mächtigen weniger, der Folgsamkeit in Ansehung der Gesetze mehr werden. Es wird etwa mehr Wohlthätigkeit, weniger Zank in Processen, mehr Zuverlässig=

besides being united, ought also to be legislative, lies at the basis of all political forms; and the body politic which, conceived in conformity to it by virtue of pure concepts of reason, signifies a Platonic Ideal (*respublica noumenon*), is not an empty chimera, but rather the eternal norm for all civil organization in general, and averts all war. A civil society organized conformably to this ideal is the representation of it in agreement with the laws of freedom by means of an example in our experience (*respublica phaenomenon*) and can only be painfully acquired after multifarious hostilities and wars; but its constitution, once won on a large scale, is qualified as the best among all others to banish war, the destroyer of everything good. Consequently, it is a duty to enter into such a system of government, but it is provisionally the duty of the monarchs, if they rule as autocrats, to govern in a republican (not democratic) way, that is, to treat the people according to principles which are commensurate with the spirit of libertarian laws (as a nation with mature understanding would prescribe them for itself), although they would not be literally canvassed for their consent.

9.

What Profit Will Progress Toward the Better Yield Humanity?

Not an ever-growing quantity of morality with regard to intention, but an increase of the products of legality in dutiful actions whatever their motives. That is, the profit (result) of man's striving toward the better can be assumed to reside alone in the good deeds of men, which will become better and better and more and more numerous; it resides alone in phenomena constituting the moral state of the human race. For we have only empirical data (experiences) upon which we are founding this prediction, namely, the physical cause of our actions as these actually occur as phenomena; and not the moral cause—the only one which can be established purely a priori—which contains the concept of duty with respect to what ought to happen.

Gradually violence on the part of the powers will diminish and obedience to the laws will increase. There will arise in the body politic perhaps more charity and less strife in lawsuits,

keit im Worthalten u. s. w. theils aus Ehrliebe, theils aus wohlverstande=
nem eigenen Vortheil im gemeinen Wesen entspringen und sich endlich
dies auch auf die Völker im äußeren Verhältniß gegen einander bis zur
weltbürgerlichen Gesellschaft erstrecken, ohne daß dabei die moralische
Grundlage im Menschengeschlechte im mindesten vergrößert werden darf;
als wozu auch eine Art von neuer Schöpfung (übernatürlicher Einfluß)
erforderlich sein würde. — Denn wir müssen uns von Menschen in ihren
Fortschritten zum Besseren auch nicht zu viel versprechen, um nicht in den
Spott des Politikers mit Grunde zu verfallen, der die Hoffnung des erste=
ren gerne für Träumerei eines überspannten Kopfs halten möchte.*)

10.
In welcher Ordnung allein kann der Fortschritt zum Besseren erwartet werden?

Die Antwort ist: nicht durch den Gang der Dinge von unten hin=
auf, sondern den von oben herab. — Zu erwarten, daß durch Bildung
der Jugend in häuslicher Unterweisung und weiterhin in Schulen, von
den niedrigen an bis zu den höchsten, in Geistes= und moralischer, durch
Religionslehre verstärkter Cultur es endlich dahin kommen werde, nicht
bloß gute Staatsbürger, sondern zum Guten, was immer weiter fortschrei=
ten und sich erhalten kann, zu erziehen, ist ein Plan, der den erwünschten
Erfolg schwerlich hoffen läßt. Denn nicht allein daß das Volk dafür hält,
daß die Kosten der Erziehung seiner Jugend nicht ihm, sondern dem

---

*) Es ist doch süß, sich Staatsverfassungen auszudenken, die den Forderun=
gen der Vernunft (vornehmlich in rechtlicher Absicht) entsprechen: aber vermessen,
sie vorzuschlagen, und strafbar, das Volk zur Abschaffung der jetzt bestehenden
aufzuwiegeln.

Platos Atlantica, Morus' Utopia, Harringtons Oceana und Allais'
Severambia sind nach und nach auf die Bühne gebracht, aber nie (Cromwells
verunglückte Mißgeburt einer despotischen Republik ausgenommen) auch nur ver=
sucht worden. — Es ist mit diesen Staatsschöpfungen wie mit der Weltschöpfung zu=
gegangen: kein Mensch war dabei zugegen, noch konnte er bei einer solchen gegen=
wärtig sein, weil er sonst sein eigener Schöpfer hätte sein müssen. Ein Staats=
product, wie man es hier denkt, als dereinst, so spät es auch sei, vollendet zu
hoffen, ist ein süßer Traum; aber sich ihm immer zu näheren, nicht allein denkbar,
sondern, so weit es mit dem moralischen Gesetze zusammen bestehen kann, Pflicht,
nicht der Staatsbürger, sondern des Staatsoberhaupts.

more reliability in keeping one's word, etc., partly out of love of honor, partly out of well-understood self-interest. And eventually this will also extend to nations in their external relations toward one another up to the realization of the cosmopolitan society, without the moral foundation in mankind having to be enlarged in the least; for that, a kind of new creation (supernatural influence) would be necessary. For we must also not hope for too much from men in their progress toward the better lest we fall prey with good reason to the mockery of the politician who would willingly take the hope of man as the dreaming of a distraught mind.*

10.

In What Order Alone Can Progress toward the Better Be Expected?

The answer is: not by the movement of things *from bottom to top*, but *from top to bottom*. To expect not simply to train good citizens but good men who can improve and take care of themselves; to expect that this will eventually happen by means of education of youth in the home, then in schools on both the lowest and highest level, in intellectual and moral culture fortified by religious doctrine—that is desirable, but its success is hardly to be hoped for. For while the people feel that the costs for

---

*It is sweet, however, to imagine constitutions corresponding to the requirements of reason (particularly in a legal sense), but rash to propose them and culpable to incite the populace to abolish what presently exists.

Plato's *Atlantica,* More's *Utopia,* Harrington's *Oceana* and Allais' *Severambia* have been successively brought on the scene, but have never so much as been tried (Cromwell's abortive monster of a despotic republic excepted).* The same goes for political creations as for the creation of the world; no human was present there, nor could he have been present at such an event, since he must have been his own creator otherwise. However late it may be, to hope someday for the consummation of a political product, as it is envisaged here, is a sweet dream; but that it is being perpetually approached is not only *thinkable,* but, so far as it is compatible with the moral law, an *obligation,* not of the citizens, but of the sovereign.

Staate zu Lasten kommen müssen, der Staat aber dagegen seinerseits zu
Besoldung tüchtiger und mit Lust ihrem Amte obliegender Lehrer kein
Geld übrig hat (wie Büsching klagt), weil er alles zum Kriege braucht:
sondern das ganze Maschinenwesen dieser Bildung hat keinen Zusammen=
hang, wenn es nicht nach einem überlegten Plane der obersten Staats=
macht und nach dieser ihrer Absicht entworfen, ins Spiel gesetzt und dar=
in auch immer gleichförmig erhalten wird; wozu wohl gehören möchte,
daß der Staat sich von Zeit zu Zeit auch selbst reformire und, statt Re=
volution Evolution versuchend, zum Besseren beständig fortschreite. Da
es aber doch auch Menschen sind, welche diese Erziehung bewirken sollen,
mithin solche, die dazu selbst haben gezogen werden müssen: so ist bei
dieser Gebrechlichkeit der menschlichen Natur unter der Zufälligkeit der
Umstände, die einen solchen Effect begünstigen, die Hoffnung ihres Fort=
schreitens nur in einer Weisheit von oben herab (welche, wenn sie uns
unsichtbar ist, Vorsehung heißt) als positiver Bedingung, für das aber,
was hierin von Menschen erwartet und gefordert werden kann, bloß ne=
gative Weisheit zur Beförderung dieses Zwecks zu erwarten, nämlich daß
sie das größte Hinderniß des Moralischen, nämlich den Krieg, der die=
sen immer zurückgängig macht, erstlich nach und nach menschlicher, darauf
seltener, endlich als Angriffskrieg ganz schwinden zu lassen sich genöthigt
sehen werden, um eine Verfassung einzuschlagen, die ihrer Natur nach,
ohne sich zu schwächen, auf ächte Rechtsprincipien gegründet, beharrlich
zum Bessern fortschreiten kann.

Beschluß.

Ein Arzt, der seine Patienten von Tag zu Tag auf baldige Gene=
sung vertröstete: den einen, daß der Puls besser schlüge; den anderen, daß
der Auswurf, den dritten, daß der Schweiß Besserung verspräche, u. s. w.,
bekam einen Besuch von einem seiner Freunde. Wie gehts, Freund, mit
eurer Krankheit? war die erste Frage. Wie wirds gehen? Ich sterbe
vor lauter Besserung! — Ich verdenke es Keinem, wenn er in An=
sehung der Staatsübel an dem Heil des Menschengeschlechts und dem
Fortschreiten desselben zum Besseren zu verzagen anhebt; allein ich ver=
lasse mich auf das heroische Arzneimittel, welches Hume anführt und eine
schnelle Cur bewirken dürfte. — „Wenn ich jetzt (sagt er) die Nationen
im Kriege gegen einander begriffen sehe, so ist es, als ob ich zwei besoffene

education of their youth ought to be borne, not by them, but by the state, the state for its part has no money left (as Busching complains) [33] for the salaries of its teachers who are capable and zealously devoted to their spheres of duty, since it uses all the money for war. Rather, the whole mechanism of this education has no coherence if it is not designed in agreement with a well-weighed plan of the sovereign power, put into play according to the purpose of this plan, and steadily maintained therein; to this end it might well behoove the state likewise to reform itself from time to time and, attempting evolution instead of revolution, progress perpetually toward the better. Nevertheless, since they are also human beings who must effect this education, consequently such beings who themselves have to be trained for that purpose, then, considering this infirmity of human nature as subject to the contingency of events which favor such an effect, the hope for its progress is to be expected only on the condition of a wisdom from above (which bears the name of Providence if it is invisible to us); but for that which can be expected and exacted from *men* in this area toward the advancement of this aim, we can anticipate only a negative wisdom, namely, that they will see themselves compelled to render the greatest obstacle to morality—that is to say war, which constantly retards this advancement—firstly by degrees more humane and then rarer, and finally to renounce offensive war altogether, in order to enter upon a constitution which by its nature and without loss of power is founded on genuine principles of right, and which can persistently progress toward the better.

Conclusion

A doctor who consoled his patients from one day to the next with hopes of a speedy convalescence, pledging to one that his pulse beat better, to another an improvement in his stool, to a third the same regarding his perspiration, etc., received a visit from one of his friends. "How's your illness, my friend," was his first question. "How should it be? I'm dying of improvement, pure and simple!" I blame no one when, considering the ills of the state, he begins to despair of the health of humanity and its progress toward the better; but I would rely on the heroic remedy which Hume prescribes and which would effect a quick cure. "If,

Kerle sähe, die sich in einem Porzellanladen mit Prügeln herumschlagen. Denn nicht genug, daß sie an den Beulen, die sie sich wechselseitig geben, lange zu heilen haben, so müssen sie hinterher noch allen den Schaden be= zahlen, den sie anrichteten." Sero sapiunt Phryges. Die Nachwehen des gegenwärtigen Krieges aber können dem politischen Wahrsager das Ge= ständniß einer nahe bevorstehenden Wendung des menschlichen Geschlechts zum Besseren abnöthigen, das schon jetzt im Prospect ist.

at the present time," he says, "I see the nations on the point of war with one another, it is as if I were seeing two besotted fellows beating each other about with cudgels in a china shop. For not only do they have to recover slowly from the bruises they administered to each other, but afterwards they must pay for the damages that they have done." [34] *Sero sapiunt Phryges.* [35] However, the painful consequences of the present war can compel the political prophet to confess a very imminent turn of humanity toward the better that is even now in prospect.

Erster Abschnitt.

Der Streit der philosophischen Facultät mit der theologischen.

The Conflict of the Philosophy Faculty with the Faculty of Medicine

Von der Macht des Gemüths

durch den bloßen Vorsatz seiner krankhaften Gefühle
Meister zu sein.

Ein Antwortschreiben an Herrn Hofrath und Professor Hufeland.

Daß meine Danksagung für das den 12ten Dec. 1796 an mich be=
stellte Geschenk Ihres lehrreichen und angenehmen Buchs „von der
Kunst das menschliche Leben zu verlängern" selbst auf ein langes
Leben berechnet gewesen sein dürfte, möchten Sie vielleicht aus dem Da=
tum dieser meiner Antwort vom Januar dieses Jahres zu schließen Ur=
sache haben, wenn das Altgewordensein nicht schon die öftere Vertagung
(procrastinatio) wichtiger Beschlüsse bei sich führte, dergleichen doch wohl
der des Todes ist, welcher sich immer zu früh für uns anmeldet, und den
man warten zu lassen an Ausreden unerschöpflich ist.

Sie verlangen von mir ein Urtheil über Ihr „Bestreben, das Physi=
„sche im Menschen moralisch zu behandeln; den ganzen, auch physischen
„Menschen als ein auf Moralität berechnetes Wesen darzustellen und die
„moralische Kultur als unentbehrlich zur physischen Vollendung der über=
„all nur in der Anlage vorhandenen Menschennatur zu zeigen", und setzen
hinzu: „Wenigstens kann ich versichern, daß es keine vorgefaßte Meinun=
„gen waren, sondern ich durch die Arbeit und Untersuchung selbst unwider=
„stehlich in diese Behandlungsart hineingezogen wurde." — — Eine sol=
che Ansicht der Sache verräth den Philosophen, nicht den bloßen Vernunft=
künstler; einen Mann, der nicht allein gleich einem der Directoren des
französischen Convents die von der Vernunft verordneten Mittel der
Ausführung (technisch), wie sie die Erfahrung darbietet, zu seiner Heil=
kunde mit Geschicklichkeit, sondern als gesetzgebendes Glied im Corps der
Ärzte aus der reinen Vernunft hernimmt, welche zu dem, was hilft, mit

ON THE POWER OF THE MIND
TO MASTER ITS MORBID FEELINGS
BY SHEER RESOLUTION

A Letter in Reply to Privy Councillor and Professor Hufeland

The fact that I am only now, in January of this year [1798], writing to thank you for the gift of your instructive and enjoyable book *On the Art of Prolonging Human Life*, which you sent me on 12 December 1796, might make you think that I am counting on a long life in which to reply. But old age brings with it the habit of postponing important decisions (*procrastinatio*)—just as we put off concluding our lives: death always arrives too soon for us, and we are inexhaustible in thinking up excuses for making it wait.

You ask for my opinion of your "attempt to treat the physical element in man morally: to present the whole man, including his physical side, as a being that is ordered to morality, and to show that moral cultivation is essential to the physical completion of human nature, which exists only in outline." And you add, "At least I can assure you that these were no preconceived opinions, and that it was my work and investigation itself that compelled me to treat human nature in this way." Such an outlook betrays a philosopher, not a mere subtle reasoner. It is the outlook of a man who is not only, as a director of the French Convention, skilled in applying the means reason prescribes, on the basis of experience (technically), to realize the ends of medical science, but who is also a legislative member of the body of doctors drawn from pure reason and has, along with the skill to prescribe what *cures*, the wisdom to prescribe what is also *duty* in itself. In this way morally practical philosophy also provides a panacea which, though it is certainly not the complete answer to every problem, must still be an ingredient in every prescription.

175

Geschicklichkeit auch das, was zugleich an sich Pflicht ist, mit Weisheit zu verordnen weiß: so daß moralisch-praktische Philosophie zugleich eine Universalmedicin abgiebt, die zwar nicht Allen für Alles hilft, aber doch in keinem Recepte mangeln kann.

Dieses Universalmittel betrifft aber nur die Diätetik, d. i. es wirkt nur negativ, als Kunst, Krankheiten abzuhalten. Dergleichen Kunst aber setzt ein Vermögen voraus, das nur Philosophie, oder der Geist der= selben, den man schlechthin voraussetzen muß, geben kann. Auf diesen be= zieht sich die oberste diätetische Aufgabe, welche in dem Thema enthal= ten ist:

Von der Macht des Gemüths des Menschen über seine krank= hafte Gefühle durch den bloßen festen Vorsatz Meister zu sein.

Die die Möglichkeit dieses Ausspruchs bestätigenden Beispiele kann ich nicht von der Erfahrung Anderer hernehmen, sondern zuerst nur von der an mir selbst angestellten, weil sie aus dem Selbstbewußtsein hervor= geht und sich nachher allererst Andere fragen läßt: ob es nicht auch sie eben so in sich wahrnehmen. — Ich sehe mich also genöthigt, mein Ich laut werden zu lassen, was im dogmatischen Vortrage*) Unbescheidenheit verräth, aber Verzeihung verdient, wenn es nicht gemeine Erfahrung, sondern ein inneres Experiment oder Beobachtung betrifft, welche ich zu= erst an mir selbst angestellt haben muß, um etwas, was nicht jedermann von selbst, und ohne darauf geführt zu sein, beifällt, zu seiner Beurthei= lung vorzulegen. — Es würde tadelhafte Anmaßung sein, Andere mit der inneren Geschichte meines Gedankenspiels unterhalten zu wollen, wel= che zwar subjective Wichtigkeit (für mich), aber keine objective (für je= dermann geltende) enthielte. Wenn aber dieses Aufmerken auf sich selbst und die daraus hervorgehende Wahrnehmung nicht so gemein ist, sondern, daß jeder dazu aufgefordert werde, eine Sache ist, die es bedarf und ver= dient, so kann dieser Übelstand mit seinen Privatempfindungen Andere zu unterhalten, wenigstens verziehen werden.

Ehe ich nun mit dem Resultat meiner in Absicht auf Diätetik ange=

---

*) Im dogmatisch-praktischen Vortrage, z. B. derjenigen Beobachtung seiner selbst, die auf Pflichten abzweckt, die Jedermann angehen, spricht der Kanzelredner nicht durch Ich, sondern Wir. In dem erzählenden aber, der Privatempfindung (der Beichte, welche der Patient seinem Arzte ablegt), oder eigener Erfahrung an sich selbst muß er durch Ich reden.

This panacea, however, is only a *regimen* to be adopted: in other words, it functions only in a *negative* way, as the art of *preventing* disease. But an art of this sort presupposes, as its necessary condition, an ability that only philosophy, or the spirit of philosophy, can give. The supreme task of the art of formulating a regimen, which refers to this spirit, is contained in the following thesis:

On the Power of the Human Mind to Master Its Morbid Feelings Merely by a Firm Resolution

My examples confirming the possibility of this proposition cannot be drawn from other peoples' experiences, but, in the first instance, only from what I have experienced in myself; for they come from introspection, and only afterwards can I ask others whether they have not noticed the same thing in themselves. I am forced, accordingly, to talk about myself; and although this would betray lack of modesty in a dogmatic treatise,* it is excusable if we are dealing, not with common experience, but with an inner experiment or observation that I had to make on myself before I could submit, for others' consideration, something that would not of itself occur to everyone unless his attention were drawn to it. To want to entertain others with the inner history of the play of my thoughts, which has subjective importance (for me) but no objective importance (valid for everyone), would be presumptuous, and I could justly be blamed for it. But if this sort of introspection and what I found by it is something rather uncommon, which it is worthwhile for everyone to try though it must be pointed out to them, the nuisance of telling others about my private feelings can at least be excused.

Before attempting to present the results of the

---

*In treatises of a dogmatic-practical nature—for example, the sort of self-examination that is directed to duties incumbent on everyone—the lecturer speaks in terms of "we," rather than "I." But if he is describing his private feelings (as a patient to his doctor), or his personal experience as such, he must speak in terms of "I."

stellten Selbstbeobachtung aufzutreten wage, muß ich noch etwas über die
Art bemerken, wie Herr Hufeland die Aufgabe der Diätetik, d. i. der
Kunst stellt, Krankheiten vorzubeugen, im Gegensatz mit der Thera=
peutik, sie zu heilen.

Sie heißt ihm „die Kunst das menschliche Leben zu verlängern."

Er nimmt seine Benennung von demjenigen her, was die Menschen
am sehnsüchtigsten wünschen, ob es gleich vielleicht weniger wünschens=
werth sein dürfte. Sie möchten zwar gern zwei Wünsche zugleich thun:
nämlich lange zu leben und dabei gesund zu sein; aber der erstere
Wunsch hat den letzteren nicht zur nothwendigen Bedingung: sondern er
ist unbedingt. Laßt den Hospitalkranken Jahre lang auf seinem Lager
leiden und darben und ihn oft wünschen hören, daß ihn der Tod je eher
je lieber von dieser Plage erlösen möge; glaubt ihm nicht, es ist nicht sein
Ernst. Seine Vernunft sagt es ihm zwar vor, aber der Naturinstinct will
es anders. Wenn er dem Tode als seinem Befreier (*Jovi liberatori*) winkt,
so verlangt er doch immer noch eine kleine Frist und hat immer irgend
einen Vorwand zur Vertagung (*procrastinatio*) seines peremtorischen
Decrets. Der in wilder Entrüstung gefaßte Entschluß des Selbstmörders,
seinem Leben ein Ende zu machen, macht hievon keine Ausnahme: denn
er ist die Wirkung eines bis zum Wahnsinn exaltirten Affects. — Unter
den zwei Verheißungen für die Befolgung der Kindespflicht („auf daß
dir es wohlgehe, und du lange lebest auf Erden") enthält die letztere die
stärkere Triebfeder, selbst im Urtheile der Vernunft, nämlich als Pflicht,
deren Beobachtung zugleich verdienstlich ist.

Die Pflicht, das Alter zu ehren, gründet sich nämlich eigentlich
nicht auf die billige Schonung, die man den Jüngeren gegen die Schwach=
heit der Alten zumuthet: denn die ist kein Grund zu einer ihnen schuldi=
gen Achtung. Das Alter will also noch für etwas Verdienstliches an=
gesehen werden, weil ihm eine Verehrung zugestanden wird. Also nicht
etwa weil Nestorjahre zugleich durch viele und lange Erfahrung erworbene
Weisheit zu Leitung der jüngeren Welt bei sich führen, sondern blos
weil, wenn nur keine Schande dasselbe befleckt hat, der Mann, welcher sich
so lange erhalten hat, d. i. der Sterblichkeit als dem demüthigendsten
Ausspruch, der über ein vernünftiges Wesen nur gefällt werden kann („du
bist Erde und sollst zur Erde werden"), so lange hat ausweichen und gleich=
sam der Unsterblichkeit hat abgewinnen können, weil, sage ich, ein solcher
Mann sich so lange lebend erhalten und zum Beispiel aufgestellt hat.

7*

self-observation I undertook with a view to a regimen, I must say something about the way Herr *Hufeland* poses the task of *formulating a regimen*, that is, of the art of *preventing* illness, as distinguished from *therapeutics* or the art of *curing* it.

He calls the art of formulating a regimen "the art of prolonging human life."

He derives this title from what men desire most ardently, even though it might not be so desirable. Men would, indeed, like to have two wishes fulfilled at the same time: *to have a long life* and to enjoy *good health* during it. But the second wish is not a necessary condition of the first: man's wish for long life is unconditioned. Take a sick man who has been lying for years in a hospital bed, suffering and indigent, and hear how often he wishes that death would come soon and deliver him from his misery. Do not believe him: he is not in earnest about it. Though his reason does prompt him to wish for death, his natural instinct is to live. When he beckons to death as his deliverer (*Jovi liberatori*), he always asks for a short respite and has some sort of pretext for *putting off* its peremptory decree *(procrastinatio)*. The fact that a man may, in a wild rage, decide to end his own life is no exception to this; for his decision results from an emotional agitation raised almost to the point of insanity. Of the two things promised to us for fulfilling our filial duty ("may you prosper and live long on earth"), the second contains the stronger incentive, even in the judgment of reason—that is to say, as a duty the observance of which is meritorious.

The duty of honoring old age, in other words, is not really based on the consideration that age, because of its frailty, can rightly claim from youth; for weakness is no reason for being entitled to respect. Old age, therefore, claims to be considered something meritorious besides, since respect is due it. And the reason for this is not that in attaining the age of Nestor one has acquired, by varied and long experience, wisdom for guiding the young; it is only that a man who has survived so long—that is, has succeeded so long in eluding mortality, the most humiliating sentence that can be passed on a rational being ("you are dust and will return to dust")—has to this extent won immortality, so to speak. This is the reason why old people should be honored, as long as no shame has stained their lives—simply because they have preserved their lives so long and set an example.

Mit der Gesundheit, als dem zweiten natürlichen Wunsche, ist es da=
gegen nur mißlich bewandt. Man kann sich gesund fühlen (aus dem be=
haglichen Gefühl seines Lebens urtheilen), nie aber wissen, daß man
gesund sei. — Jede Ursache des natürlichen Todes ist Krankheit: man mag
sie fühlen oder nicht. — Es giebt viele, von denen, ohne sie eben verspotten
zu wollen, man sagt, daß sie für immer kränkeln, nie krank werden
können; deren Diät ein immer wechselndes Abschweifen und wieder Ein=
beugen ihrer Lebensweise ist, und die es im Leben, wenn gleich nicht den
Kraftäußerungen, doch der Länge nach weit bringen. Wie viel aber meiner
Freunde oder Bekannten habe ich nicht überlebt, die sich bei einer einmal
angenommenen ordentlichen Lebensart einer völligen Gesundheit rühmten:
indessen daß der Keim des·Todes (die Krankheit), der Entwickelung nahe,
unbemerkt in ihnen lag, und der, welcher sich gesund fühlte, nicht wußte,
daß er krank war; denn die Ursache eines natürlichen Todes kann man
doch nicht anders als Krankheit nennen. Die Causalität aber kann man
nicht fühlen, dazu gehört Verstand, dessen Urtheil irrig sein kann; indessen
daß das Gefühl untrüglich ist, aber nur dann, wenn man sich krankhaft
fühlt, diesen Namen führt; fühlt man sich aber so auch nicht, doch gleich=
wohl in dem Menschen verborgenerweise und zur baldigen Entwickelung
bereit liegen kann; daher der Mangel dieses Gefühls keinen andern Aus=
druck des Menschen für sein Wohlbefinden verstattet, als daß er schein=
barlich gesund sei. Das lange Leben also, wenn man dahin zurücksieht,
kann nur die genossene Gesundheit bezeugen, und die Diätetik wird vor
allem in der Kunst das Leben zu verlängern (nicht es zu genießen)
ihre Geschicklichkeit oder Wissenschaft zu beweisen haben: wie es auch Herr
Hufeland so ausgedrückt haben will.

Grundsatz der Diätetik.

Auf Gemächlichkeit muß die Diätetik nicht berechnet werden; denn
diese Schonung seiner Kräfte und Gefühle ist Verzärtelung, d. i. sie hat
Schwäche und Kraftlosigkeit zur Folge und ein allmähliges Erlöschen der
Lebenskraft aus Mangel der Übung; so wie eine Erschöpfung derselben
durch zu häufigen und starken Gebrauch derselben. Der Stoicism als
Princip der Diätetik (sustine et abstine) gehört also nicht bloß zur prak=
tischen Philosophie als Tugendlehre, sondern auch zu ihr als Heil=
kunde. — Diese ist alsdann philosophisch, wenn bloß die Macht der

On the other hand, it is always uncertain whether man's second natural wish, for good health, is fulfilled. He can *feel* well (to judge by his comfortable feeling of vitality), but he can never *know* that he is healthy. The cause of natural death is always illness, whether one feels it or not. There are many people of whom one can say, without really wanting to ridicule them, that they are always *sickly* but can never be *sick*. Their regimen consists in constantly deviating from and returning to their way of life, and by this they manage to get on well and live a long, if not a robust life. I have outlived a good many of my friends or acquaintances who boasted of perfect health and lived by an orderly regimen adopted once and for all, while the seed of death (illness) lay in them unnoticed, ready to develop. They *felt* healthy and did not *know* they were ill; for while the cause of natural death is always illness, *causality* cannot be felt. It requires understanding, whose judgment can err. Feeling, on the other hand, is infallible; but we do not call a man ill unless he *feels* ill, although a disease which he does not *feel* may lie hidden in him, about to come forth. Hence if he does not feel ill, he is entitled to express his well-being only by saying that he is *apparently* in good health. So a long life, considered in retrospect, can testify only to the health one *has enjoyed*, and the art of a regimen will have to prove its skill or science primarily in the art of *prolonging* life (not enjoying it). This is what Herr *Hufeland*, too, wanted to say.

The Principle of the Regimen

A regimen for prolonging man's life must not aim at a life of *ease*; for by such indulgence toward his powers and feelings he would spoil himself. In other words, it would result in frailty and weakness, since his vital energy can be gradually extinguished by lack of exercise just as it can be drained by using it too frequently and too intensely. Hence the *Stoic* way of life (*sustine et abstine*) belongs, as the principle of a regimen, to practical *philosophy* not only as the *doctrine of virtue* but also as the *science of medicine*. Medical science is *philosophical* when the sheer power

Vernunft im Menschen, über seine sinnliche Gefühle durch einen sich selbst gegebenen Grundsatz Meister zu sein, die Lebensweise bestimmt. Dagegen, wenn sie diese Empfindungen zu erregen oder abzuwehren die Hülfe außer sich in körperlichen Mitteln (der Apotheke, oder der Chirurgie) sucht, sie bloß empirisch und mechanisch ist.

Die Wärme, der Schlaf, die sorgfältige Pflege des nicht Kranken sind solche Verwöhnungen der Gemächlichkeit.

1) Ich kann der Erfahrung an mir selbst gemäß der Vorschrift nicht beistimmen: man soll Kopf und Füße warm halten. Ich finde es dagegen gerathener, beide kalt zu halten (wozu die Russen auch die Brust zählen), gerade der Sorgfalt wegen, um mich nicht zu verkälten. — Es ist freilich gemächlicher im laulichen Wasser sich die Füße zu waschen, als es zur Winterszeit mit beinahe eiskaltem zu thun; dafür aber entgeht man dem Übel der Erschlaffung der Blutgefäße in so weit vom Herzen entlegenen Theilen, welches im Alter oft eine nicht mehr zu hebende Krankheit der Füße nach sich zieht. — Den Bauch, vornehmlich bei kalter Witterung, warm zu halten, möchte eher zur diätetischen Vorschrift statt der Gemächlichkeit gehören: weil er Gedärme in sich schließt, die einen langen Gang hindurch einen nicht=flüssigen Stoff forttreiben sollen; wozu der sogenannte Schmachtriemen (ein breites den Unterleib haltendes und die Muskeln desselben unterstützendes Band) bei Alten, aber eigentlich nicht der Wärme wegen gehört.

2) Lange oder (wiederholentlich, durch Mittagsruhe) viel schlafen ist freilich eben so viel Ersparniß am Ungemache, was überhaupt das Leben im Wachen unvermeidlich bei sich führt, und es ist wunderlich genug, sich ein langes Leben zu wünschen, um es größtentheils zu verschlafen. Aber das, worauf es hier eigentlich ankommt, dieses vermeinte Mittel des langen Lebens, die Gemächlichkeit, widerspricht sich in seiner Absicht selbst. Denn das wechselnde Erwachen und wieder Einschlummern in langen Winternächten ist für das ganze Nervensystem lähmend, zermalmend und in täuschender Ruhe krafterschöpfend: mithin die Gemächlichkeit hier eine Ursache der Verkürzung des Lebens. — Das Bett ist das Nest einer Menge von Krankheiten.

3) Im Alter sich zu pflegen oder pflegen zu lassen, blos um seine Kräfte durch die Vermeidung der Ungemächlichkeit (z. B. des Ausgehens in schlimmem Wetter) oder überhaupt die Übertragung der Arbeit an Andere, die man selbst verrichten könnte, zu schonen, so aber das Leben

of man's reason to master his sensuous feelings by a self-imposed principle determines his manner of living. On the other hand, if medical science seeks the help of external physical means (drugs or surgery) to stimulate or ward off these sensations, it is merely empirical and mechanical.

Warmth, sleep, and *pampering* ourselves when we are not ill are some of these bad habits of a life of ease.

1) From my own experience, I cannot agree with the rule that the head and feet should be kept warm. I find it more advisable to keep them both cold (the Russians include the chest as well), just as a precaution *against being cold.* Granted it is more comfortable, in winter, to wash one's feet in tepid water than in water that is almot ice-cold: using cold water prevents a slackening of the blood vessels in members far removed from the heart—a condition which, in old age, often results in an incurable disease of the feet. It may be a precept of a regimen, rather than of comfort, to keep the abdomen warm, especially in cold weather; for it contains the intestines, which have to carry a non-liquid material over a long course. This, rather than warmth itself, is the reason for using what is called a supporting belt in old age (a wide band that holds in the abdomen and supports its muscles).

2) To sleep a *long time* or a *great deal* (intermittently, by siestas) is, admittedly, to spare ourselves just this much of the inconvenience that waking life inevitably brings with it—and it is rather odd to want a long life in order to sleep most of it away. But what is really to the point here is that this supposed means to a long life, comfort, contradicts its own purpose. For alternate waking and falling asleep again in long winter nights cripples, depresses, and exhausts the entire nervous system in a mere illusion of rest. So in this case comfort contributes to shortening one's life. The bed is a nest for a whole flock of illnesses.

3) Some elderly people *coddle* themselves, or let themselves be coddled, because they think they can prolong their lives if they *conserve* their energy by avoiding discomfort (for example, going out in bad weather) or, in general, by relegating to others work they could do themselves. But their solicitude for themselves brings about the direct opposite: premature old age

zu verlängern, diese Sorgfalt bewirkt gerade das Widerspiel, nämlich das
frühe Altwerden und Verkürzung des Lebens. — — Auch daß sehr alt ge=
wordene mehrentheils verehelichte Personen gewesen wären, möchte
schwer zu beweisen sein. — In einigen Familien ist das Altwerden erblich,
und die Paarung in einer solchen kann wohl einen Familienschlag dieser
Art begründen. Es ist auch kein übles politisches Princip, zu Beförde=
rung der Ehen das gepaarte Leben als ein langes Leben anzupreisen; ob=
gleich die Erfahrung immer verhältnißweise nur wenig Beispiele davon
an die Hand giebt von solchen, die neben einander vorzüglich alt geworden
sind; aber die Frage ist hier nur vom physiologischen Grunde des Alt=
werdens — wie es die Natur verfügt, nicht vom politischen, wie die Con=
venienz des Staats die öffentliche Meinung seiner Absicht gemäß gestimmt
zu sein verlangt. — Übrigens ist das Philosophiren, ohne darum eben
Philosoph zu sein, auch ein Mittel der Abwehrung mancher unangenehmer
Gefühle und doch zugleich Agitation des Gemüths, welches in seine Be=
schäftigung ein Interesse bringt, das von äußern Zufälligkeiten unabhängig
und eben darum, obgleich nur als Spiel, dennoch kräftig und inniglich ist
und die Lebenskraft nicht stocken läßt. Dagegen Philosophie, die ihr
Interesse am Ganzen des Endzwecks der Vernunft (der eine absolute Ein=
heit ist) hat, ein Gefühl der Kraft bei sich führt, welches die körperliche
Schwächen des Alters in gewissem Maße durch vernünftige Schätzung des
Werths des Lebens wohl vergüten kann. — Aber neu sich eröffnende Aus=
sichten zu Erweiterung seiner Erkenntnisse, wenn sie auch gerade nicht zur
Philosophie gehörten, leisten doch auch eben dasselbe, oder etwas dem Ähn=
liches; und sofern der Mathematiker hieran ein unmittelbares Inter=
esse (nicht als an einem Werkzeuge zu anderer Absicht) nimmt, so ist er
in sofern auch Philosoph und genießt die Wohlthätigkeit einer solchen Er=
regungsart seiner Kräfte in einem verjüngten und ohne Erschöpfung ver=
längerten Leben.

Aber auch bloße Tändeleien in einem sorgenfreien Zustande leisten,
als Surrogate, bei eingeschränkten Köpfen fast eben dasselbe, und die mit
Nichtsthun immer vollauf zu thun haben, werden gemeiniglich auch alt.
— Ein sehr bejahrter Mann fand dabei ein großes Interesse, daß die vielen
Stutzuhren in seinem Zimmer immer nach einander, keine mit der andern
zugleich schlagen mußten; welches ihn und den Uhrmacher den Tag über
genug beschäftigte und dem letztern zu verdienen gab. Ein Anderer fand
in der Abfütterung und Cur seiner Sangvögel hinreichende Beschäftigung,

and a shorter life. Again, it might be hard to prove that *married* people have a *better chance* of living to a very old age. In some families longevity is hereditary, and intermarriage in such a family may well establish a family trait of this kind. Again, it is not a bad political principle to promote marriage by commending married life as a long life, although experience provides relatively few examples of married couples who have lived to an exceptionally old age together. But here we are concerned only with the physiological cause of longevity according to the order of nature, not with the cause that might be assigned to it for political reasons, that is, with what the state's interests require in the way of public opinion. Again, *philosophizing*, in a sense that does not involve being a philosopher, is a means of warding off many disagreeable feelings and, besides, a *stimulant* to the mind that introduces an interest into its occupations—an interest which, just because it is independent of external contingencies, is powerful and sincere, though it is merely in the nature of a game, and keeps the vital force from running down. On the other hand *philosophy*, whose interest is the entire final end of reason (an absolute unity), brings with it a feeling of power which can well compensate to some degree for the physical weaknesses of old age by a rational estimation of life's value. But opening new prospects for increasing our knowledge, even if they do not belong directly to philosophy, serves the same function, or one similar to it; and to the extent that the mathematician takes an *immediate* interest in mathematics (and does not consider it instrumental to some other end), he is also a philosopher and enjoys the benefit of having his powers stimulated in this way, in a life that is rejuvenated and prolonged without exhaustion.

But for people of limited intelligence, merely puttering about in a carefree situation is a substitute that serves almost the same function, and those who are always busy doing nothing are usually long-lived as well. A very old man found a great interest in making the numerous clocks in his room strike always one after another, never at the same time—an interest that gave both him and the watchmaker more than enough to do all day and earned the watchmaker a living. For another, feeding and caring for his songbirds served to keep him busy from his own mealtime

um die Zeit zwischen seiner eigenen Abfütterung und dem Schlaf auszufüllen. Eine alte begüterte Frau fand diese Ausfüllung am Spinnrade unter dabei eingemischten unbedeutenden Gesprächen und klagte daher in ihrem sehr hohen Alter, gleich als über den Verlust einer guten Gesellschaft, daß, da sie nunmehr den Faden zwischen den Fingern nicht mehr fühlen könnte, sie vor langer Weile zu sterben Gefahr liefe.

Doch damit mein Discurs über das lange Leben Ihnen nicht auch lange Weile mache und eben dadurch gefährlich werde, will ich der Sprachseligkeit, die man als einen Fehler des Alters zu belächeln, wenn gleich nicht zu schelten pflegt, hiemit Grenzen setzen.

1.
Von der Hypochondrie.

Die Schwäche, sich seinen krankhaften Gefühlen überhaupt, ohne ein bestimmtes Object, muthlos zu überlassen (mithin ohne den Versuch zu machen über sie durch die Vernunft Meister zu werden), — die Grillenkrankheit (hypochondria vaga),*) welche gar keinen bestimmten Sitz im Körper hat und ein Geschöpf der Einbildungskraft ist und daher auch die dichtende heißen könnte — wo der Patient alle Krankheiten, von denen er in Büchern liest, an sich zu bemerken glaubt, ist das gerade Widerspiel jenes Vermögens des Gemüths über seine krankhafte Gefühle Meister zu sein, nämlich Verzagtheit, über Übel, welche Menschen zustoßen könnten, zu brüten, ohne, wenn sie kämen, ihnen widerstehen zu können; eine Art von Wahnsinn, welchem freilich wohl irgend ein Krankheitsstoff (Blähung oder Verstopfung) zum Grunde liegen mag, der aber nicht unmittelbar, wie er den Sinn afficirt, gefühlt, sondern als bevorstehendes Übel von der dichtenden Einbildungskraft vorgespiegelt wird; wo dann der Selbstquäler (heautontimorumenos), statt sich selbst zu ermannen, vergeblich die Hülfe des Arztes aufruft: weil nur er selbst durch die Diätetik seines Gedankenspiels belästigende Vorstellungen, die sich unwillkürlich einfinden, und zwar von Übeln, wider die sich doch nichts veranstalten ließe, wenn sie sich wirklich einstellten, aufheben kann. — Von dem, der mit dieser Krankheit behaftet, und so lange er es ist, kann man nicht verlangen, er solle seiner krankhaften Gefühle durch den bloßen Vorsatz Meister werden. Denn

---

*) Zum Unterschiede von der topischen (hypochondria intestinalis).

to his bedtime. A wealthy old lady found a way to fill her time with idle chatter at the spinning wheel; and when she was very old she complained, just as if she had lost a good companion, that she was in danger of dying from boredom now that she could no longer feel the thread between her fingers.

But since I am afraid that my discourse on longevity may be boring, and so dangerous, to you, I shall put a limit on the garrulity that earns amused toleration, if not censure, as a fault of old age.

1.
On Hypochondria

The exact opposite of the mind's power to master its pathological feelings is *hypochondria*, the weakness of abandoning oneself despondently to general morbid feelings that have no definite object (and so making no attempt to master them by reason). Since this sort of melancholia (*hypochondria vaga*)* has no definite seat in the body and is a creature of the imagination, it could also be called *fictitious* disease, in which the patient finds in himself symptoms of every disease he reads about in books. The opposite of the mind's self-mastery, in other words, is fainthearted brooding about the ills that could befall one, and that one would not be able to withstand if they should come. It is a kind of insanity; for though some sort of unhealthy condition (such as flatulence or constipation) may be the source of it, this state is not felt immediately, as it affects the senses, but is misrepresented as impending illness by inventive imagination. And then the self-tormenter (*heautontimorumen-os*), instead of pulling himself together, summons the doctor's help. But this does no good, since only he himself, by disciplining the play of his thoughts, can put an end to these harassing notions that arise involuntarily—notions, indeed, of diseases that could not be prevented if they were really forthcoming. As long as a man is afflicted with this sickness we cannot expect him to master his morbid feelings by sheer resolution; for if he could

---

*As distinguished from *localized* hypochondria (*hypochondria intestinalis*).

wenn er dieses könnte, so wäre er nicht hypochondrisch. Ein vernünftiger Mensch statuirt keine solche Hypochondrie: sondern wenn ihm Beängstigungen anwandeln, die in Grillen, d. i. selbst ausgedachte Übel, ausschlagen wollen, so fragt er sich, ob ein Object derselben da sei. Findet er keines, welches gegründete Ursache zu dieser Beängstigung abgeben kann, oder sieht er ein, daß, wenn auch gleich ein solches wirklich wäre, doch dabei nichts zu thun möglich sei, um seine Wirkung abzuwenden, so geht er mit diesem Anspruche seines inneren Gefühls zur Tagesordnung, d. i. er läßt seine Beklommenheit (welche alsdann bloß topisch ist) an ihrer Stelle liegen (als ob sie ihm nichts anginge) und richtet seine Aufmerksamkeit auf die Geschäfte, mit denen er zu thun hat.

Ich habe wegen meiner flachen und engen Brust, die für die Bewegung des Herzens und der Lunge wenig Spielraum läßt, eine natürliche Anlage zur Hypochondrie, welche in früheren Jahren bis an den Überdruß des Lebens gränzte. Aber die Überlegung, daß die Ursache dieser Herzbeklemmung vielleicht bloß mechanisch und nicht zu heben sei, brachte es bald dahin, daß ich mich an sie gar nicht kehrte, und während dessen, daß ich mich in der Brust beklommen fühlte, im Kopf doch Ruhe und Heiterkeit herrschte, die sich auch in der Gesellschaft nicht nach abwechselnden Launen (wie Hypochondrische pflegen), sondern absichtlich und natürlich mitzutheilen nicht ermangelte. Und da man des Lebens mehr froh wird durch das, was man im freien Gebrauch desselben thut, als was man genießt, so können Geistesarbeiten eine andere Art von befördertem Lebensgefühl den Hemmungen entgegen setzen, welche bloß den Körper angehen. Die Beklemmung ist mir geblieben; denn ihre Ursache liegt in meinem körperlichen Bau. Aber über ihren Einfluß auf meine Gedanken und Handlungen bin ich Meister geworden durch Abkehrung der Aufmerksamkeit von diesem Gefühle, als ob es mich gar nicht anginge.

2.
Vom Schlafe.

Was die Türken nach ihren Grundsätzen der Prädestination über die Mäßigkeit sagen: daß nämlich im Anfange der Welt jedem Menschen die Portion zugemessen worden, wie viel er im Leben zu essen haben werde, und, wenn er seinen beschiedenen Theil in großen Portionen verzehrt, er auf eine desto kürzere Zeit zu essen, mithin zu sein sich Rechnung machen

do this, he would not be hypochondric. A reasonable man *vetoes* any such hypochondria; if uneasiness comes over him and threatens to develop into melancholia—that is, self-devised illness—he asks himself whether his anxiety has an object. If he finds nothing that could furnish a valid reason for his anxiety, or if he sees that, were there really such a reason, nothing could be done to prevent its effect, he goes on, despite this claim of his inner feeling, to his agenda for the day—in other words, he leaves his oppression (which is then merely local) in its proper place (as if it had nothing to do with him), and turns his attention to the business at hand.

I myself have a natural disposition to hypochondria because of my flat and narrow chest, which leaves little room for the movement of the heart and lungs; and in my earlier years this disposition made me almost weary of life. But by reflecting that, if the cause of this oppression of the heart was purely mechanical, nothing could be done about it, I soon came to pay no attention to it. The result was that, while I felt the oppression in my chest, a calm and cheerful state prevailed in my mind, which did not fail to communicate itself to society, not by intermittent whims (as is usual with hypochondriacs), but purposely and naturally. And since our *joie de vivre* depends more on what we freely *do* with life than on what we *enjoy* as a gift from it, mental work can set another kind of heightened vital feeling against the limitations that affect the body alone. The oppression has remained with me, for its cause lies in my physical constitution. But I have mastered its influence on my thoughts and actions by diverting my attention from this feeling, as if it had nothing to do with me.

2.

On Sleep

The Turks, with their fatalism, have a saying about moderation: that at the beginning of the world each man had allotted to him the portion he would have to eat during his lifetime, and to the degree that he squanders his ration in very large meals, he can count on a shorter time *to eat* and so *to exist*.

könne: das kann in einer Diätetik als Kinderlehre (denn im Genießen
müssen auch Männer von Ärzten oft als Kinder behandelt werden) auch
zur Regel dienen: nämlich daß jedem Menschen von Anbeginn her vom
Verhängnisse seine Portion Schlaf zugemessen worden, und der, welcher
von seiner Lebenszeit in Mannsjahren zu viel (über das Dritttheil) dem
Schlafen eingeräumt hat, sich nicht eine lange Zeit zu schlafen, d. i. zu
leben und alt zu werden, versprechen darf. — Wer dem Schlaf als süßen
Genuß im Schlummern (der Siesta der Spanier) oder als Zeitkürzung
(in langen Winternächten) viel mehr als ein Dritttheil seiner Lebenszeit
einräumt, oder ihn sich auch theilweise (mit Absätzen), nicht in einem Stück
für jeden Tag zumißt, verrechnet sich sehr in Ansehung seines Lebens=
quantum theils dem Grade, theils der Länge nach. — Da nun schwerlich
ein Mensch wünschen wird, daß der Schlaf überhaupt gar nicht Bedürfniß
für ihn wäre (woraus doch wohl erhellt, daß er das lange Leben als eine
lange Plage fühlt, von dem, so viel er verschlafen, eben so viel Mühselig=
keit zu tragen er sich erspart hat), so ist es gerathener fürs Gefühl sowohl
als für die Vernunft, dieses genuß= und thatleere Drittel ganz auf eine
Seite zu bringen und es der unentbehrlichen Naturrestauration zu über=
laffen: doch mit einer genauen Abgemessenheit der Zeit, von wo an und
wie lange sie dauern soll.

Es gehört unter die krankhaften Gefühle zu der bestimmten und ge=
wohnten Zeit nicht schlafen, oder auch sich nicht wach halten zu können;
vornehmlich aber das erstere, in dieser Absicht sich zu Bette zu legen und
doch schlaflos zu liegen. — Sich alle Gedanken aus dem Kopf zu schlagen,
ist zwar der gewöhnliche Rath, den der Arzt giebt: aber sie oder andere
an ihre Stelle kommen wieder und erhalten wach. Es ist kein anderer
diätetischer Rath, als beim inneren Wahrnehmen oder Bewußtwerden
irgend eines sich regenden Gedanken die Aufmerksamkeit davon sofort ab=
zuwenden (gleich als ob man mit geschlossenen Augen diese auf eine andere
Seite kehrte): wo dann durch das Abbrechen jedes Gedanken, den man
inne wird, allmählig eine Verwirrung der Vorstellungen entspringt, da=
durch das Bewußtsein seiner körperlichen (äußeren) Lage aufgehoben wird,
und eine ganz verschiedene Ordnung, nämlich ein unwillkürliches Spiel
der Einbildungskraft (das im gesunden Zustande der Traum ist), eintritt,
in welchem durch ein bewundernswürdiges Kunststück der thierischen Or=

This saying can also serve as a rule in a regimen, when we put this in the form of *elementary school teaching* (for in questions of pleasure, doctors must often treat men as if they were children): the rule, namely, that fate in the beginning assigned to each man his portion of *sleep*, and that one who has given too much of his adult life (more than one-third of it) to sleep cannot expect a long time for sleeping, that is, for living and growing old. If, in order to enjoy the sweet luxury of dozing (the Spanish *siesta*) or to pass the time (in long winter nights), a man allots much more than a third of his lifetime to sleep, or if he metes it out bit by bit, in naps instead of in one continuous period each day, he miscalculates seriously regarding the *quantity of life* at his disposal, both as to the level and the length of it. Now hardly anyone would wish that he could dispense with sleep entirely (which shows that we regard a long life as a long drudgery, and the part of it spent in sleep as an escape from this much hardship). So it is more advisable, for both feeling and reason, to set aside completely this third that is empty of enjoyment and activity, and relinquish it to the necessary restoration of nature. However, one should regulate exactly the time it is to begin and how long it is to last.

To be unable to sleep at one's fixed and habitual time, or also unable to stay awake, is a kind of morbid feeling. But of these two, insomnia is worse: to go to bed intending to sleep, and yet lie awake. Doctors usually advise a patient to drive all *thoughts* from his head; but they return, or others come in their place, and keep him awake. The only disciplinary advice [for the insomniac] is to turn away his attention as soon as he perceives or becomes conscious of any thought stirring (just as if, with his eyes closed, he turned them to a different place). This interruption of any thought that he is aware of gradually produces a confusion of ideas by which his awareness of his physical (external) situation is suspended; and then an altogether different order sets in, an involuntary play of imagination (which, in a state of health, is *dreaming*). Dreaming is an

ganisation der Körper für die animalischen Bewegungen ab gespannt, für die Vitalbewegung aber innigst agitirt wird und zwar durch Träume, die, wenn wir uns gleich derselben im Erwachen nicht erinnern, gleichwohl nicht haben ausbleiben können: weil sonst bei gänzlicher Ermangelung derselben, wenn die Nervenkraft, die vom Gehirn, dem Sitze der Vorstellungen, ausgeht, nicht mit der Muskelkraft der Eingeweide vereinigt wirkte, das Leben sich nicht einen Augenblick erhalten könnte. Daher träumen vermuthlich alle Thiere, wenn sie schlafen.

Jedermann aber, der sich zu Bette und in Bereitschaft zu schlafen gelegt hat, wird bisweilen bei aller obgedachten Ablenkung seiner Gedanken doch nicht zum Einschlafen kommen können. In diesem Fall wird er im Gehirn etwas Spastisches (Krampfartiges) fühlen, welches auch mit der Beobachtung gut zusammenhängt: daß ein Mensch gleich nach dem Erwachen etwa $1/_2$ Zoll länger sei, als wenn er sogar im Bette geblieben und dabei nur gewacht hätte. — Da Schlaflosigkeit ein Fehler des schwächlichen Alters und die linke Seite überhaupt genommen die schwächere ist,*) so fühlte ich seit etwa einem Jahre diese krampfichte Anwandelungen und sehr empfindliche Reize dieser Art (obzwar nicht wirkliche und sichtbare Bewegungen der darauf afficirten Gliedmaßen als Krämpfe), die ich nach der Beschreibung anderer für gichtische Zufälle halten und dafür einen Arzt suchen mußte. Nun aber, aus Ungeduld, am Schlafen mich gehindert zu fühlen, griff ich bald zu meinem stoischen Mittel, meinen Gedanken mit

---

*) Es ist ein ganz unrichtiges Vorgeben, daß, was die Stärke im Gebrauch seiner äußern Gliedmaßen betrifft, es bloß auf die Übung, und wie man frühe gewöhnt worden, ankomme, welche von beiden Seiten des Körpers die stärkere oder schwächere sein solle; ob im Gefechte mit dem rechten oder linken Arm der Säbel geführt, ob sich der Reiter, im Steigbügel stehend, von der Rechten zur Linken oder umgekehrt aufs Pferd schwinge, u. dgl. Die Erfahrung lehrt aber, daß, wer sich am linken Fuße Maß für seine Schuhe nehmen läßt, wenn der Schuh dem linken genau anpaßt, er für den rechten zu enge sei, ohne daß man die Schuld davon den Eltern geben kann, die ihre Kinder nicht besser belehrt hätten; so wie der Vorzug der rechten Seite vor der linken auch daran zu sehen ist, daß der, welcher über einen etwas tiefen Graben schreiten will, den linken Fuß ansetzt und mit dem rechten überschreitet; widrigenfalls er in den Graben zu fallen Gefahr läuft. Daß der preußische Infanterist geübt wird, mit dem linken Fuße anzutreten, widerlegt jenen Satz nicht, sondern bestätigt ihn vielmehr; denn er setzt diesen voran, gleich als auf ein Hypomochlium, um mit der rechten Seite den Schwung des Angriffs zu machen, welchen er mit der rechten gegen die linke verrichtet.

admirable device of our animal organization by which the body is relaxed for animal movement but stimulated within for vital movement; so, even if we do not remember our dreams when we wake up, they must still have occurred; for otherwise, if they were totally lacking—if the nervous energy that proceeds from the brain, the seat of representations, did not work in unison with the muscular power of the viscera—life could not maintain itself for an instant. This is why we presume that all animals dream when they sleep.

But it can happen to anyone, now and then, that when he lies down in bed ready to sleep he cannot fall asleep, even by diverting his thoughts in this way. When this happens he will feel a kind of spasm (like a cramp) in his brain—a feeling quite consistent with the observation that a man upon awakening is some half-inch taller than if he had only remained in bed awake. Since insomnia is a failing of weak old age, and since the left side is generally weaker than the right,* I felt, perhaps a year ago, these cramplike seizures and quite sensible stimuli of this kind (though they were not, like cramps, actual visible movements of the affected limb); and from other people's descriptions I had to take them for attacks of gout and consult a doctor about them. But, impatient at feeling my sleep interfered with, I soon had recourse to my Stoic remedy of fixing my thought forcibly on

---

*It is sometimes said that exercise and early training are the only factors determining which side of a man's body will be stronger or weaker, as far as the use of his external members is concerned—whether in combat he will handle the sabre with his right arm or with his left, whether the rider standing in his stirrup will vault onto his horse from right to left or vice-versa, and so forth. But this assertion is quite incorrect. Experience teaches that if we have our shoe measurements taken from our left foot, and the left shoe fits perfectly, the right one will be too tight; and we can hardly lay the blame for this on our parents, for not having taught us better when we were children. The advantage of the right side over the left can also be seen from the fact that, if we want to cross a deep ditch, we put our weight on the left foot and step over with the right; otherwise we run the risk of falling into the ditch. The fact that Prussian infantrymen are trained to *start out* with the left foot confirms, rather than refutes, this assertion; for they put this foot in front, as on a fulcrum, in order to use the right side for the impetus of the attack, which they execute with the right foot against the left.

Anstrengung auf irgend ein von mir gewähltes gleichgültiges Object, was es auch sei, (z. B. auf den viel Nebenvorstellungen enthaltenden Namen Cicero) zu heften: mithin die Aufmerksamkeit von jener Empfindung ab=zulenken; dadurch diese dann und zwar schleunig stumpf wurde, und so die Schläfrigkeit sie überwog, und dieses kann ich jederzeit bei wieder=kommenden Anfällen dieser Art in den kleinen Unterbrechungen des Nacht=schlafs mit gleich gutem Erfolg wiederholen. Daß aber dieses nicht etwa bloß eingebildete Schmerzen waren, davon konnte mich die des andern Morgens früh sich zeigende glühende Röthe der Zehen des linken Fußes überzeugen. — Ich bin gewiß, daß viele gichtische Zufälle, wenn nur die Diät des Genusses nicht gar zu sehr dawider ist, ja Krämpfe und selbst epileptische Zufälle (nur nicht bei Weibern und Kindern, als die dergleichen Kraft des Vorsatzes nicht haben), auch wohl das für unheilbar verschriene Podagra bei jeder neuen Anwandlung desselben durch diese Festigkeit des Vorsatzes (seine Aufmerksamkeit von einem solchen Leiden abzuwenden) abgehalten und nach und nach gar gehoben werden könnte.

3.
Vom Essen und Trinken.

Im gesunden Zustande und der Jugend ist es das Gerathenste in Ansehung des Genusses, der Zeit und Menge nach, bloß den Appetit (Hunger und Durst) zu befragen; aber bei den mit dem Alter sich ein=findenden Schwächen ist eine gewisse Angewohnheit einer geprüften und heilsam gefundenen Lebensart, nämlich wie man es einen Tag gehalten hat, es eben so alle Tage zu halten, ein diätetischer Grundsatz, welcher dem langen Leben am günstigsten ist; doch unter der Bedingung, daß diese Abfütterung für den sich weigernden Appetit die gehörige Ausnahmen mache. — Dieser nämlich weigert im Alter die Quantität des Flüssigen (Suppen oder viel Wasser zu trinken) vornehmlich dem männlichen Ge=schlecht: verlangt dagegen derbere Kost und anreizenderes Getränk (z. B. Wein), sowohl um die wurmförmige Bewegung der Gedärme (die unter allen Eingeweiden am meisten von der vita propria zu haben scheinen, weil sie, wenn sie noch warm aus dem Thier gerissen und zerhauen werden, als Würmer kriechen, deren Arbeit man nicht bloß fühlen, sondern sogar hören kann) zu befördern und zugleich solche Theile in den Blutumlauf zu

some neutral object that I chose at random (for example, the name Cicero, which contains many associated ideas), and so diverting my attention from that sensation. The result was that the sensation was dulled, even quickly so, and outweighed by drowsiness; and I can repeat this procedure with equally good results every time that attacks of this kind recur in the brief interruptions of my night's sleep. It occurred to me that these might be merely imaginary pains; but the fact that the toes of my left foot were bright red the next morning convinced me that they were not. I am sure that many attacks of *gout* could be checked in the same way, provided one's diet of food and drink is not too great an obstacle, and even *cramps* and *epileptic* seizures (though this does not apply to women and children, who do not have the necessary strength of resolution). Indeed, even cases of *podagra* that have been given up as incurable could be controlled, at each new attack, by a firm resolution (to divert one's attention from the pain), and, indeed, gradually cured.

3.
On Food and Drink

When a man is healthy and young, his best guide to when and how much to eat and drink is simply his *appetite* (hunger and thirst). But when the weaknesses of old age set in, he can best prolong his life by a disciplinary principle of making a *habit*, to a certain extent, of a manner of living that he has tested and found beneficial; in other words, by uniformity in his daily routine—provided that his diet allows for suitable exceptions when his appetite balks at it. More specifically, an elderly person's appetite, and especially a man's, refuses large quantities of liquids (soup, or too much drinking water); on the other hand, it demands more stimulating drink (wine, for example) and heartier food, both to bring into the circulatory system stimulating elements which help to keep the machinery of blood circulation working, and to promote the *vermicular* movement of the intestines (which, of all the viscera, seem to have the most *vita propria*; for if they are removed still warm from an animal

bringen, die durch ihren Reiz das Geräder zur Blutbewegung im Umlauf zu erhalten beförderlich sind.

Das Wasser braucht aber bei alten Leuten längere Zeit, um, ins Blut aufgenommen, den langen Gang seiner Absonderung von der Blutmasse durch die Nieren zur Harnblase zu machen, wenn es nicht dem Blute assimilirte Theile (dergleichen der Wein ist), und die einen Reiz der Blutgefäße zum Fortschaffen bei sich führen, in sich enthält; welcher letztere aber alsdann als Medicin gebraucht wird, dessen künstlicher Gebrauch eben darum eigentlich nicht zur Diätetik gehört. Der Anwandelung des Appetits zum Wassertrinken (dem Durst), welche großentheils nur Angewohnheit ist, nicht sofort nachzugeben, und ein hierüber genommener fester Vorsatz bringt diesen Reiz in das Maß des natürlichen Bedürfnisses des den festen Speisen beizugebenden Flüssigen, dessen Genuß in Menge im Alter selbst durch den Naturinstinct geweigert wird. Man schläft auch nicht gut, wenigstens nicht tief bei dieser Wasserschwelgerei, weil die Blutwärme dadurch vermindert wird.

Es ist oft gefragt worden: ob, gleich wie in 24 Stunden nur Ein Schlaf, so auch in eben so viel Stunden nur Eine Mahlzeit nach diätetischer Regel verwilligt werden könne, oder ob es nicht besser (gesunder) sei, dem Appetit am Mittagstische etwas abzubrechen, um dafür auch zu Nacht essen zu können. Zeitkürzender ist freilich das letztere. — Das letztere halte ich auch in den sogenannten besten Lebensjahren (dem Mittelalter) für zuträglicher; das erstere aber im späteren Alter. Denn da das Stadium für die Operation der Gedärme zum Behuf der Verdauung im Alter ohne Zweifel langsamer abläuft, als in jüngeren Jahren, so kann man glauben, daß ein neues Pensum (in einer Abendmahlzeit) der Natur aufzugeben, indessen daß das erstere Stadium der Verdauung noch nicht abgelaufen ist, der Gesundheit nachtheilig werden müsse. — Auf solche Weise kann man den Anreiz zum Abendessen nach einer hinreichenden Sättigung des Mittags für ein krankhaftes Gefühl halten, dessen man durch einen festen Vorsatz so Meister werden kann, daß auch die Anwandelung desselben nachgerade nicht mehr verspürt wird.

and cut into pieces, they crawl like worms, and one can not only feel but even hear them working).

With elderly people, water, once in the blood stream, takes longer to complete the long process of separation from the blood mass through the kidneys to the bladder when it does not contain elements which are assimilated to the blood and stimulate the blood vessels to eliminate it (as wine does). But in this case wine is used medicinally, and because of this its artificial use is not really part of a preventive regimen. Attacks of the appetite for water (thirst) are, for the most part, only habit; and by not giving in to them at once, and adopting a firm resolution about this, one reduces this stimulus to the level of a natural need to add liquids to solid foods. Even natural instinct denies elderly people the use of liquids in great quantities. Moreover, drinking water to excess lowers the temperature of the blood and so prevents one from sleeping well, or at least deeply.

The question is often raised, whether the rules of a regimen permit only one meal, as well as only one period of sleep, in twenty-four hours, or whether it would not be *better* (more healthful) to stint the appetite somewhat at the midday meal and eat something at night. Having an evening meal is, admittedly, better for passing the time; and I also consider it more beneficial in the so-called best years of life (middle age). But in later years it is better to eat only at midday; for since the stages of the digestive process in the intestines undoubtedly take longer to complete in old age, there is reason to believe that setting nature a new task (by an evening meal) when the first stage of digestion is still going on is prejudicial to health. For this reason, an impulse to have an evening meal after an adequate and satisfying one at midday can be considered a pathological feeling; and one can master it so completely by a firm resolution that one gradually ceases to feel these attacks at all.

4.

Von dem krankhaften Gefühl aus der Unzeit im Denken.

Einem Gelehrten ist das Denken ein Nahrungsmittel, ohne welches, wenn er wach und allein ist, er nicht leben kann; jenes mag nun im Lernen (Bücherlesen) oder im Ausdenken (Nachsinnen und Erfinden) bestehen. Aber beim Essen oder Gehen sich zugleich angestrengt mit einem bestimmten Gedanken beschäftigen, Kopf und Magen oder Kopf und Füße mit zwei Arbeiten zugleich belästigen, davon bringt das eine Hypochondrie, das andere Schwindel hervor. Um also dieses krankhaften Zustandes durch Diätetik Meister zu sein, wird nichts weiter erfordert, als die mechanische Beschäftigung des Magens oder der Füße mit der geistigen des Denkens wechseln zu lassen und während dieser (der Restauration gewidmeten) Zeit das absichtliche Denken zu hemmen und dem (dem mechanischen ähnlichen) freien Spiele der Einbildungskraft den Lauf zu lassen; wozu aber bei einem Studirenden ein allgemein gefaßter und fester Vorsatz der Diät im Denken erfordert wird.

Es finden sich krankhafte Gefühle ein, wenn man in einer Mahlzeit ohne Gesellschaft sich zugleich mit Bücherlesen oder Nachdenken beschäftigt, weil die Lebenskraft durch Kopfarbeit von dem Magen, den man belästigt, abgeleitet wird. Eben so, wenn dieses Nachdenken mit der krafterschöpfenden Arbeit der Füße (im Promeniren)*) verbunden wird. (Man kann das Lucubriren noch hinzufügen, wenn es ungewöhnlich ist.) Indessen sind die krankhaften Gefühle aus diesen unzeitig (invita Minerva) vorgenommenen Geistesarbeiten doch nicht von der Art, daß sie sich unmittelbar durch den bloßen Vorsatz augenblicklich, sondern allein durch Entwöhnung vermöge eines entgegengesetzten Princips nach und nach heben lassen, und von den ersteren soll hier nur geredet werden.

---

*) Studirende können es schwerlich unterlassen, in einsamen Spaziergängen sich mit Nachdenken selbst und allein zu unterhalten. Ich habe es aber an mir gefunden und auch von andern, die ich darum befrug, gehört: daß das angestrengte Denken im Gehen geschwinde matt macht; dagegen, wenn man sich dem freien Spiel der Einbildungskraft überläßt, die Motion restaurirend ist. Noch mehr geschieht dieses, wenn bei dieser mit Nachdenken verbundenen Bewegung zugleich Unterredung mit einem Andern gehalten wird, so daß man sich bald genöthigt sieht, das Spiel seiner Gedanken sitzend fortzusetzen. — Das Spazieren im Freien hat gerade die Absicht durch den Wechsel der Gegenstände seine Aufmerksamkeit auf jeden einzelnen abzuspannen.

4.

On Pathological Feelings that Come from Thinking at Unsuitable Times

Thinking—whether in the form of *study* (reading books) or *reflection* (meditation and discovery)—is a scholar's food; and when he is wide awake and *alone*, he cannot live without it. But if he taxes his energy by occupying himself with a specific thought when he is eating or walking, he inflicts two tasks on himself at the same time—on the head and the stomach or on the head and the feet; and in the first case this brings on hypochondria, in the second, vertigo. To master these pathological states by a regimen, then, all he has to do is alternate the mechanical occupation of the stomach or the feet with the mental occupation of thinking and, while he is eating or taking a walk (restoring himself), check deliberate thought and give himself over to the free play of imagination (a quasi-mechanical activity). But, in the scholar's case, this requires the adoption, in a general way, of a firm resolution to go on a *diet with regard to thinking*.

The practice of occupying oneself with reading or reflecting when dining alone provokes pathological feelings; for intellectual work diverts vital energy from the stomach and bothers it. Reflecting while taking a walk also brings on these feelings, since the work the feet are doing is already draining one's energy.* (The same thing holds true of *studying by artificial light*, if one is not used to it.) However, these pathological feelings arising from intellectual work undertaken at the wrong time (*invita Minerva*) are not the kind that can be eliminated directly and at once by sheer resolution. One can get rid of them only gradually, by breaking the habit through a principle opposed to it. And here we should be speaking only of those that can be mastered immediately.

---

*When a man of studious habits goes for a walk alone, it is hard for him to refrain from entertaining himself with his own reflections. But if he engages in strenuous thinking during his walk, he will soon be exhausted, whereas if he gives himself over to the free play of imagination, the motion will refresh him—the reports of others whom I asked about this confirm my own experience. If in addition to thinking he also engages in conversation while he is walking, he will be even more fatigued, so that he will soon have to sit down to continue with his play of thought. The purpose of walking in the open air is precisely to keep one's attention moving from one object to another and so *to keep it from becoming fixed* on any one object.

5.
Von der Hebung und Verhütung krankhafter Zufälle durch den Vorsatz im Athemziehen.

Ich war vor wenigen Jahren noch dann und wann vom Schnupfen und Husten heimgesucht, welche beide Zufälle mir desto ungelegener waren, als sie sich bisweilen beim Schlafengehen zutrugen. Gleichsam entrüstet über diese Störung des Nachtschlafs entschloß ich mich, was den ersteren Zufall betrifft, mit fest geschlossenen Lippen durchaus die Luft durch die Nase zu ziehen; welches mir anfangs nur mit einem schwachen Pfeifen und, da ich nicht absetzte oder nachließ, immer mit stärkerem, zuletzt mit vollem und freiem Luftzuge gelang, es durch die Nase zu Stande zu brin= gen, darüber ich dann sofort einschlief. — Was dies gleichsam convulsivi= sche und mit dazwischen vorfallendem Einathmen (nicht wie beim Lachen ein continuirtes) stoßweise erschallende Ausathmen, den Husten, betrifft, vornehmlich den, welchen der gemeine Mann in England den Altmanns= husten (im Bette liegend) nennt, so war er mir um so mehr ungelegen, da er sich bisweilen bald nach der Erwärmung im Bette einstellte und das Einschlafen verzögerte. Dieses Husten, welches durch den Reiz der mit offenem Munde eingeathmeten Luft auf den Luftröhrenkopf erregt wird,*)

---

*) Sollte auch nicht die atmosphärische Luft, wenn sie durch die Eustachische Röhre (also bei geschlossenen Lippen) circulirt, dadurch, daß sie auf diesem dem Gehirn nahe liegenden Umwege Sauerstoff absetzt, das erquickende Gefühl gestärkter Lebensorgane bewirken, welches dem ähnlich ist, als ob man Luft trinke; wobei diese, ob sie zwar keinen Geruch hat, doch die Geruchsnerven und die denselben nahe liegende einsaugende Gefäße stärkt? Bei manchem Wetter findet sich dieses Erquickliche des Genusses der Luft nicht: bei anderem ist es eine wahre Annehm= lichkeit sie auf seiner Wanderung mit langen Zügen zu trinken: welches das Ein= athmen mit offenem Munde nicht gewährt. — — Das ist aber von der größten diätetischen Wichtigkeit, den Athemzug durch die Nase bei geschlossenen Lippen sich so zur Gewohnheit zu machen, daß er selbst im tiefsten Schlaf nicht anders verrichtet wird, und man sogleich aufwacht, sobald er mit offenem Munde geschieht, und dadurch gleichsam aufgeschreckt wird; wie ich das anfänglich, ehe es mir zur Gewohnheit wurde auf solche Weise zu athmen, bisweilen erfuhr. — Wenn man genöthigt ist stark oder bergan zu schreiten, so gehört größere Stärke des Vorsatzes dazu von jener Regel nicht abzuweichen und eher seine Schritte zu mäßigen, als von ihr eine Ausnahme zu machen; ingleichen, wenn es um starke Motion zu thun ist, die etwa ein Erzieher seinen Zöglingen geben will, daß dieser sie ihre Bewe= gung lieber stumm, als mit öfterer Einathmung durch den Mund machen lasse.

5.

On Overcoming and Preventing Pathological Seizures by a Resolution about Breathing

A few years ago I suffered occasionally from catarrh and cough, and these attacks were all the more troublesome because they sometimes occurred when I was going to sleep. Indignant, so to speak, at having my night's sleep disturbed, I resolved, with regard to the attacks of catarrh, to keep my lips closed tight and to breathe only through my nose. At first I could manage only a thin, whistling breath; but as I did not give up or relax my efforts, my breathing grew continually stronger until finally I could inhale fully and freely through my nose. And when I reached this point, I fell asleep at once. As for *coughing*—a spasm, so to speak, of loud exhalations broken by gasps (not continuous, like laughter)—I was bothered especially by what the ordinary Englishman calls an old man's cough (since the attacks come when one is lying in bed), which was all the more annoying since it sometimes came just after I had got warm in bed, and delayed my sleep. Since this kind of cough is brought on when air breathed through the mouth irritates the larynx,* no mechanical

---

*Is it not likely that atmospheric air circulating through the Eustachian tubes (when the lips are kept closed) produces the refreshing feeling of increased vigor in the vital organs by depositing oxygen as it makes this circuit that brings it near the brain—a feeling as if one were *drinking* air? And that air, though it has no odor of its own, in this way strengthens the olfactory nerves and the adjacent vessels which absorb it? In some kinds of weather one does not get this refreshment from drinking air; but in others, it is a real pleasure to drink it in long draughts as one strolls along, a pleasure one does not get from inhaling through the mouth. But it is of the utmost importance, in a regimen, to become so *accustomed* to inhaling through the nose, with closed lips, that one cannot do otherwise, even in the deepest sleep, and wakes up at once, startled out of sleep, so to speak, as soon as one inhales through the mouth. This sometimes happened to me at first, before I made it a habit to breathe in this way. When one has to walk rapidly or uphill, one needs greater strength of resolution not to depart from this rule, and to moderate one's steps rather than make an exception to the rule. The same thing is true of vigorous exercise; and a teacher who is directing his pupils' exercise should have them do it in silence rather than inhale frequently through the mouth. My young

nun zu hemmen, bedurfte es einer nicht mechanischen (pharmaceutischen), sondern nur unmittelbaren Gemüthsoperation: nämlich die Aufmerk=samkeit auf diesen Reiz dadurch ganz abzulenken, daß sie mit Anstren=gung auf irgend ein Object (wie oben bei krampfhaften Zufällen) gerichtet und dadurch das Ausstoßen der Luft gehemmt wurde, welches mir, wie ich es deutlich fühlte, das Blut ins Gesicht trieb, wobei aber der durch denselben Reiz erregte flüssige Speichel (saliva) die Wirkung dieses Rei=zes, nämlich die Ausstoßung der Luft, verhinderte und ein Herunter=schlucken dieser Feuchtigkeit bewirkte. — Eine Gemüthsoperation, zu der ein recht großer Grad des festen Vorsatzes erforderlich, der aber darum auch desto wohlthätiger ist.

6.
Von den Folgen dieser Angewohnheit des Athemziehens mit geschlossenen Lippen.

Die unmittelbare Folge davon ist, daß sie auch im Schlafe fort=währt, und ich sogleich aus dem Schlafe aufgeschreckt werde, wenn ich zu=fälligerweise die Lippen öffne und ein Athemzug durch den Mund ge=schieht; woraus man sieht, daß der Schlaf und mit ihm der Traum nicht

Meine jungen Freunde (ehemalige Zuhörer) haben diese diätetische Maxime als probat und heilsam gepriesen und sie nicht unter die Kleinigkeiten gezählt, weil sie bloßes Hausmittel ist, das den Arzt entbehrlich macht. — Merkwürdig ist noch: daß, da es scheint, beim lange fortgesetzten Sprechen geschehe das Einathmen auch durch den so oft geöffneten Mund, mithin jene Regel werde da doch ohne Schaden überschritten, es sich wirklich nicht so verhält. Denn es geschieht doch auch durch die Nase. Denn wäre diese zu der Zeit verstopft, so würde man von dem Redner sagen, er spreche durch die Nase (ein sehr widriger Laut), indem er wirklich nicht durch die Nase spräche, und umgekehrt, er spreche nicht durch die Nase, indem er wirklich durch die Nase spricht: wie es Hr. Hofr. Lichtenberg launicht und richtig bemerkt. — Das ist auch der Grund, warum der, welcher lange und laut spricht (Vorleser oder Prediger), es ohne Rauhigkeit der Kehle eine Stunde lang wohl aushalten kann: weil nämlich sein Athemziehen eigent=lich durch die Nase, nicht durch den Mund geschieht, als durch welchen nur das Ausathmen verrichtet wird. — Ein Nebenvortheil dieser Angewohnheit des Athemzuges mit beständig geschlossenen Lippen, wenn man für sich allein wenigstens nicht im Discurs begriffen ist, ist der: daß die sich immer absondernde und den Schlund befeuchtende Saliva hiebei zugleich als Verdauungsmittel (stomachale), vielleicht auch (verschluckt) als Abführungsmittel wirkt, wenn man fest genug ent=schlossen ist, sie nicht durch üble Angewohnheit zu verschwenden.

(pharmaceutical) remedy is needed to check it; a mental action can stop it directly—the action, namely, of completely diverting one's attention from this irritation by directing it forcibly to some other object (as with convulsive seizures, which I have already discussed), which stops the expulsion of air. I clearly felt it drive the blood to my face. But the flow of saliva brought on by this irritation checked its effect, the expulsion of air, and the saliva subsided. Such a mental operation requires a very high degree of firmness in one's resolution, but this makes it all the more beneficial.

6.

On the Results of This Habit of Breathing with Closed Lips

The *immediate* result is that the habit carries over into sleep, and I am startled out of my sleep as soon as I happen to open my lips and draw a breath through my mouth. This shows that sleep, and with it dreaming, is not such a complete absence of the

---

friends (former students) have commended this disciplinary maxim as proved and beneficial, and have not belittled it because it is a simple household remedy by which we can dispense with the doctor's services. A further point should be noted: though it might seem that one who *speaks* for a long time *inhales* through his mouth every time he opens it and so breaks the rule with impunity, this is not really so; for even then he inhales through his *nose*. For when the speaker's nose is stopped up, we say that he speaks through his nose (a very disagreeable sound) because he is not really speaking through his nose; and vice-versa, he does not "speak through his nose" when he is really speaking through his nose, as Privy Councillor *Lichtenberg* notes humorously and correctly. It is for the same reason that people who have to speak for a long time and in a loud voice (lecturers and preachers) can keep it up for an hour without getting hoarse: namely, that they inhale through the nose and merely *exhale* through the mouth. An incidental advantage of habitually inhaling with closed lips, when one is alone or at least not engaged in conversation, is that saliva, which is constantly secreted and moistens the throat, is also made to act as a digestive agent (*stomachale*) and perhaps also (when swallowed) as a laxative, if one's decision not to waste it is firm enough.

eine so gänzliche Abwesenheit von dem Zustande des Wachenden ist, daß sich nicht auch eine Aufmerksamkeit auf seine Lage in jenem Zustande mit einmische: wie man denn dieses auch daraus abnehmen kann, daß die, welche sich des Abends vorher vorgenommen haben früher als gewöhnlich (etwa zu einer Spazierfahrt) aufzustehen, auch früher erwachen; indem sie vermuthlich durch die Stadtuhren aufgeweckt worden, die sie also auch mitten im Schlaf haben hören und darauf Acht geben müssen. — Die mittelbare Folge dieser löblichen Angewöhnung ist: daß das unwillkür= liche abgenöthigte Husten (nicht das Aufhusten eines Schleims als be= absichtigter Auswurf) in beiderlei Zustande verhütet und so durch die bloße Macht des Vorsatzes eine Krankheit verhütet wird. — — Ich habe sogar gefunden, daß, da mich nach ausgelöschtem Licht (und eben zu Bette gelegt) auf einmal ein starker Durst anwandelte, den mit Wassertrinken zu löschen ich im Finstern hätte in eine andere Stube gehen und durch Herumtappen das Wassergeschirr suchen müssen, ich darauf fiel, verschie= bene und starke Athemzüge mit Erhebung der Brust zu thun und gleich= sam Luft durch die Nase zu trinken; wodurch der Durst in wenig Se= cunden völlig gelöscht war. Es war ein krankhafter Reiz, der durch einen Gegenreiz gehoben ward.

Beschluß.

Krankhafte Zufälle, in Ansehung deren das Gemüth das Vermögen besitzt, des Gefühls derselben durch den bloßen standhaften Willen des Menschen, als einer Obermacht des vernünftigen Thieres, Meister werden zu können, sind alle von der spastischen (krampfhaften) Art: man kann aber nicht umgekehrt sagen, daß alle von dieser Art durch den bloßen festen Vorsatz gehemmt oder gehoben werden können. — Denn einige derselben sind von der Beschaffenheit, daß die Versuche sie der Kraft des Vorsatzes zu unterwerfen das krampfhafte Leiden vielmehr noch verstärken; wie es der Fall mit mir selber ist, da diejenige Krankheit, welche vor etwa einem Jahr in der Kopenhagener Zeitung als „epidemischer, mit Kopfbe= drückung verbundener Katarrh" beschrieben wurde,*) (bei mir aber wohl ein Jahr älter, aber doch von ähnlicher Empfindung ist) mich für eigene Kopfarbeiten gleichsam desorganisirt, wenigstens geschwächt und stumpf gemacht hat und, da sich diese Bedrückung auf die natürliche Schwäche

---

*) Ich halte sie für eine Gicht, die sich zum Theil aufs Gehirn geworfen hat.

waking state as to exclude attention to one's situation in sleep. The fact that a man does awaken earlier than usual if, the preceding evening, he decided to get up earlier (to go for a walk, perhaps) leads to the same conclusion; for he is presumably awakened by the clocks of the city, which he must have heard and paid attention to in his sleep. The *mediate* result of this laudable habit is that it prevents involuntary, forced coughing (as distinguished from deliberate coughing to discharge phlegm) in one's sleep as well as when one is awake, so that sheer force of resolution averts an illness. I have found that it has even further results. Once, after I had put out the light and gone to bed, I suddenly felt an intense thirst and went, in the dark, to another room to get a drink of water. While I was groping about for the water pitcher, I hit upon the idea of *drinking* air through my nose, so to speak, by taking several deep breaths and expanding my chest. Within a few seconds this quenched my thirst completely. The thirst was a pathological stimulus, which was neutralized by a counteracting stimulus.

Conclusion

All pathological attacks in which man's mind can master these feelings by sheer steadfast will, as the superior power of a rational animal, are convulsive (cramplike) in nature. But we cannot convert this proposition and say that every convulsive seizure can be checked or eliminated merely by a firm resolution. For some of them are such that an attempt to subject them to the force of one's resolution aggravates the convulsive ailment. This was true in my own case, when I contracted an illness that the *Cophenhagen Newspaper* described, about a year ago, as "an epidemic of catarrh accompanied by *distress in the head*" (I came down with it a year before this, but the symptoms were similar).* The result of it was that I felt disorganized—or at least weakened and dulled—in my intellectual work; and since this ailment has attached itself to the natural weaknesses of my old age, it will end only with life itself.

---

*I think it is a kind of gout that has to some extent penetrated the brain.

des Alters geworfen hat, wohl nicht anders als mit dem Leben zugleich aufhören wird.

Die krankhafte Beschaffenheit des Patienten, die das Denken, in so= fern es ein Festhalten eines Begriffs (der Einheit des Bewußtseins ver= bundener Vorstellungen) ist, begleitet und erschwert, bringt das Gefühl eines spastischen Zustandes des Organs des Denkens (des Gehirns) als eines Drucks hervor, der zwar das Denken und Nachdenken selbst, inglei= chen das Gedächtniß in Ansehung des ehedem Gedachten eigentlich nicht schwächt, aber im Vortrage (dem mündlichen oder schriftlichen) das feste Zusammenhalten der Vorstellungen in ihrer Zeitfolge wider Zerstreuung sicheren soll, bewirkt selbst einen unwillkürlichen spastischen Zustand des Gehirns, als ein Unvermögen, bei dem Wechsel der auf einander folgen= den Vorstellungen die Einheit des Bewußtseins derselben zu erhalten. Daher begegnet es mir: daß, wenn ich, wie es in jeder Rede jederzeit ge= schieht, zuerst zu dem, was ich sagen will, (den Hörer oder Leser) vorbe= reite, ihm den Gegenstand, wohin ich gehen will, in der Aussicht, dann ihn auch auf das, wovon ich ausgegangen bin, zurückgewiesen habe (ohne welche zwei Hinweisungen kein Zusammenhang der Rede Statt findet) und ich nun das letztere mit dem ersteren verknüpfen soll, ich auf einmal meinen Zuhörer (oder stillschweigend mich selbst) fragen muß: Wo war ich doch? Wovon ging ich aus? welcher Fehler nicht sowohl ein Fehler des Geistes, auch nicht des Gedächtnisses allein, sondern der Geistes= gegenwart (im Verknüpfen), d. i. unwillkürliche Zerstreuung und ein sehr peinigender Fehler ist, dem man zwar in Schriften (zumal den phi= losophischen: weil man da nicht immer so leicht zurücksehen kann, von wo man ausging) mühsam vorbeugen, obzwar mit aller Mühe nie völlig ver= hüten kann.

Mit dem Mathematiker, der seine Begriffe oder die Stellvertreter derselben (Größen= und Zahlenzeichen) in der Anschauung vor sich hin= stellen, und daß, so weit er gegangen ist, alles richtig sei, versichert sein kann, ist es anders bewandt, als mit dem Arbeiter im Fache der vornehm= lich reinen Philosophie (Logik und Metaphysik), der seinen Gegenstand in der Luft vor sich schwebend erhalten muß und ihn nicht bloß theilweise sondern jederzeit zugleich in einem Ganzen des Systems (d. r. V.) sich darstellen und prüfen muß. Daher es eben nicht zu verwundern ist, wenn ein Metaphysiker eher invalid wird, als der Studirende in einem ande= ren Fache, ingleichen als Geschäftsphilosophen; indessen daß es doch einige

This pathological condition of the patient, which accompanies and impedes his thinking, in so far as thinking is holding firmly onto a concept (of the unity of ideas connected in his consciousness), produces the feeling of a spasmic state in his organ of thought (his brain). This feeling, as of a burden, does not really weaken his thought and reflection itself, or his memory of preceding thoughts; but when he is setting forth his thoughts (orally or in writing), the very need to guard against distractions which would interrupt the firm coherence of ideas in their temporal sequence produces an involuntary spasmic condition of the brain, which takes the form of an inability to maintain unity of consciousness in his ideas, as one takes the place of the preceding one. In every discourse I first prepare (the reader or the audience) for what I intend to say by indicating, in prospect, my destination and, in retrospect, the starting point of my argument (without these two points of reference a discourse has no consistency). And the result of this pathological condition is that when the time comes for me to connect the two, I must suddenly ask my audience (or myself, silently): now where was I? where did I start from? This is a defect, not so much of the mind or of the memory alone, as rather of *presence of mind* (in connecting ideas)—that is, an involuntary *distraction*. It is a most distressing feeling, which one can guard against in writing, though only with great labor (especially in philosophical writing, where it is not always easy to look back to one's starting point); but despite all one's efforts, one can never obviate it completely.

It is different with the mathematician, who can hold his concepts or their substitutes (symbols of quantity or number) before him in intuition and assure himself that, as far as he has gone, everything is correct. But the worker in the field of philosophy, especially pure philosophy (logic and metaphysics), must hold his object hanging in midair before him, and must always describe and examine it, not merely part by part, but within the totality of a system as well (the system of pure reason). Hence it is not surprising if metaphysicians are incapacitated sooner than scholars in other fields or in applied philosophy. Yet

derer geben muß, die sich jenem ganz widmen, weil ohne Metaphysik über=
haupt es gar keine Philosophie geben könnte.

Hieraus ist auch zu erklären, wie jemand für sein Alter gesund zu
sein sich rühmen kann, ob er zwar in Ansehung gewisser ihm obliegenden
Geschäfte sich in die Krankenliste mußte einschreiben lassen. Denn weil
das Unvermögen zugleich den Gebrauch und mit diesem auch den Ver=
brauch und die Erschöpfung der Lebenskraft abhält, und er gleichsam nur
in einer niedrigeren Stufe (als vegetirendes Wesen) zu leben gesteht,
nämlich essen, gehen und schlafen zu können, was für seine animalische
Existenz gesund, für die bürgerliche (zu öffentlichen Geschäften verpflichtete)
Existenz aber krank, d. i. invalid, heißt: so widerspricht sich dieser Candi=
dat des Todes hiemit gar nicht.

Dahin führt die Kunst das menschliche Leben zu verlängern: daß
man endlich unter den Lebenden nur so geduldet wird, welches eben nicht
die ergötzlichste Lage ist.

Hieran aber habe ich selber Schuld. Denn warum will ich auch der
hinanstrebenden jüngeren Welt nicht Platz machen und, um zu leben, mir
den gewöhnten Genuß des Lebens schmälern: warum ein schwächliches
Leben durch Entsagungen in ungewöhnliche Länge ziehen, die Sterbe=
listen, in denen doch auf den Zuschnitt der von Natur Schwächeren und
ihre muthmaßliche Lebensdauer mit gerechnet ist, durch mein Beispiel in
Verwirrung bringen und das alles, was man sonst Schicksal nannte (dem
man sich demüthig und andächtig unterwarf), dem eigenen festen Vorsatze
unterwerfen; welcher doch schwerlich zur allgemeinen diätetischen Regel,
nach welcher die Vernunft unmittelbar Heilkraft ausübt, aufgenommen
werden und die therapeutische Formeln der Officin jemals verdrängen
wird?

Nachschrift.

Den Verfasser der Kunst das menschliche (auch besonders das literäri=
sche) Leben zu verlängern darf ich also dazu wohl auffordern, daß er wohl=
wollend auch darauf bedacht sei, die Augen der Leser (vornehmlich der
jetzt großen Zahl der Leserinnen, die den Übelstand der Brille noch härter
fühlen dürften) in Schutz zu nehmen, auf welche jetzt aus elender Ziererei
der Buchdrucker (denn Buchstaben haben doch als Malerei schlechterdings
nichts Schönes an sich) von allen Seiten Jagd gemacht wird: damit nicht,
so wie in Marokko durch weiße Übertünchung aller Häuser ein großer

some people must devote themselves entirely to metaphysics, because without it there would be no philosophy at all.

This also explains how a person can boast of being healthy *for his age* though he must put himself on the sick list with regard to certain affairs incumbent on him. For as his *inability* to discharge this business prevents him from using his vital energy, it also prevents him from expending and consuming it. He admits that he is living only on a lower level, so to speak (vegetating): namely, that he can eat, walk, and sleep; and since a state of health in relation to his animal existence can be one of illness in relation to his civil existence (in which he is obliged to transact certain public business), this candidate for death does not contradict himself in the least.

So the art of prolonging human life leads to this: that in the end one is tolerated among the living only because of the animal functions one performs—not a particularly amusing situation.

But in this respect I myself am guilty. For why am I not willing to make way for younger people who are struggling upward, and why do I curtail the enjoyment of life I am used to just to stay alive? Why do I prolong a feeble life to an extraordinary age by self-denial, and by my example confuse the obituary list, which is based on the average of those who are more frail by nature and calculated on their life expectancy? Why submit to my own firm resolution what we used to call fate (to which we submitted humbly and piously)—a resolution which, in any case, will hardly be adopted as a universal rule of regimen by which reason exercises direct healing power, and which will never replace the prescriptions the pharmacist dispenses?

Postscript

I might also suggest that the author of the art of prolonging human life (and in particular, literary life) kindly consider the protection of readers' eyes (especially the now large number of women readers, who may feel more strongly about the nuisance of glasses). At present our eyes are harassed from all sides by the wretched affectations of book printers (for letters, considered as

Theil der Einwohner der Stadt blind ist, dieses Übel aus ähnlicher Ur=
sache auch bei uns einreiße, vielmehr die Buchdrucker desfalls unter Poli=
zeigesetze gebracht werden. — Die jetzige Mode will es dagegen anders;
nämlich:

1) Nicht mit schwarzer, sondern grauer Tinte (weil es sanfter und
lieblicher auf schönem weißen Papier absteche) zu drucken.

2) Mit Didotschen Lettern von schmalen Füßen, nicht mit Breit=
kopfschen, die ihrem Namen Buchstaben (gleichsam bücherner Stäbe zum
Feststehen) besser entsprechen würden.

3) Mit lateinischer (wohl gar Cursiv=)Schrift ein Werk deutschen
Inhalts, von welcher Breitkopf mit Grunde sagte: daß niemand das Lesen
derselben für seine Augen so lange aushalte, als mit der deutschen.

4) Mit so kleiner Schrift, als nur möglich, damit für die unten etwa
beizufügende Noten noch kleinere (dem Auge noch knapper angemessene)
leserlich bleibe.

Diesem Unwesen zu steuern, schlage ich vor: den Druck der Berliner
Monatsschrift (nach Text und Noten) zum Muster zu nehmen; denn man
mag, welches Stück man will, in die Hand nehmen, so wird man die durch
obige Leserei angegriffene Augen durch Ansicht des letzteren merklich ge=
stärkt fühlen.*)

---

*) Unter den krankhaften Zufällen der Augen (nicht eigentlichen Augen-
krankheiten) habe ich die Erfahrung von einem, der mir zuerst in meinen Vierziger-
jahren einmal, späterhin mit Zwischenräumen von einigen Jahren dann und wann,
jetzt aber in einem Jahre etlichemal begegnet ist, gemacht; wo das Phänomen
darin besteht: daß auf dem Blatt, welches ich lese, auf einmal alle Buchstaben
verwirrt und durch eine gewisse über dasselbe verbreitete Helligkeit vermischt und
ganz unleserlich werden: ein Zustand, der nicht über 6 Minuten dauert, der einem
Prediger, welcher seine Predigt vom Blatte zu lesen gewohnt ist, sehr gefährlich sein
dürfte, von mir aber in meinem Auditorium der Logik oder Metaphysik, wo nach
gehöriger Vorbereitung im freien Vortrage (aus dem Kopfe) geredet werden kann,
nichts als die Besorgniß entsprang, es möchte dieser Zufall der Vorbote vom Er-
blinden sein; worüber ich gleichwohl jetzt beruhigt bin: da ich bei diesem jetzt öfter
als sonst sich ereignenden Zufalle an meinem Einen gesunden Auge (denn das linke
hat das Sehen seit etwa 5 Jahren verloren) nicht den mindesten Abgang an Klar-
heit verspüre. — Zufälligerweise kam ich darauf, wenn sich jenes Phänomen er-
eignete, meine Augen zu schließen, ja um noch besser das äußere Licht abzuhalten,
meine Hand darüber zu legen, und dann sah ich eine hellweiße, wie mit Phosphor
im Finstern auf einem Blatt verzeichnete Figur, ähnlich der, wie das letzte Viertel
im Kalender vorgestellt wird, doch mit einem auf der convexen Seite ausgezackten

8*

pictures, have no intrinsic beauty at all). In Moroccan cities, a large percentage of the inhabitants are blind because all the houses are whitewashed; and to prevent this evil from spreading among us from a similar cause, printers should be subjected to police regulations in this respect. The current *fashion* in printing, however, would have it otherwise. It dictates:

1) That the text be printed with *gray* ink instead of black (because the contrast of gray ink on fine white paper is softer and more agreeable).

2) That it be printed in *Didot* characters with narrow feet, instead of *Breitkopf* characters, which would correspond better to the name *Buchstaben* [letters]—(*bucherner Stabe* [beechwood staffs], as it were, for steadying oneself).

3) That works in the German language be printed with *Roman* (and even italic) type, although, as Breitkopf [36] rightly said, this tires the eyes more quickly than does Gothic type.

4) That printers use the smallest possible type that will allow still smaller letters (even harder on the eyes) to remain legible when used in footnotes.

To control this abuse, I suggest that printers take as their model the *Berlin Monthly* (both its text and its notes); for no matter what page one opens it to, the sight of it will strengthen the eyes perceptibly when they have been strained by reading the kind of print described above.*

---

*When I was forty years old I experienced the first attack of a *pathological condition* of the eyes (not really an opthalmic disease), which used to recur, from time to time, at intervals of some years but now comes several times within a year. The phenomenon is that, when I am reading, a certain brightness suddenly spreads over the page, confusing and mixing up all the letters until they are completely illegible. This condition, which does not last longer than six minutes, could be very risky for a preacher who is in the habit of reading off his sermons from pages. But since, in my courses in logic and metaphysics, I can lecture freely (from my head) after a suitable preparation, my own concern was that these attacks might be the precursor of blindness. But I am no longer worried about this; for, although the attacks now come more frequently than usual, I do not notice any loss of acuity in my one good eye (I lost the sight in my left eye some five years ago). Once when this phenomenon happened, it occurred to me to close my eyes and even hold my hand over them to keep out external light even better; and then I saw in the darkness a luminous figure outlined in phosphorous, so to speak, on a page,

Rande, welche allmählich an Helligkeit verlor und in obbenannter Zeit verschwand. — Ich möchte wohl wissen: ob diese Beobachtung auch von Andern gemacht, und wie diese Erscheinung, die wohl eigentlich nicht in den Augen — als bei deren Bewegung dies Bild nicht zugleich mit bewegt, sondern immer an derselben Stelle gesehen wird —, sondern im Sensorium commune ihren Sitz haben dürfte, zu erklären sei. Zugleich ist es seltsam, daß man ein Auge (innerhalb einer Zeit, die ich etwa auf 3 Jahre schätze) einbüßen kann, ohne es zu vermissen.

J. Kant.

similar to the one that represents the last quarter in the calendar but with a jagged border on the convex side. After gradually diminishing in brightness, it disappeared within six minutes. I should like to know whether other people have had the same experience and how we can explain this appearance, [37] which might well have its source in the *sensorium commune* rather than in the eyes—for when I moved my eyes, this picture did not move with them: I saw it always in the same place. It is also curious that one can *lose* the sight in one eye without *noticing* it (I estimate the period, with regard to my left eye, at about three years).

I. Kant

Notes

1. Although Kant is probably referring primarily to Frederick William's rigid orthodoxy and intolerance of dissent, he may also have in mind the King's mystical tendencies and the series of sexual escapades that culminated in his bigamous marriage to the Countess of Dehnhof. Kant's former pupil J.G. Kiesewetter, who became tutor to the royal children in Berlin, kept Kant informed of events at court. See for example, his letter of June 14, 1791 (XI, 264-66): "The King has already had several visions of Jesus. . . . He is weak in body and soul now, and he sits for hours, weeping. Dehnhof has fallen from grace and gone to her sister-in-law, but the King has written to her again and in all probability she will come back soon. Rietz [another of the King's mistresses] is still an influential woman. The people who tyrannize over the King are Bischofswerder, Woellner, and Rietz."

2. In keeping with tradition, Frederick William was crowned in Koenigsberg. As rector of the university at the time, Kant shared the responsibility for the coronation ceremonies and was publicly praised by the new King. I have been unable to discover what additional "expressions of his favor" Kant is referring to in this passage.

3. Johann Cristoph Woellner (1732-1800). On Woellner's role in the suppression of religious discussion, see the translator's introduction.

4. Vorlaender, in his notes to the *Akademie* text, cites Arthur Warda's view that the friend Kant mentions is Wasianski, his later biographer. However, Biester's letter to Kant of December 17, 1794, shows that he has read Kant's reply to Frederick William and regrets the promise made to refrain from writing on religion (XI, 535-36).

215

5. Kant's original draft of this letter, which is worded somewhat differently from the version published here, is to be found in the *Akademie* edition, XI, 508-11.

6. Johann David Michaelis (1717-91) was a Professor of Theology in Goettingen and a colleague of C.F. Staeudlin, to whom *The Conflict of the Faculties* was dedicated. His writings on moral philosophy were published posthumously, in 1792, by Staeudlin. The practice Kant is referring to is summarized by Michaelis on page 5 of this work: "Here I can furnish no proof from the Bible; and should I want to quote it, this would have to be only by way of illustration, or in the same way that any other human book—juridical, moral, or historical—is cited."

7. Since the *Akademie* text here seems contrary to the sense of the paragraph, I have followed the *Philosophische Bibliothek* edition, ed. Klaus Reich (1959), which reads *"nicht nach ihrem theoretischen Vermogen, sondern nach dem, was sie als zu thun vorschreibt..."*

8. Eberhard Julius von Massow, who in 1798 was appointed Minister of Justice, head of the state department of church and schools, and *Ober-Kurator* of the universities. The draft of a letter which Kant wrote to him as *Regierungspraesident* in 1797, recommending a former pupil for a vacant professorship, mentions that von Massow had honored Kant with a visit "a few years ago" and was well-disposed toward him (XII, 187-88).

9. Claudius Salmasius (1588-1655), a French historian and jurist, published in 1648 a work entitled *De annis climacteriis et de antiqua astrologia.*

10. According to August Oncken in *Die Maxime laissez faire et laissez passez* (Bern, 1886), this story, in which Colbert was the French Minister, was the source of the maxim "laissez faire."

11. See John, 5:39. The text reads: "Search the scriptures; for in them ye think ye have eternal life."

12. Following Vorlaender's emendation of the text. He states: "I believe that Kant wrote: *'weil, was aus Schriftstellen fur die Religion auszumitteln sei, blos ein Gegenstand der Vernunft sein kann, auch....'*" (VII, 349).

13. Guillaume Postel, a famous orientalist and visionary, was born in 1505 or 1510 at Dolerie near Barenton and died in Paris in 1581. The book referred to is his *Les très merveilleuses victoires des femmes du nouveau-monde, et comment elles doivent à tout le monde par raison commander, et même à ceux qui auront la monarchie du monde vieil.*

14. Emanuel Swedenborg (1688-1772), the Swedish religious writer whose views Kant compared with the "dreams" of rationalist metaphysicians in his satirical *Dreams of a Spirit-Seer* (1766).

15. According to Vorlaender, Kant is probably referring to a work by Wieland published in 1791.

16. In his work *Jerusalem oder uber religiose Macht und Judentum.*

17. Lazarus Ben David (1762-1832) was noted for his role in propagating Kant's philosophy in Vienna during the period from 1794 to 1797. He was originally from Berlin.

18. Phillip J. Spener (1635-1705), whose *Pia desideria* (1675) became the program of Pietism.

19. A.H. Franck (1663-1727), a pastor and professor in Halle, was one of the leaders of the Pietist movement, noted especially for the charitable organizations he established.

20. Count Nikolaus Ludwig von Zinzendorf (1700-1760), German leader of a sect which was established in Bohemia in 1467 as the Bohemian Brethren and reconstituted in 1722 as the Moravian Brethren.

21. Johann Georg Hamann (1730-88), a critic of the Enlightenment as an attempt to divorce reason from tradition, history, and the particularity of experience. In his introduction to the *Philosophische Bibliothek* edition of *Der Streit der Fakultaten* (pp. XII-XIII), Klaus Reich quotes at length the correspondence between Hamann and Kant which led Kant to take this famous dictum in an essentially moral sense, notably in his *Metaphysic of Morals* (VI, 440).

22. Christian Friedrich Nicolai (1733-1811) was a highly successful publisher, editor of various literary journals, novelist, and "popular philosopher." One of his best-known works was a twelve-volume study of the economic, social, cultural and religious life of Germany and Switzerland entitled *Description of a Journey through Germany and Switzerland in 1781*.

23. Pierre La Coste, a pastor of the Reformed Church in Leipzig, whose sermons appeared in a German translation in 1756.

24. Denis Petau (1583-1652), a French Jesuit theologian, wrote several chronological works, most notably an *Opus de doctrina temporum*.

25. Johann Bengel (1687-1752), a theologian of Wuerttemberg, wrote a work entitled *Ordo temporum a principio per periodos oeconomiae divinae historicus atque propheticus*, in which he gave the year 1836 as the beginning of the millenium.

26. Johann Georg Frank (1705-1784) published in 1774 a mystical chronology with a very long title, *Praeclusio chronologiae fundamentalis...: in cyclo Jobeleo biblico detectae et ad chronologiam tam sacram quam profanam applicatae*. As for Kant's question: "What are we to say to this?" the answer can be found in his *Anthropology from a Pragmatic Point of View*, under the heading "On the Power of Using Signs" (VII, 194 ff.): "We should, further, take note here of a strange way in which man's imagination plays with him by confusing signs with things, or putting an intrinsic reality into signs, as if things must conform to them. . . . "

27. Kant and Wilmans carried on a rather one-sided correspondence between September 1797 and May 1799 (see XII, 202, 207, 230, 259, 277, 279). Of these letters, only the present one and the final exchange have been preserved. In his final letter to Wilmans Kant explains his oversight in failing to answer Wilman's letter of October 28, 1798, which had apparently asked why Kant could not completely endorse his position. Kant replies that Wilmans' view of understanding and its relation to reason makes unity of consciousness in one and the same subject impossible. In the missing documents, Wilmans had apparently elaborated his view that understanding, which contains all the manifold of representation, is purely material and totally distinct from reason.

27a. Johann Christian Reil (1759-1813, Professor of Medicine in Halle and later in Berlin, founded the *Archiv fur Physiologie* in 1796.·

28. Abdera, center of the Atomic School of philosophy in the ancient world. Beside the metaphors which suggest the philosophy of Democritus, Kant may also have had in mind the ancient canard that the air of Abdera makes men silly. Wieland's *Die Geschichte der Abderiten* (1774), a popular satire comparing modern Biberach with ancient Abdera in point of silliness, made the name readily understandable to Kant's readers.

29. Refers to the Danish astronomer, Tycho Brahe (1546-1601), who sought a *via media* between the Ptolemaic and Copernican systems by advancing the theory in his work, *Astronomiae Instauratae Progymnasmata*, Vol. II (1588), that the five planets then known, excluding earth, revolve around the sun, but the sun and solar system simultaneously revolve about the earth once annually.

30. The French Revolution.

30a. "When it met the divine Vulcanian armour, the mortal blade, like brittle ice, snapped in the stroke . . ." Refers to Meliscus' sword, the weapon Aeneas snatched in his battle with Turnus (Virgil, *Aeneid* XII, 739ff, trans. J.W. Mackail, "Modern Library" edn.).

31. Kant's reference is to a work of Johann B. Erhard (1766-1827), *Über das Recht des Volkes zu einer Revolution* (Jena and Leipzig, 1795), p. 189.

32. Kant's references are to the work of Petrus Camper (1722-89), *Über den natürlichen Unterschied der Gesichtszüge* (Berlin, 1792), and to the *Handbuch der Naturgeschichte* (Göttingen, 1779) by Johann F. Blumenbach (1752-1840).

32a. Sir Thomas More's political satire was published in 1516 in Latin, was translated into English in 1551. The *Oceana* contained Harrington's exposition of an ideal constitution, the law-giver supposedly Oliver Cromwell, whose protectorate over England lasted from 1653-58. The *Histoire des Severambes* appeared first in English, 1675, then in French, 1677 and 1679, and is supposed to derive from a certain Vairasse d'Allais.

33. Anton F. Büsching (1724-93) was the author of extensive writings on geography, history, education and religion, as well as the editor of the *Magazin für die neue Historie und Geographie* (23 vols., 1767-93) and *Wochentl. Nachrichten von neuen Landkarten* (Berlin, 1773-87).

34. Hume wrote: "I must confess, when I see princes and states fighting and quarrelling, amidst their debts, funds, and public mortgages, it always brings to my mind a match of cudgel-playing fought in a China shop." "Of Public Credit," in *Essays, Moral, Political and Literary*, eds. Green and Grose (London, 1898). The "heroic remedy" Hume refers to is the refusal to support war through contracting public debts. Kant proposed the same in *Perpetual Peace*, see above, p.88.

35. "The Phrygians are wise too late" (Cicero, *ad fam.* VII. 16).

36. Johann Gottlieb Breitkopf (1719-94), of Leipzig, advocated the development of Gothic type, whereas the Didot firm in Paris had, since 1713, published its *Antiqua* in very small type.

37. Hufeland here added a note, confirming Kant's view that this condition, which is becoming more common, is not an opthalmic disease, and suggesting that it results from some transient circulatory or gastric irritation, or perhaps from general weakness. Vorlaender's notes to the *Akademie* edition of the text quote several of Hufeland's comments (VII, 346-47).

An S. Karabel Production